THE VIŚIṢṬĀDVAITA VEDĀNTA OF RĀMĀNUJA

(A Comparative and Critical Study)

S. R. Bhatt

MOTILAL BANARSIDASS
INTERNATIONAL
DELHI

Reprint Edition : Delhi, 2023
First Edition : 1975

ISBN : 978-81-19394-22-7

Also available at

MOTILAL BANARSIDASS INTERNATIONAL

H. O. : 41 U.A. Bungalow Road, (Back Lane)Jawahar Nagar, Delhi - 110 007
4261 (basement) Lane #3,Ansari Road, Darya Ganj, New Delhi - 110 002
203 Royapettah High Road, Mylapore, Chennai - 600 004
12/1A, 2nd Floor, Bankim Chatterjee Street, Kolkata - 700 073
Stockist : Motilal Books, Ashok Rajpath, Near Kali Mandir, Patna - 800 004

Printed & Bound by
MOTILAL BANARSIDASS INTERNATIONAL

To
My Revered Teacher
Professor A.G. Javadekar

PREFACE

The present work is a comparative and critical study of some of the fundamental metaphysical problems discussed in the philosophies of Rāmānuja, Pāñcarātra school and the Āḷvārs. Since the philosophy of Rāmānuja is developed in direct opposition to, and by way of criticism of, the Advaita philosophy, and since the Pāñcarātra philosophy is in many respects similar to that of the Advaita, the latter has also been taken into consideration,

The main idea that has prompted this study is an examination of the view held by many scholars that the philosophy of Rāmānuja is a direct outcome of his conscious effort to blend the Vedāntic metaphysics with the Vaiṣṇavite religion of the Pāñcarātra school and the Āḷvārs. It has also been intended to show that Rāmānuja's teachings are entirely based on the Vedic scriptures, and that his organicismic interpretation of the Vedānta philosophy offers a bold, and in no way less important, contrast to the absolutistic interpretation of Śankara and his followers.

To my knowledge this is the first work of its kind which aims at a comparative and critical study of the philosophies of Rāmānuja, the Advaita School, the Pāñcarātra school and the Āḷvārs along the lines of treatment here followed.

As regards the philosophy of Rāmānuja the results of my comparative study have shown that it does not seems to have been influenced by the Pāñcarātra school and the Āḷvārs, Though such a position may appear starting and unpalatable to many writers on, and the followers of, the Viṣiṣṭādvaita and Śrī-vaiṣṇavism, it is the logical outcome of the glaring contradictions that prevail between the views of Rāmānuja on the one hand and those of the Pāñcarātra school and the Āḷvārs on the other. I have also ventured to call into question the ascription of a number of doctrines to Rāmānuja based on misunderstanding caused by a failure to dissociate his philosophy from the Viṣiṣṭādvaita of his followers.

So far as the exposition of the philosophy of the Pāñcarātra school is concerned, I have not dealt with it in details as I have already done so in a separate work, entitled 'The Philosophy of Pāñcarātra', published by Ganesh & Co., Madras, 1968.

As regards the philosophical implications of the religion of the Āḷvārs I had to rely on secondary sources because of my lack of knowledge of Tamil and other southern languages. I am, however, confident that my account of their philosophical position is quite a fair representation of their views.

This work is a revised form my thesis submitted to the M. S. University of Baroda under the guidance of Prof. A. G. Javadekar. But for his critical and constructive suggestions the work would have been what it is. I express my gratefulness to him. I am also grateful to Dr. C. P. Brahmo, Dr. B. L. Atreya and Dr. S. L. Bhyrappa for their valuable suggestions and guidance offered from time to time. I am further thankful to Swami B. H. Bon Maharaj, Rector, Institute of Oriental Philosophy, Vrindaban, for appointing me as research fellow on Rāmānuja chair at the said Institute for the year 1960-61.

My thanks are due to Shri J. P. Jain & Mr. Abhishek Jain, Partners, Motilal Banarsidass International, who undertook the publication of this work. I must thank my wife Smt. Annapurna for making all possible efforts to provide an Ideal atmosphere conducive to creative writing. Lastly my indebtedness is due to all the scholars whose works I have freely quoted and consulted.

S. R. Bhatt
September' 2023.

CONTENTS

INTRODUCTION

The object of the present work being a comparative study of the metaphysical doctrines of Rāmānuja, Pāñcarātra school and Āḷvārs, we propose to start with a historical introduction to each of these.

I

Rāmānuja as a Vedāntic ācārya

To start with Rāmānuja[1], it can easily be discerned that his philosophy has its roots in the Vedāntic tradition. Ever since the dawn of thought the Indian mind is distinguished for its natural inclination for spiritualistic metaphysical reflections the culmination of which is reached in the Vedānta system. So much was the prominence attained by the Vedānta that many of the prominent thinkers of India took pride in being the commentators on the basic Vedānta texts.

Prasthāna-traya as foundational texts of Vedānta

The philosophy of Vedānta is contained in the Upaniṣads, the Bhagavadgītā and the Brahma-sūtras, technically known as 'prasthāna-traya' teaching the same philosophical truth respectively in mystical, moral and metaphysical forms. These three together constitute its foundation as well as supreme authority. The Upaniṣads are the pioneer works of the Vedānta system. Since they seem to teach apparently contradictory doctrines, a need was felt to attempt to systematise their teachings, as a result of which the Brahma-sūtras and the Gītā came into existence.

Commentators on Prasthāna-traya

The ambiguity which prevailed in the Upaniṣads and which necessitated the composition of the Brahma-sūtras and the Gītā, was also found to prevail in the latter two. Consequently all the subsequent Vedāntic ācāryas were obliged to write commentaries on the prasthāna-traya, specially on the Brahma-sūtras which was regarded as the most systematic exposition of the Vedānta philosophy. The chief commentators, whose works are known to us, are Śankara, Bhāskara, Rāmānuja. Nimbārka, Madhva, Vallabha, Śrīkaṇṭha and Baladeva. All these ācāryas attempt to expound the Sūtras in a coherent and systematic way claiming to satisfy the triple tests of scriptural support (śruti), logicality (yukti) and experiential certainty (anubhava). Starting with different philosophical standpoints, all of them interpret the Sūtras differently, so much so that no two commentators agree with each other. Each commentator professes that he alone has arrived at the true and genuine meaning of the Sūtras.

Śankara and Rāmānuja as most outstanding commentators.

Among these commentators Śankara's Advaita, also known as Kevalādvaita, and Rāmānuja's Viśiṣṭādvaita are the most popular and ingenious expositions. Śankara, as has been universally recognised, has evolved one of the most compact and finished systems of thought. But Rāmānuja's panentheistic interpretion of the Vedānta philosophy offers a bold, and in no way less important, contrast to the absolutistic position of Śankara. There are differences of opinion among the scholars as to who is nearer to the true spirit of the triple texts, yet it remains indisputable that Rāmānuja's system is an equally significant expression of the Vedāntic thought. Dr. Keith remarks that Rāmānuja's attempt in the Śrī-Bhāṣya 'in substantial merit and completeness far outdid any previous effort to find in the Brahma-sūtras a basis for monotheism'.[2]

Viśiṣṭādvaita of Rāmānuja.

The system of philosophy associated with the name of Rāmānuja is known as Viśiṣṭādvaita. Though this word does not occur in his works, it truly represents the panentheistic or organicismic idea of his system. He has not developed any new system of thought, nor does he claim originality. He accepts the authority of an ancient and weighty Vedāntic tradition established by his Viśiṣṭādvaitic precursors like Bodhāyana, and developed by the 'pūrvācāryas' (ancient teachers) like Ṭaṇka, Dramiḍa, Guhadeva, Kapardin, Bhāruci and others.[3] His genius lies in the systematic and masterly presentation of the Viśiṣṭādvaita, and thereby controverting the Advaita at a highly needed time. He does so by emphasising the spiritual experience without ignoring the critical requirements of philosophy. He provides the love of God with a convincing philosophy, and philosophy with a sublime love of God. The ideas of grace of God and the doctrine of devotion, adumbrated in the Vedic hymns and developed in the Upaniṣads and the Gītā, blossom forth fully in him through the Viṣṇupurāṇa.[4]

Yāmuna's Criticism of Advaita

The polemic against Advaita by Rāmānuja is not the first of its kind. It seems that Yāmuna[5] —the author of 'Siddhi-traya' and 'Gītārtha Samgraha' —was the first thinker of the Viśiṣṭādvaita school who sought to controvert the advaitic view by dialectical method. In his 'Siddhi-traya', under Ātma-siddhi which is devoted to a comparative and critical discussion of the individual self and Supreme Self from different standpoints, he subjects to a critical examination the advaitic theory of the self as pure consciousness as set forth in the Iṣṭa-siddhi of Vimuktātman. Under Samvitsiddhi he repudiates other important advaitic doctrines such as the unity of the self, the illusoriness of the universe, the concept of avidyā and the like. After Yāmuna Rāmānuja carried forward this task with greater fervour as Māyāvāda had become more pronounced in his time.

Rāmānuja's polemic against Advaita

The chief aim of Rāmānuja, as is evident from the very first adhikaraṇa of the Śrī Bhāṣya and the second introductory verse of the Vedārtha Samgraha, is to controvert the doctrines of the Advaita school, with a view to establish the teachings of the Viśiṣṭādvaita school on a sound logical basis. His attack is directed mainly against the central doctrine of the Advaita that Brahman, which is attributeless pure consciousness devoid of all determinations, constitutes the sole reality and the manifoldness of the world and everything other than Brahman are not real. The doctrine of Māyā, which is unique to the Advaita school, suffers the heavy brunt of his attack.

It is not difficult to understand as to why Rāmānuja devoted greater attention to the refutation of the Advaita school than to that of any other school of thought. It was not because the philosophy of Advaita was holding an unquestionable sway at his time but because the absolutistic ideologies of the later advaitins, under the influence of Gauḍapāda and Buddhism, had reached the verge of agnosticism and were thought to have been endangering the existence of theism.

Works of Rāmānuja

The first work written by Rāmānuja is the Vedārtha Samgraha where he reinterprets the principal Upaniṣadic texts which, as the advaitins claim, lend themselves to advaitic interpretation. He establishes the unsoundness of their alleged advaitic leaning and expounds them in accordance with the teachings of the Viśiṣṭādvaita. Then he writes his magnum opus, the *Śrī Bhāṣya*, a commentary on the Brahma-sūtras. After this he composes two epitomes of the Śrī Bhāṣya, the Vedānta Sāra, a short and simple gloss, and the Vedānta Dīpa, a work on the same model but fuller in discussion and more exhaustive in exposition. Lastly, he writes a commentary on the Gītā, which is a work of great merit and a result of considerable thought.

Apart from the above works, two other works viz., Gadya-trayam and Nitya-granthas, are also ascribed to him but the authenticity of this ascription is quite doubtful. They vary from his other works in style as well as in subject matter. The Nitya-grantha, which deals with the routine of a devotee and with devotional lyrics, contains no philosophy. The Gadya-trayam, described as 'exercises in bhakti'[6], seems to be an imitation, by some later hand, of Rāmānuja's introduction to the Gītā Bhāṣya.

Sources of Rāmānuja's Philosophy

The main sources for the philosophy of Rāmānuja are the prasthāna-traya. Unlike Śankara, he makes unsparing use of illustrative and corroborative evidences from the Mahābhārata, Rāmāyaṇa and Viṣṇupurāṇa. Sometimes he also derives support from Smṛtis, Dharma Śāstras, Brāhmaṇas and Āraṇyakas which are all strictly brāhmaṇical works.

It has often been said, rather taken for granted, that Rāmānuja was essentially and substantially influenced and inspired by the Pāñcarātra Saṃhitās and the works of the Āḻvārs. Our comparative study in the present work will show that this view does not seem to be valid.[7]

II

Pāñcarātra school as a branch of Āgama

Now we come to the Pāñcarātra school.[8] The Pāñcarātra school, also known as Bhāgavata or Sāttvata or Ekāntic school, occupies a unique and significant place in Vaiṣṇavism. It forms an important part of the Hindu Āgama religion which has yielded an unmitigated influence all over India, and has contributed a lot in the making of living Hindu religion in the different parts of India under different names.

Origin and antiquity of Pāñcarātra school

From the information available about the Pāñcarātra school it is very difficult to decide precisely its antiquity as a school of thought and a body of people practicing a mode of religion in conformity thereto. But it seems to be of considerable antiquity, and its earliest literature must have been composed, perhaps in the North, long before the great epics. Though we do not have any literary evidence as to the train of reasoning by which the doctrines of this school came to be formulated and reached the present form, yet we may believe that there must have been a body of the Pāñcarātra teachings handed down from teacher to pupil, and practised more or less generally by the people, before the general teachings got formulated in handbooks.[9]

Sources and extent of Pāñcarātra literature

The earliest available record of the Pāñcarātra thought is contained in the Nārāyaṇīya section of the Śānti parva of the

Mahābhārata. But there it does not seem to appear in its original form, because the sectaries have preserved for us not so much the opinion actually held by the people as much the opinion the sectaries wished them to hold.

Apart from the Nārāyaṇīya we find an exposition of the Pāñcarātra doctrines in a voluminous literature variously named as Pāñcarātra Upaniṣads, Pāñcarātra Tantras, Pāñcarātra Āgamas etc., but popularly known as Pāñcarātra Samhitās, a major portion of which has fallen now into oblivion or extinction. The extensive nature of the Pāñcarātra literature can be gauged from what Dr. Schrader has opined that 'the Samhitā literature of the Pāñcarātra must have once amounted to not less but probably more than one and a half million ślokas'[10]

Principal subjects treated in Pāñcarātra literature

The teachings of the Pāñcarātra school, and in general of the whole Āgama literature, generally fall into four sections, according to the four main themes treated, which are as follows : (i) Jñāna – It comprises philosophical doctrines regarding God, nature, individual soul, process of creation, means of liberation etc. It also includes occultism containing the knowledge of the secret powers of letters, syllables, formulas and figures.

(ii) Yoga :—It means meditation or concentration, specially with a view to acquire magic powers or to attain release.

(iii) Kriyā :—It includes the rules to be followed in the making of idols, and in the construction and consecration of temples.

(iv) Caryā :—It deals with the rules of conduct regarding worship, rites, festivals and social duties.

Dr. Schrader mentions ten principal subjects[11] but suggests that the name Pāñcarātra must have come from the five principal subjects treated in it, which are tattva (ontology), muktiprada (liberation), bhaktiprada (devotion), yogic (Yoga) and vaiṣayika (objects of senses). This suggestion we meet with in the Nārada-Pāñcarātra and Ahirbudhnya Samhitā.[12]

The major part of the Pāñcarātra literature, however, comprises kriyā and caryā. As a matter of fact there is very little philosophy in them, because their main concern is to describe the rules about the various rites and rituals of the sect. Interspersed with these are philosophical doctrines which form the basis of the later Śrīvaiṣṇava philosophy and religion of the followers of Rāmānuja.

Prevalence of Tāntric element in Pāñcarātra

A notable feature and dominant element of the Pāñcarātra Samhitās seems to be prevalence of tāntrism. It is not definitely known how and when tāntrism arose, but that it is of considerable antiquity, no one can deny. It seems to be of a non-Vedic origin. In one of its phases of development its ideas and practices were frankly anti-Vedic. In its early character it does not seem to have recognised the authority of the Vedas, though in later times it could not ignore them.[13]

The extant Samhitās are the earliest available records of the tāntric influence. How deeply tāntric ideas and practices influenced the Pāñcarātra could be seen from an examination of the contents of the Samhitās like Jayākhya, Pārameśvara, Ahirbudhnya etc. which are the most ancient and authoritative Pāñcarātra works.[14]

Nature of Pāñcarātra Philosophy

(i) *In the Nārāyaṇīya*—The Pāñcarātra philosophy in the Nārāyaṇīya is less complicated than what it is in the Samhitās. It is free from the ritualistic and tāntric details, the kriyā and caryā portions, which occupy more than three-fourth of the Samhitā literature. This seems to be due to its early origin. Whatever little ritualistic element is found in the Nārāyaṇīya, it is brāhmaṇical in nature. The Nārāyaṇīya thought contains a curious combination of upaniṣadic mysticism, along with the popular worship of a personal god in an ardently devotional atmosphere with all its paraphernalia of mythological fancy. The speculative side which is meant to supply a philosophical background to the religion is an inadequate medley of various ideas, sometimes unrelated and incongruous.[15]

(ii) *In the Samhitās*—The primary concern of the Pāñcarātra school in the Samhitā literature seems to be the sādhanā or the practical method of realising the Ultimate Reality. Their aim is not to establish any definite system of thought. That is why abstract metaphysical speculations could not find prominence in them. The philosophical portions introduced here and there with a view to explain the various practices and rituals could not successfully do so, and they are not always relevant to them. The Samhitās incorporate the fundamental tenets of other schools (darśanas), mainly of the Vedānta and the Sāmkhya-yoga, and apply them to the practical effort for the realisation of the supreme goal.

The Pāñcarātra school, like other tantras, believes in one, ultimate, non-dual Reality, which possesses in its fundamental nature two aspects, viz., static (nivṛtti) and dynamic (pravṛtti), represented respectively by Brahman and Its Śakti. In the description of the former we find an unmistakable influence of the advaitic tendency, and in the latter that of the Sāmkhya. The Ultimate Reality is described, in the manner of the Upaniṣads, as an attributeless conscious substance, always escaping the grasp of intellectual comprehension and verbal expression. This attitude of silence and ineffability is perfectly in line with its predominating advaitic tendency. One cannot, therefore, but believe that the philosophy of the Pāñcarātra school is much nearer the Advaita than to the Viśiṣṭādvaita.

III

Āḷvārs as passionate devotees of Viṣṇu

Now we turn to the Āḷvārs.[16] The rise of the line of Āḷvārs, Tāmil vaiṣṇava poet-saints, is one of the most notable events in the history of Vaiṣṇava religion and bhakti movement. The Āḷvārs, twelve of whom have obtained canonical recognition, were mostly low caste people, but pure in heart and intensely devoted to Viṣṇu. They were in the real and the fullest sense God-intoxicated, God-enamoured and God-absorbed mystics. The word 'Āḷvār' itself means 'one who is lost in the ineffable splendour and mystery of the Lord'. As Dr. Dasgupta has put it, 'The word Āḷvār means one who has a deep intuitive knowledge of God and one who is immersed in the contemplation of Him'.[17]

Works of Āḷvārs

The Āḷvārs were the divers in the ocean of God-consciousness. Their intense religious fervour, 'fervent glow of emotion'[18], and passionate devotion to the Deity are reflected in a collection of verses called 'Nālāyira Prabandham' which even today is revered by the Śrī-vaiṣṇava community as a sacred canon and is recited in worship and other festivals. These verses are valuable not for any new philosophical conception of the Deity, but for the fact that they reveal the depth of religious feeling to which the view of a loving and endearing Deity has given rise. They may be described as welling with a genuine and devoted love of an intense degree bordering on a maddening intoxication and ecstasy. The unalloyed devotion of the Āḷvārs finds vent and is exhibited to the fullest in these poems of artistic merit which speak of devotee's indissoluble affiliation to the Deity.

Chronology of Āḷvārs

The traditional dates ascribed to the Āḷvārs are quite fanciful and varied.[19] Modern researches on this subject bring down their dates from 4203 B.C.[20] to a period not earlier than 7th or 9th century A.D.[21] In the beginning it was believed that they were the disciples of Rāmānuja, but later on it was contended that the reverse should be the case. From the material available to us it is difficult to determine with any exactitude the dates of the Āḷvārs. It seems more probable that they were posterior to Rāmānuja or even some of them his younger contemporaries. This may be supported by the fact that the Prabandham contains in it a centum on Rāmānuja composed by one who calls himself in the course of the work as a disciple of Rāmānuja's chief disciple Kuruṭṭāḷvār.[22] This may further be supported by the comparative studies in the meditative bhakti of Rāmānuja and the emotional bhakti of the Ālvārs. The latter bears an explicit impact of the Bhāgavata Purāṇa whereas the former is uninfluenced by it.

Āḷvārs as mystics and not philosophers

The main feature of the Āḷvār movement is that it is emotional and not contemplative. It is not the philosophic spirit but the religious need that is strong in them. It is therefore quite natural that philosophical speculation concerning the nature of Reality or an investigation into the logical and epistemological position of the religion preached by them, cannot be found in their works. Since theirs is a religion and not a philosophy, it is difficult to build a systematic philosophy out of their devotional utterances. Of all the Āḷvārs, Nāmmāḷvār is the most philosophic. In h s hymns we find a philosophical approach to the concept of Deity.

Mysticism of Āḷvārs

The Āḷvārs, as we have said, are the mystics par excellence, in whom the 'mystic germ' is fully developed. The dominant traits of their mysticism are its emotional nature and the mingling of the erotic and mystic elements which find expression in an amorous language. In the deliverances of their mystic consciousness, we find three characteristics. The first is the maddening divine intoxication which turns them into 'sick-souls' suffering 'mystic pains', a state which may be compared with the 'dark night of the soul' as described by Saint Teresa. The second is imaginary identifications with the legendary associates of Kṛṣṇa, their beloved. This element is peculiar to the Āḷvārs and is rare in other mystics of the world. The last is their devotion to the Deity resulting in total surrender. Here we shall deal with the first two characteristics and take up the third one subsequently in the chapter on the means of emancipation.

Maddening divine intoxication of Āḷvārs

The Āḷvārs, like other mystics, wish to experience a constant companionship with God in a state of delirious and rapturous reciprocation of ravishing love. Their hearts overwhelm with a constant whirling emotion of love. They are like the love-stricken lovers who cannot afford to lose sight of the beloved, and who are ready to fight the world and endure all privations and persecution for the sake of the beloved. They forget everything that arouses the sense of separateness, and always occupy themselves with the Lord. They feel helpless and restless, and experience extreme uneasiness and great misery when they lose the presence of God, because nothing else can satisfy them. In many of their hymns we find the longing and the cry of their hearts for union with God, the pangs of separation and the consequent sense of desolation, and the anticipated joy of reunion[23] Nāmmāḷvār in a pathetic language portrays the melancholy and miserable condition of a devotee who like a lover pining for his beloved lord steals into the darkness of the night, when all the world is asleep.[24]

We find the best exposition of such an attitude in Mrs. Sarojini Naidu's poem, 'The Flute-player of Vrindaban', where the devotee, even if, is sundered from the Lord through many insurmountable difficulties, and is obstructed with innumerable and unsurpassable hindrances, so that the reunion may seem remote, yet he cannot afford to lose the Lord, and at the risk of losing everything keeps alive the eternal link of love which cannot be broken away even by the Lord Himself. Nāmmāḷvār also under a different context declares in a similar vein,

> 'God ! I have now clasped thy feet firmly.
> Try if Thou canst spurn me and shake Thyself off from me.'

In this way the passionate devotion in the Āḷvārs is realised as a maddening intoxication associated with tears, cries, pining and languishing.[25]

Imaginary identifications of Āḷvārs

In the intensity of devotion and exuberance of feeling the Āḷvārs are so absorbed that in pondering over the incidents connected with the life of Kṛṣṇa, as described in the Bhāgavata Purāṇa, they identify themselves with those who had deep love for Kṛṣṇa, and they behave with, and address, the Deity accordingly[26]. Thus Nāmmāḷvār regards himself as a gopī, lover of Kṛṣṇa, and expresses his concern lest Kṛṣṇa should come to grief at the hands of demons.[27] He represents himself as a maiden disconsolate and pining for Kṛṣṇa, her absent lover. Then, like a gopī, he ardently desires to be embraced by Kṛṣṇa.[28] Similarly, Āndāl, the lady Āḷvār, imagines herself a gopī, who rising in the morning wakes up other gopis and goes with them to arouse the sleeping Kṛṣṇa.[29] This identification is further extended to Yaśodā, Kṛṣṇa's foster mother. Thus Periyāḷvār requests the moon to come to the infant Kṛṣṇa who longs to play with it.[30]

This sort of emotional identification is something peculiar to the Āḷvārs. Regarding the novelty of this identification Dr. Das Gupta remarks, 'Even in the Bhāgavata Purāṇa we hear of devotional intoxication through intense emotion, but we do not hear of any devotees identifying themselves with the legendary personages associated with the life of Kṛṣṇa, and expressing their sentiment of love as proceeding out of such imaginary identification. We hear of the Gopī's love for Kṛṣṇa, but we do not hear of any person identifying himself with Gopī and expressing his sorrow of separation.'[31] He further writes, 'But the idea that the legend of Kṛṣṇa should have so much influence on the devotees as to infuse them with the characteristic spirits of the legendary personages in such a manner as to transform their lives after their pattern is probably a new thing in the history of devotional development in any religion.'[32] Again he writes, 'It seems fairly certain that the Āḷvārs were the earliest devotees who moved forward in the direction of such emotional transformation.'[33]

The devotional songs of the Āḷvārs show an intimate familiarity with the various events of the legendary life of Kṛṣṇa. They vividly describe his pranks, amusements and frolics. All these betray an intimate knowledge and influence of the Bhāgvata Purāṇa, where devotion has an unrestrained tendency of extravagant enthusiasm, of a surging emotion which thrills the body, chokes the speech and leads to trance.

References and footnotes :—

1. For the life-history of Rāmānuja see the following works :
   (a) A. Govindacharya, *The life of Rāmānuja*,
   (b) S. Krishnaswami Aiyangar, *Śrī Rāmānuja*,
   (c) T. Rajagopalacharya, *The Vaiṣṇavite Reformers of India*,
   (d) Swami Ramakrishnananda, *Life of Śrī Rāmānuja*.
2. Hasting's *Encyclopaedia of Religion and Ethics*, Vol. X. P. 572.
3. Cf. the first line of *Śrī-bhāṣya*; *Vedārtha Samgraha*, Section, 93.
4. Cf. Bhatt, S. R., 'Bhakti as Means of Emancipation in Rāmānuja', *Vedanta Kesari*, January, 1965.
5. This Yāmuna should not be confused with the Śrī-vaiṣṇava Yāmuna to whom the works like 'Āgama Prāmāṇya' are ascribed. Cf. Bhatt. S.R., 'Did Rāmānuja Advocate Pāñcarātra and Śrī-vaiṣṇavism ?, *Philosophical Quarterly*, April, 1963.
6. J.A.B. Van Buitenen, *Vedārtha Samgraha*, Introduction, p. 32.

7. Ibid, pp. 38-39.
8. Bhatt, S.R., *The Philosophy of the Pāñcarātra.*
9. F. Otto Schrader, *An introduction to the Pāñcarātra and Ahirbudhnya Samhitā.*
10. Ibid, pp. 6-12, 14.
11. Ibid, p. 26.
12. 'Rātram ca jñāna vacanam jñānam pañcavidham smṛtam' Ahirbudhnya Samhitā, 1.64.
13. Bhatt, S. R., *The Philosophy of the Pāñcarātra*, Loc. cit., pp. 10 ff.
14. Bhatt, S.R., Smṛti kāla me vedika aur pāñcarātra, vicāradhārā Kā sambandha, *Kashi Nagari Pracharani Patrika*, Samvat 2021, Anka, 3.
15. Mrnal Dasgupta, *Indian Historical Quarterly*, 1931, pp. 346-58; 655-79; 1932, pp. 64-84.
16. For the life-history of the Āḷvārś see the following works;
    (i) A Govindacharya, *The Holy Lives of the Azvars*
    (ii) S. Krishnaswami Aiengar, *Ancient India*
17. A History of Indian Philosophy, vol. III, p. 68.
18. Hooper, Hymns of the Āḷvārs, p. 30.
19. See Dasgupta, S.N., Loc, cit, pp. 63-68; S.K. Aiengar, *Early History of Vaiṣṇavism in South India*, pp. 4-13;R.G.Bhandarkar, *Vaiṣṇavism, Śaivism* etc. pp. 68-69.
20. This is the date ascribed to the first Āḷvār in one of the guruparamparās.
21. See Dasgupta, S.N., Loc. cit., p. 64.
22. See Gopinath Rao, T. A., *History of Śrī-vaiṣṇavism*, Sri Subramanyam Lectures, 1923, pp. 29-31, p. 60; Aiengar, S.K., Loc. Cit. pp. 4-5.
23. Aiengar, S.K., Loc. cit., pp. 17.
24. See J.S.M. Hooper 'Hymns of the Āḷvārs' pp. 61-88. See also Dasgupta, Loc. cit, pp. 78ff.

    It would suffice here to give two instances of the same.

    The mistress' friend despairs at the sight of her languishing.

    (a) Day and night she knows not sleep,
    In floods of tears her eyes do swim,
    Lotus-like eyes she weeps and reels,

Ah ! how without Thee can I bear;
She pants and feels all earth for Him.

(b) ……Ah as she sobs and lisps
The Cloud- hued's names; I know not if she'll live
Or if her frame and spirit mild must pass !

25. See the quotation from Tiruvaymoli II. I in Kumarappa's *'The Hindu conception of the Deity'*, p. 133.
26. See the further description and analysis of and remarks about this element of the mysticism of the Āḷvārs in DasGupta, Loc. cit, pp. 79, 83-84.
27. He prays, 'O My Lord ! Go not Thou to tend the cows. Many asuras set up by Kamsa take alluring forms and wander about in Thy meadows and entice thee. If they succeed many evils will come upon Thee. I implore you to listen to me.' (C. 10.3.9)
28. See Tiruvaymoli c. 10.3.5 and 6-quoted by Kumarappa, Loc. cit, pp. 129-130.
29. Kumarappa, Ibid, pp. 130, 131.
30. Ibid, p. 130.
31. Loc cit, p. 81.
32. Ibid, p. 81.
33. Ibid, p. 82.

CHAPTER I

APPROACH TO REALITY

Introduction

The history of mankind reveals a constant recurrence of some fundamental problems which have agitated human mind right from the dawn of human civilization. One of such perennial problems is the nature of Reality. The demand for some kind of universally acceptable conception of the Reality is one which human mind cannot help making. But no two human minds have ever agreed with each other in their pronouncements on the same. The conclusions of reason and reflection lead us to the idea of one Being, an all-inclusive Absolute. But the facts of life and experience, on the other hand, compel us to admit a plurality of existence which cannot be confined within the narrow walls of rigid identity. We cannot help believing in the existence of one fundamental all-inclusive unity, but at the same time we cannot deny the existence of the manifest plurality.

Such a baffling situation gives rise to a number of problems. For example, in what relation does the plurality stand to the all-inclusive Unity ? Is the Unity the sole reality and the plurality mere nugatory ? Or, otherwise, is the plurality the real Reality and the Unity mere abstraction and the super-imposition of the mind ? To put the same problem in a more concrete way, what is the status of the world of animate beings and inanimated things ?

Is this world a real entity existing in its own right, or is it but a mode of a unitary Absolute, the only Reality there is or can be ?

A corollary of the problem of the nature of Reality is the issue whether the Absolute of Philosophy is the same as God of Religion. In other words, the problem is, does the Absolute denote a personal Being who thinks and loves, or is it an undifferentiated impersonal pure thought ? Another supplementary problem that confronts us is with regard to the knowability or otherwise of Reality.

In view of our avowed purpose we shall confine our treatment of these problems to the views of Rāmānuja, Pāñcarātra School and Āḷvārs. Since the philosophy of Rāmāṇuja is developed in direct opposition to, and by way of criticism of, the Advaita School, and since the Pāñcarātra thought is similar to the Advaitic view in many respects, the latter will also be taken into consideration.

Knowability of the Ultimate Reality

The Ultimate Reality in the metaphysical categorisation is named alike by these thinkers and schools as Brahman. With regard to the knowledge of Brahman they are unanimous in saying that It is beyond human understanding. Such an agnosticism is noticeable in the Upaniṣads as well.[1] However, it has been maintained by all that Brahman can be known in a different sense and through a different way. To make this clear we shall give below an individual accout of their views.

(a) *Advaitic view*

The Advaita school denies the possibility of our having any conceptual knowledge of Brahman. The moment we attempt to do so, it is contended, Brahman is brought down to the position of finite.[2] It can, however, be known or realised intuitively, but such a knowledge is altogether different from the ordinary ratiocinative knowledge based on subject-object dualism. The knowledge of Brahman advocated in this school is in the form of identity-consciousness which means realising oneself as identical with Brahman.

(b) *Rāmānuja's view*

Rāmānuja is also categorical in holding that neither perception based on outer sense organ or internal organ or on yoga, nor inferenec, nor any form of human experience can give us the knowledge of Brahman. No amount of generalisation based on the characteristics exhibited by the material world can suffice to prove Its existence. He considers in detail and refutes the various arguments put forth to establish by empirical means the existence of Brahman.[3]

On the authority of the Sūtrakāra Rāmānuja contends that with regard to supersensuous matters scripture alone is authoritative and reasoning is to be applied only to support the scripture.[4] Scriptures declare that Brahman is unknowable by any means of proof,[5] but It is visible and manifest to the 'subtle seers'[6] or to him whom It chooses.[7] In the Gītā we learn that through the grace of God, Arjuna was given a special eye whereby he was able to see the universal form of the Deity.[8] Accordingly Rāmānuja maintains that Brahman can be known by bhakti or upāsanā, and through Its grace.[9] Regarding the place of scripture in this respect, Rāmānuja maintains that it is only a means to the direct knowledge or intuition of Brahman.[10]

(c) *Pāñcarātra view*

The Pāñcarātra school, like the Advaita, regards the Ultimate Reality as unknown and unknowable. Brahman is regarded as having a transcendent nature which is beyond human understanding 'whose middle is unmanifest; whose end is unmanifest; who is beyond the ken of logic or argument; who is unknowable.'[11] At times in the manner of the Upaniṣads 'Brahman is defined as "that who cannot be seen with the eye, touched with the sense of touch, smelt with the sense of smell' and who is 'beyond the ken of the sense of taste.'[12] Though Brahman is thus beyond the ken of eyes, It can be intuited directly like the fragrance of the flower.[13] This intuitive knowledge, like that of the Advaita, is also nothing other than realising oneself as identical with Brahman.[14]

Though the transcendent aspect of Brahman is unknowable through empirical means, the immanent aspect is not so. But it must be noted that this immanent aspect is not ultimately real.[15] The Nārāyaṇīya declares that the Deity reveals Himself to His devotees.[16] For instance, the unmanifest God becomes manifest for the sake of Nārada[17] and Uparicara,[18] but He was not seen by the priest Bṛhaspati, who was indignant at seeing Him. He was told that only he can see God to whom He becomes gracious.[19] Ekata, Dvita and Trita practised austerities for four thousand years, but could not see Him and were told that He cannot be seen by one who is destitute of devotion.[20]

In this way the Pāñcarātra school believes that the unknown and incomprehensible becomes known and comprehensible, appears in human form and speaks through human tongue solely out of urge of love and surge of grace. This is the wonder of wonders, the great mystery hidden from great thinkers, but revealed to great devotees like Nārada. It should however be noted that Śankara, the great Advaitin, also dwells on the love of, and devotion to, the Deity (Īśvara).[21]

(d) Āḷvārs' view

For the Āḷvārs the existence of God is a supreme fact. His existence should be experienced; it cannot be perceived or proved. The categories of reason cannot apprehend Him. Therefore, Nāmmāḷvār declares, 'It is impossible to declare that He has this not that. He cannot be reached by any thought either on earth or in the heavens'[22]. 'It is impossible even for gods to know His real nature...He is beyond the beyond.'[23]

Though God cannot be known through reason, and no one can behold Him with the eye, yet He can be apprehended by the devotees through their devotion resulting in the grace of God. Thus Nāmmāḷvār declares that though He is unknown to others, 'Yet He is to me of a definite nature'.[24] 'He is very easily accessible to His devotees. His ways are very mysterious to others.'[25]

From the foregoing it is obvious that the possibility of the empirical knowledge of the Ultimate Reality is denied by all these thinkers. The Advaita and the Pāñcarātra schools advocate an intuitive knowledge of the Ultimate Reality which means being one with it. Rāmānuja and the Āḷvārs however do not favour this view. According to them one can know God through devotion and through His grace. This knowledge does not mean being one with Him, though in some of the Āḷvārs we do find a tendency towards absolute identity. In the Advaita and the Pāñcarātra schools there is a place for devotion and love, but that is at the immanent or phenomenal level only.

Relation between Absolute of Philosophy and God of Religion

The Advaita and the Pāñcarātra schools make a distinction between the Absolute of philosophy and God of religion, the indeterminate Brahman and the determinate Brahman, the intuitional Highest and the logical Highest. This distinction is very sharp in the Advaita. But Rāmānuja not only does not agree with this but he is quite vehement in opposing it. The Āḷvārs, somehow, are too absorbed in the immanent God to bother about the transcendent Absolute. We shall give below an account of their views on this problem.

(a) Advaitic view

According to the Advaita school the Absolute of Philosophy (nirguṇa Brahman) is the only Reality, and God of Religion (saguṇa Iśvara) is the Absolute cast in the moulds of thought. The God of religion is nothing but a projection of, or concession to, the ignorant and empirical mind, and hence is not real. This distinction, it should be made clear, is conceptual only, and does not mean that there are two Brahmans, to wit, Saguṇa and Nirguṇa. The one and the same Brahman is experienced differently at two different levels of reality.

(b) Pāñcarātra view

Like the Advaita, the Pāñcarātra school also draws a distinction between the transcendent and the immanent aspects of Reality, but no fixed boundary is drawn between the two. The only Supreme Being the Pāñcarātra thinkers know about is the Transcendent One. But, somehow, they could not rest satisfied with this aspect and soon recognised that aspect also with which It stands related, though not directly, to the universe. Of these two aspects the transcendent one is undoubtedly real, but it is not clear as to whether both of them are equally real, or the former alone is real. Nor is it clear whether the personal God has a being for Himself and an appearance for others. In the Nārāyaṇīya, as we have said,[26] we come across a passage wherein it is stated that the later personal appearance of Brahman is due to māyā and should not be regarded as real. In the Samhitās we do not find any such clear statement. Yet on the basis of the general drift of the school, which is manifestly advaitic, we may believe that the personal form is regarded as real from the meditational standpoint only.

(c) Rāmānuja's view

Rāmānuja, on the contrary, does not see eye to eye with this sort of distinction. For him the Absolute and God, the nirguṇa Brahman and the saguṇa Brahman, have no distinction, conceptual or metaphysical. Both stand for the same Reality. One and the same Reality is both immanent and transcendent, and both these aspects have the same ontological status.

Āḷvārs' view

The Āḷvārs share the same view. Though they declare that 'God has a form and He has no form'[27] yet they are quite clear in saying that both personal and the impersonal forms are of one and the same Deity. They have not said anything about the ontological status of the two, nor should we expect so from them, because they are essentially devotees and not philosophers. But from their writings this much we can make out that for them both the forms are equally real.

Ontological approach to Reality

The basic ontological problem has been the riddle of 'one and many'. Different theories have been put forth to solve this riddle. On the ground that one and many are incompatibles, some thinkers affirm one and deny many. Some who do not fight shy of this incompatibility accept both as real but ascribe different degrees of importance to each of them. Here we shall consider the Advaitic and Rāmānuja's position on this problem. The Pāñcarātra view will not be discussed separately for it is the same as the Advaitic one. Since the Āḷvārs did not concern themselves with this problem, we shall not deal with them too.

Advaitic approach to Reality

The most distinguishing feature of the Advaita school on its metaphysical side is the advocacy of the doctrine of nirguṇa Brahman. The one and the only Reality admitted is the pure Brahman devoid of all determinations. Accordingly all differences are denied in the Absolute Unity. It finds no room for many in the unity of pure non-differentiated Brahman. To it unity defies logically all differences. Thus failing to reconcile the unity with multiplicity, it negates the latter to posit the former. The Absolute for it is not a synthetic unity but an abstract identity. The world of animate and inanimate objects, then, is but a transient mode of the eternal, immutable and unitary Absolute. There is nothing like a real existence, a real summum bonum, for the finite being. Within the range of the finite it can never experience that the ultimate end has been really secured. The end of all existence consists merely in removing the illusion under which all finite spirits live and which makes the end seem yet unaccomplished. As a matter of fact there is nothing like finite spirits, because they are no other than the One Absolute. This leaves no room for doubt that the worldly progress and achievements are but appearances of an eternally perfect Absolute which has no unfulfilled purposes and unsolved problems.

Criticism of Advaitic view

Thus the Brahman of the Advaita is exclusively a principle of rigid identity. To borrow Hegel's criticism of Schelling's Absolute 'it is like a lion's den to which many paths lead, but from which none leads back'. But Reality is too rich and complex to be confined within the narrow limits of rigid identity. Even Śankara, the most logical of all the Advaitins, though feels shy in giving place to multiplicity at the transcendental plane, he also feels that the multiplicity cannot be dismissed as mere nugatory. It is mithyā but not tuccha. It has an existence, though apparent one. He cannot outrightly reject the many, nor can he find a place for it in the One. Though he is wise enough to leave the problem as almost inexplicable under a good reason that human understanding is incompetent to comprehend how one becomes many, yet to conceive an end of an existence, however apparent, that has no beginning, is certainly a strain upon thought. The taxing problem remains as to why the unity should even in appearance be broken up into multiplicity, why the infinite appears in the guise of innumerable finites, why this world of illusion be here at all.

Further, the ontological position of the Advaita is based on an untenable epistemological position, that thought is identical with Reality. But our point is, if the thought is identical with Reality, knowledge is needless and if it is altogether different from Reality, knowledge is impossible. As a matter of fact every judgement is an affirmation of Reality and not mere apprehension of identity devoid of contents. It is true that knowledge-relation cannot be established between two altogether different terms, but it is also meaningless to talk of such a relation between two exactly identical terms. Though every judgement affirms identity, there is also another equally important factor viz., difference. Thought qualifies Reality and presupposes a distinction between subject and object, which are integrally united and not isolated bits. Therefore, Reality is not bare undifferentiated unity, but a unity that contains and admits of differences which are all real. All determinations, limitations and differences are *in* it, but not *of* it. They are not left unorganised but coordinated. These differences which are accommodated in this unifying principle do not vanish at any time. They are coeval and coeternal with the unity, even though subject to change from subtle to gross state and *vice versa.* Thus alone can we meet with the demands of reason as well as experience.

Statement of Organicism — a more satisfactory view

A true system of thought, therefore, is that which recognises both the opposite elements (one and many) and yet rises above them to a higher principle, a synthesis in which the opposition is reconciled. Organicism is a theory which fulfils this task by postulating a unity which expresses itself in and through the diversity of forms and functions. The idea of a living organism is not that of a barren unity of an abstraction which is bereft of multiplicity of its organs, but that of a concrete unity which realises itself in and through that multiplicity. Just as a part is not intelligible except through the idea of the whole of which it is a part, and just as a whole is not conceivable without any reference to its constituent parts, so also the organs are not intelligible except by the idea of the organism, and the organism also is not conceivable without any reference to its organs. Thus Organicism regards one and many as members of an organic whole, each having a being of its own, but a being that implies a relation to the other.

The Advaitin cannot speak of such a world of mutual appreciation and organic relation, for there is no such thing as a society of selves in his philosophy. He tells of a state of existence which is not a society of selves, but the only Self, one without a second, resting in its own glory. Here there is no manifoldness, but solid singleness. So he cannot entertain the idea of mutual give and take which is the core of Organicism. The chief value of Organicism lies in the fact that it recognises the inalienable individuality and the reality of the manifold finite spirits and matter, and assigns them a proper place, function and value in the unifying conception of an all-embracing unity (or Absolute) without in any way destroying its supreme perfection. The Absolute though differentiates Itself into matter and spirits, is not exhausted by them nor does It become completely identified with them, but reserves an inexhaustible amount of reality, whereby It transcends them. The multiplicity of finite spirits and matter also, instead of being annihilated in the all-absorbing unity of the Absolute, enjoys a relative reality, derives its being, discharges its functions and realises its value within the concrete unity of the Absolute. Both are necessary to each other and realise themselves in and through the other.

Organicism of the Upaniṣads

The Upaniṣads have developed this theory and Rāmānuja has presented it in a systematic and well-thought-out form, and therefore, it calls for our consideration.

The problem of one and many has been one of the central issues of inquiry in the Upaniṣads. There the disciple puts forth a query before the preceptor, 'Kena ekena vijñātena sarvam vijñātam bhavati ?' (i.e. by knowing which One everything else can be known ?) And the answer that he gets is, 'Ekena brahmavijñātena sarvam vijñātam bhavati' (i.e. by knowing One Brahman everything else can be known). The Brahman of the Upaniṣads is the all-pervading Supreme Reality which contains within Itself all finit spirits and matter. All sentient beings and non-sentient things live, move and have their being in it, who originates, accommodates and assimilates them within Its organic unity. This truth is expressed in the Upaniṣadic sayings like 'Tajjalān' (Chād. III. 14.1), 'yato vā imāni bhūtāni jāyante yena jātāni jīvanti yat prayantyabhisamviśanti tadvijijñāyasva tadbrahmeti' (Tait. III. I) 'Sanmūlāsomyemāṇ prajāssadāyatanāssatpratiṣṭhitāḥ' (Chand. VI. 8. 6) and the like. The Śvetāśvatara abounds with such passages, which need not be reproduced here.

The Bṛhadāraṇyaka in an oft-recurring simile tells us how God is the Supreme Soul. 'Just as the spokes of a wheel are held together in the navel of the wheel, similarly in this Supreme Soul are centred all these beings, all gods, all worlds and all individual souls. The Supreme Soul is the king of all.' (III.5.15). In another passage the same Upaniṣad tells us by a change of expression that 'Just as little sparks come out of fire, even so from the Supreme Soul all prānas, all worlds, all gods, all beings come out.' (II.I.10) The same is corroborated in the Gītā. (VII.7). The doctrine of Brahman as Antaryāmin, advanced in the Bṛhadāraṇyaka by Yājñavalkya in conversation with Uddālaka Āruṇi gives a classical exposition of this view. Uddālaka puts a query before Yājñavalkya, 'pray tell me what is that thread by which this universe and the other universe, and all the things therein, are held together? Do tell me also who is the controller of the thread of this universe and the other universe and all the things therein?' The answer given is, 'who dwells in the earth and within the earth, whom the earth does not know, whose body the earth is, who from within controls the earth, He is thy soul, the Inner Controller, the Immortal'. (III.7). In the Taittirīya we find a remarkable passage wherein it is described how God, the One, transformed Himself into the manifold world. This passage is notable because of its reconcilliation of the contradictories, and because it tells that contradictions are also real. It runs as follows, 'Having created the universe He entered into it, became both this and that, the defined and the undefined, the supported and the supportless, the knowledge and the not-knowledge, the reality and the unreality, yea, He became the reality, it is for this reason that all this is really called real.'

Rāmānuja's approach to Reality

Like the Upaniṣads, Rāmānuja solves the problem of one and many not by denying many and affirming one, nor by denying one and affirming many but by making many the predicate of one. As a matter of fact one and many had never posed any problem to him, because he starts with the position that one, by its very nature or immanent necessity, is impregnated with the many.

Rāmānuja is not content with a mystery hidden in the clouds of negatives. He does not deprive the Absolute of all determinations and reduce It to bare abstraction by ruthless logic of negative method. Like the advaitin, he rejects the view of mere plurality, and admits the existence of one Being only, but he further adds that all finite beings are real expressions of this Supreme Being. He is a monist no less than the advaitin but his monism is concrete one. He is as emphatic as the advaitin in declaring that there is nothing other than Brahman but adds that by 'other' he means heterogeneous and homogeneous differences only and not the internal ones.

The absolute of Rāmānuja is a living reality with a creative urge. It is a synthesis which does not deny differentiations, but expresses itself through them only. It is a whole that does not deny its parts, a substance that does not oust its attributes, a ground which does not negate its consequent, an integrity that does not shut itself of fulness. It is a concrete Being which contains the finite as moments of Its own existence, through which it transcends its own initial abstract character.

Thus Rāmānuja believes in the existence of a complex whole which includes both unity and diversity as integral elements. God is such a complex whole of which cit and acit constitute the modes. This idea is the very life blood of his philosophy. It is very well expressed by the term 'Viśiṣṭādvaita' which is a name assigned to his system. The underlying idea can be explained by the illustration of a fruit wherein the pulp and the peel, fiber and the form, the taste and the smell etc. all together constitute the fruit ; and though inseparable, all are mutually different and distinguishable having their own specific inalienable characteristics. Likewise God comprehends within His organic fold all matter and souls which are His attributes, modes, accessories, accidents, powers, bodies, forms, organs etc.[28] He is above all, in all, and through all. All are in Him, out of Him and unto Him.

Concept of God as Śārīrin

The sum and substance of the organicismic view of Rāmānuja lies in the idea of God as Śārīrin, which may be regarded as the raison d'être of his system. This is the solution the Bṛhadāraṇyaka Upaniṣad has offered for the vexed problem of One and many. Accordingly, God is regarded by Rāmānuja as the Supreme Embodied Soul, because the entire complex of intelligent beings and non-intelligent things constitute His body. He is indwelling (antaryāmin), supporting (ādhāra), controlling (niyantā) and final cause (śeṣi, Lit. utiliser). The body is, therefore, defined by Rāmānuja as 'Any substance which a sentient soul is capable of completely controlling and supporting for its own purposes, and which stands to the soul in an entirely subordinate relation.' Thus Rāmānuja maintains that the Absolute is a supreme organism consisting of a cosmic soul and its dependent bodily parts (the world and the selves) which serve Its purpose. The bodily parts, or the modes, are identical (ananya) with God as they are one with Him in their substance. But they are also different from God, just as the body is different from its soul. Though the modes are thus different from God, they do not create any division in the integrity of His being, for He realises His synthetic character through them only. The modes also, in the synthetic totality, lose the sense of isolated and independent units, keeping up their individuality. This model dependence of the world and the finite selves, however, does not rule out their monadic uniqueness. They do not have a distinctive existence of their own, and what makes them adjectives or modes is the fact that they cannot be understood without reference to God, their substance.[29]

Apṛthaksiddhi—a theory of relation

The relation between the substance (God) and the modes (world and finite selves) is regarded by Rāmānuja as one of 'inseparability' (apṛthaksiddhi). Describing the nature of this relation Prof. Hiriyanna observes,[30] 'It connotes that one of the two entities related is dependent upon the other in the sense that one cannot exist without the other also existing and that it cannot be rightly known without the other also being known at the same time'. This negative way of indicating the relation emphasises the identity of Being and its attributes and at the same time retains the conception of relation in the integrity of Being by rejecting the absolute oneness and identity of the Śankarites.'[31] Prof. Hiriyanna regards this relation to be 'the pivot on which his (Rāmānuja's) whole philosophy turns'.[32]

Advaitic denial of relation

The incompatibility between the absolutistic dogma and the dualistic requirement of relation leads advaitic thinkers to deny relation altogether. It has a place in empirical consciousness, but it cannot be applied to the absolute. It is something mysterious. It has an appearance but no reality. Criticising the naiyāyika concept of samavāya the advaitin points out that a system of relation leads to an infinite regress. In the dynamic character of being, Rāmānuja, on the contrary, finds the possibility of inner relation without involving any infinite regress.

Apṛthaksiddhi compared with Samavāya of Nyāya-Vaiśeṣika

According to the Nyāya school samavāya relation is a real entity intervening between two terms, or the relata, as a tertium quid (padārthāntara), or as a distinct 'link' connecting them into a relational unity.[33] Samavāya is usually regarded as an internal relation,[34] but Prof. Hiriyanna has rightly pointed out that it is external only. He writes, 'Even samavāya, it is necessary to add, has to be explained as an external relation, although it is usual to represent it as internal in modern works on Nyāya-Vaiśeṣika'.[35] He elsewhere writes, 'The very fact that it is independent and relates ultimately simple factors, shows that it cannot be an internal one'.[36]

The apṛthaksiddhi of Rāmānuja is similar to the samavāya of Nyāya in regard to its recognition of the reality, mutual necessity and the distinctiveness of the relata in it. But it is different from the samavāya in three respects. First, unlike samavāya, apṛthaksiddhi is not a separate entity (or category) external to the relata. Secondly, the relata in samavāya remain mutually external although they are held together in an 'intrinsic' unity by samavāya. In order that samavāya may hold good there should be two genuinely different entities. But the apṛthaksiddha relation, as we have seen, rejects alike identity and difference. The third and the last point of difference, which is a consequence of the second is that while samavāya is an external relation, apṛthaksiddha is an internal one.

Principle of Sāmānādhikaraṇya

How the Absolute is related to the so-called manifold appearance, or, in other words, how the one contains the many, has been a problem for the philosophers. Bradley, in the West, confesses the inability of human thought in this respect. He writes, 'We do not know why and how the Absolute divides itself into centres, or the way in which so divided, it still remains one. The relation of the many experiences to the single experience and so to one another is, in the end, beyond us.'[37]

But for Rāmānuja this is not a difficult problem. He rejects the absolutistic principle of bare identity and discovers a living principle of differentiation at the very heart of identity. This principle of differentiation within the unity of the Absolute, he interpreted in terms of sāmānādhikaraṇya, a grammatical principle of the coordination of words in a sentence, with the help of which he throws away both the concepts of bheda and abheda and institutes instead the concept of Viśeṣaṇa (predication).

On the basis of the principle of sāmānādhikaraṇya, Rāmānuja holds that unity and diversity can co-exist and be in intimate relation to each other.[38] The two are distinct and not contradictories, and can be reconciled in a synthetic unity. Rāmānuja, thus, does not deny many but makes it a predicate of one with the help of the adjectival principle.

Different applications of the principle of Sāmānādhikaraṇya

Rāmānuja has made different constructive as well as polemic uses of this principle. The advaitin resorts to lakṣaṇā in order to prove that Brahman is non-differentiated Reality. But Rāmānuja repudiates the advaitin's distinction of primary and secondary meanings of the texts, and with the help of the principle of sāmānādhikaraṇya, interprets the texts in an altogether different way and thereby proves that Brahman cannot be regarded as non-differentiated. The second use made of this principle is for proving the reality of the finite self and the world. Lastly he uses it to prove the distinctness of Brahman from the finite self and the world.

To prove that Brahman is differentiated

Rāmānuja differs fundamentally with regard to the interpretation of the Upaniṣadic text, 'Satyam, jñānam, anantam brahma' (Tait. II. 1) The main issue is whether in this text the terms in question denote the very being (svarūpa) of Brahman or His characteristics. The advaitin develops the view that the viśeṣaṇas (satyam, jñānam and anantam) have here not an attributive but a definitive function (lakṣaṇārtha). Attributes, he argues, serve the purpose of specifying members of the same particular class, but Brahman does not belong to any class. Therefore, these attributes do not have any attributive function. At the most they can have a negative or an indirect attributive function. That is to say, the term 'anantam' denies to Brahman the properties of phenomenal objects. The terms satyam and jñānam cannot be taken negatively, but only indirectly. The Advaitin further maintains that these terms which are found in coordination or apposition (sāmānādhikaraṇya) convey an impartite and non-relational sense only. That is to say, the text in question is understood to mean that Brahman is Truth, Knowledge and Infinitude, and not that it is possessed of these three characteristics. In order to explain this he takes the help of an illustration 'So'yam Devadattaḥ' in which on the basis of jahadajahallakṣanā, the two terms 'that Devadatta' and 'this Devadatta' which stand in coordination are regarded to convey the idea of one individual. He further adds that though these terms refer to the same non-differentiated object, viz., Brahman, yet they are not synonymous.

Criticising the advaitin Rāmānuja maintains that sentence, where the terms stand in coordination, does not convey an impartite and non-relational sense, but, on the contrary, it denotes one entity as qualified by the characteristics connoted by the terms of the sentence. For his support Rāmānuja quotes the definition of coordination given by the grammarians. It is the application to one thing of several words, for the application of each of which there is a different [motive. It means that though the terms of a proposition have different connotation, they can yet denote one and the same thing. Thus, for instance, in the judgement 'blue lotus' the term 'blue' has a different connotation from that of 'lotus' and yet the two terms refer to one object, viz., 'lotus'.

Rāmānuja further argues that the three terms in the text in question do not have one purport only. By the very nature of the principle of coordination we must admit a plurality of causes for the application of those several terms to one thing. If it is still insisted that they do have one purport only, then, Rāmānuja replies that in that case the three terms would not but be synonymous, and as such the employment of more than one term would be superfluous. If it is further said that it is not superfluous because there is a difference in respect of their connotations (nimitta bheda), then in that case Rāmānuja refuses to admit that a number of terms can refer to a non-differentiated object even if they be mere apophatic.

Regarding the applicability of the illustration 'So' yam Devadattaḥ' which, according to the advaitin is an identity-judgement and predicates no attributes to the subject, Rāmānuja replies that the Devadatta of 'here and now' cannot be wholly identical with the Devadatta of 'then and there', because then and there he had different attributes than here and now.

In the end Rāmānuja reminds the advaitin that the distinction of several attributes predicated to one thing does not imply distinction in the thing itself. Even though the characteristics connoted by the several terms found in coordination are different, the object denoted remains one and the same, without losing its integrity. The mere fact that an object is related to several characteristics would not mean that the object itself is not an integral whole. One and the same entity may be related to several characteristics without in any way impairing its integrity. Thus the true meaning of sāmānādhikaraṇya is not absolute identity but the relation of a thing to its attributes.[39]

To prove the reality of the finite self

According to the basic premises of the Advaita school, true self is one only, and the plurality of individual selves is not ultimately real. In order to support his contention he takes the help of the famous scriptural text 'Tattvamasi' which, as he declares, equates the finite self with Brahman. Śankara, in the Upadeśasahasri,[40] declares that when we establish the sense of 'tvam' by means of anvaya (positive) and vyatireka (negative) formulations the sense of the judgement 'tattvamasi' becomes clear. The terms 'anvaya' and 'vyatireka' which also occur in the Naiṣkarmyasiddhi of Sureśvara, are explained by Prof. Hiriyanna as 'method of agreement' and 'method of difference'.[41] J.A.B. Van Buitenen explains Śankara's meaning in the following way, 'The proposition is first considered positively by anvaya, whereby the connexion is realised between that in 'tat' which is in 'tvam' and contrariwise; then it is considered negatively by vyatireka, whereby that in 'tvam' which is not in 'tat' is excluded from 'tvam' and contrariwise.'[42]

Rāmānuja, on the basis of the principle of coordination, points out that in all cases of predication what is predicated is not a bare identity but a substance which is characterised by different attributes, so that the 'tvam' cannot be entirely identical with 'tat'. The coordination here is not meant to convey the idea of the absolute unity of a non-differentiated substance. On the contrary, the words 'tat' and 'tvam' denote Brahman distinguished by difference. The word 'tat' refers to Brahman, Omniscient, etc. and the word 'tvam' which stands in coordination to 'tat' conveys the idea of Brahman in so far as having for its body the individual souls. 'This' he writes, 'is in accordance with the general principle that coordination is meant to express one thing subsisting in a two-fold form. If such doubleness of form were abandoned there could be no difference of aspects giving rise to the application of different terms, and the entire principle of coordination too would be given up.[43]

To explain the relation of Brahman to matter and souls

Rāmānuja further applies this principle to explain the relation of Brahman to matter and souls. He maintains that all scriptural teachings with regard to Brahman as cause and the world as effect, or Brahman as soul and the world as body imply in the end that Brahman is the substance and the world is its attribute.[44] Therefore, he writes, 'All things thus are predicative to, or modes of, Paramapuruṣa; hence Paramapuruṣa alone exists, adjectivated by everything else. All terms are thus connotations of Him by the rule of Sāmānādhikaraṇya, or the rule which expresses the insepa-rable relation existing between substance and attribute, or the invariable co-existence of subject and predicate.'[45]

With the help of the principle of coordination Rāmānuja provides the necessary distinction between Brahman (the substance) and the world (the mode) so that neither the reality of the world, nor the perfection of Brahman is in danger of being sacrificed. What makes a thing a mode is not sameness of character but complete dependence.[46]

Nature of Ultimate Reality

One of the central problems of ontology is that of the nature of Reality. The answer to it depends mainly upon one's approach to Reality. In the preceding section we have seen the advaitic and Rāmānuja's contrasting ontological approaches. From this stems their diverse ontological positions, which we shall now discuss. We shall also deal separately with the accounts of the Pāñcarātra school and the Āḻvārs.

Advaitic view

The most distinguishing feature of the Advaita school is the advocacy of the doctrine of Nirviśeṣa or Nirguṇa Brahman. The Ultimate Reality is one only without a second, pure, undifferentiated consciousness. As Thibaut has put it, 'whatever is, is in reality one; there truly exists only one universal being called Brahman or Paramātman, the highest self. This being is of an absolute homogeneous nature; it is pure 'Being', or, which comes to the same, pure intelligence or thought (caitanya, jñāna). Intelligence or thought is not to be predicated of Brahman as its attribute, but it constitutes its substance; Brahman is not a thinking being, but thought itself. It is absolutely destitute of qualities; whatever qualities or attributes are conceivable, can only be denied of it... Brahman...is associated with a certain power called Māyā or avidyā to which the appearance of this entire world is due'[47] Rāmānuja in his mahāpūrvapakṣa summarises the advaitic position thus, 'Brahman as pure intelligence, entirely divested of any kind of forms, is the Ultimate Reality and all differences of the knower, the known, and the diverse forms of knowledge are fictitiously superimposed on It owing to a certain defect.'[48]

Rāmānuja's criticism of advaitic position

The concept of God advocated by Rāmānuja, which he derived from Bodhāyana and other Vedāntic teachers, is in direct opposition to the above advaitic view. Therefore before he could develop and systematise the views set forth by Bodhāyana etc., he had to refute the advaitic view, and to prove that the scriptures admitted a very different interpretation.

The polemic against the advaitic concept of Reality as a homogeneity of consciousness, exclusive of determinations, is divided by Rāmānuja into two parts. First, he tries to prove that Reality is not undifferentiated. Then he attempts to prove that it is also not pure consciousness.

Reality not undifferentiated

In maintaining that Reality cannot be undifferentiated Rāmānuja argues that those who assert that Reality can be undifferentiated, have really no means to prove so, for all proofs are based on the assumption of some qualified character.[49] He offers the following arguments in support of his contention:

(1) No proof in experience :—There is no proof of undifferentiated substance in our experience (or consciousness). Even if some one tries to prove that one's own experience, which is really qualified in nature, is unqualified, he will have to pick up some special trait in it in virtue of which he will maintain that it is unqualified ; but by that very fact his attempt will be defeated, for that special trait will make it qualified. Further, the advaitin himself admits that 'to consciousness there actually belong different attributes such as permanency, oneness, self-luminousness etc. in general'. Lastly, the very attempt of the advaitin to prove differences between his view and other views, implies that Reality is affected with difference.[50]

(2) Nor in Śabda :—There is no proof of undifferentiated substance in speech (śabda). Speech operates with words and sentences. The plurality of words is based on plurality of meanings.

The sentence, therefore, which is an aggregate of words, expresses some special meanings of words, and hence has no power to denote a thing devoid of all difference.[51]

(3) Nor in perception :—Perception also does not prove it. As regards the determinate perception it is well established that it manifests an entity with its characters ; but even indeterminate perception manifests some character, for its indeterminateness means only the exclusion of some particular character. All apprehension of consciousness takes place by means of some distinction like 'this is such and such'. The first apprehension of object (prathama piṇḍa grahaṇa) is not devoid of difference, but in it only some specific characters are discerned. When it is perceived again the characters discerned before are revived in the mind, and by comparison the specific characters are properly assimilated. This is what we call determinate perception.[52]

(4) Nor in inference :—Inference also being based on perception, cannot reveal a thing undifferentiated. It may be argued that even in opposition to perception, inference may establish that all differences are unreal. This is not possible, says Rāmānuja, for to do so inference will have to establish that reality is different from what it is revealed to be in perception, and in this very fact it will be admitting the reality of differences. Further, it is impossible to say that, though perception reveals differences as real, inference may come to a contrary conclusion ; for to do so inference will have to contradict itself. It will have to establish that differences are unreal on the ground that they are real (i.e., on the ground of perception on which inference ultimately rests). Rāmānuja thus concludes that 'a person who maintains the existence of a thing devoid of difference, on the ground of differences affecting that very thing, simply contradicts himself without knowing what he does.'[53]

(5) Nor in the nature of knowledge :—Rāmānuja further argues that all knowledge is differentiated. Every thought is an affirmation of reality and not mere apprehension of identity devoid of differentiation. The very nature of thought as a synthetic activity propounds at once its relational character.[54]

(6) Nor in Śruti :—Scriptures do not teach that Brahman is devoid of all differentiations. Rāmānuja criticises the advaitin for bifurcating scriptural texts as nirguṇa śruti and saguṇa śruti. He insists that all texts are equally important and they should be interpreted in a synthetic manner. Accordingly the passage 'Being only was there in the beginning...' does not mean that Brahman is a pure unity devoid of all differences, otherwise how can attributes like eternity be predicated to It. What it really means is that It is one like whom there is none other, and that It is the Alpha and the Omega of the universe. Similarly the passage of the Mundaka (1.i.5) which denies qualities to Brahman, negates only the undesirable qualities and not all the qualities.

In a similar way Rāmānuja at many places interprets a host of texts and concludes that what the scriptures teach is that Brahman has many excellent qualities, and is not undifferentiated.[55]

(7) Nor in Smṛtis and Purāṇas :—Rāmānuja lastly derives support from the Smṛtis and Purāṇas, which, he says, also teach that Brahman is 'essentially free from all imperfections whatsoever and comprises within Itself all auspicious qualities.'[56]

From all this Rāmānuja concludes that there is no proof anywhere of a substance devoid of all differences. Or, stated positively, the only Real revealed by the means of knowledge is one characterised by differences. This conclusion is so important for Rāmānuja that he erects his entire philosophy on its foundation.

Reality not pure consciousness

Rāmānuja now proceeds to refute the second part of the advaitic thesis, viz., the Ultimate Reality, which is pure undifferentiated being, is identical with pure consciousness.[57] He argues that since everything experienced is found to display differences within itself, and since all proofs rest on experience, the advaitin cannot prove his undifferentiated pure consciousness to be real. 'Consciousness is either proved or not. If it is proved, it follows that it possesses attributes; if it is not, it is something absolutely nugatory, like a skyflower, and similar purely imaginary things.'

Rāmānuja further argues that the advaitin himself predicates certain attributes such as eternity, oneness and self-luminousness to

Brahman, so that even on his hypothesis Brahman is not pure attributeless consciousness. Nor can he argue against this that all these attributes are in reality mere consciousness, for they are essentially distinct. Even if it is said that these qualities are not positive attributes existing within the nature of consciousness, but merely indicate absence in consciousness of qualities opposed to them, and hence are to be described as negative attributes of consciousness, that they do qualify the nature of consciousness, and hence are attributes, is proved by the fact that otherwise it would be possible to ascribe non-eternity, non-oneness and the like to consciousness.'[58]

Reality cannot be impersonal

Thus controverting advaitic thesis of regarding Brahman as attributeless pure consciousness, Rāmānuja now attempts to prove that Brahman must be regarded as a self or person. The advaitin equates consciousness with Brahman. But Rāmānuja argues that consciousness, regarded as a proof in itself by the advaitin, must be a proof of something to some one; that is, it inevitably presupposes a self on the one hand and objects on the other. And if it thus presupposes a self to which it belongs, it is clear that it is this self which is the agent in consciousness and not consciousness itself. That is why we say 'I experience' (anubhavāmyaham). The essential character of consciousness is that by its very existence it renders things capable of being objects. That such is the essential nature of consciousness the advaitin himself admits, for he proves thereby the self-luminosity of the consciousness which thus clearly presents itself as the attribute of an agent.

That consciousness is an activity of the self is further established from the fact that it consists of momentary mental states which require a permanent self as their substrate and relating principle. From the fact of recognition we further clearly see that this agent is permanent while its attribute, i.e., consciousness, changes.

Moreover, the grammarians tell us that words such as consciousness are relative. We cannot use the expression 'He knows' without reference to an object known and the subject who knows.[59]

From the foregoing examination and refutation of the fundamental advaitic position Rāmānuja concludes that Brahman, the highest Reality, is not a pure substance destitute of all qualities, or a consciousness void of attributes. His analysis of the nature of consciousness further leads him to the conclusion that consciousness presupposes a conscious self and is different from it. Brahman, to whom consciousness is predicated, cannot be mere non-differentiated consciousness, but must be a self characterised by consciousness.

Rāmānuja's view

Rāmānuja describes Brahman as the highest Person, charac terised by an infinite number of excellent qualities, and piles adjectives on adjectives describing the divine attributes. He defines Brahman as 'that highest Person who is the ruler of all, whose nature is antagonistic to all evil, whose purposes come true, who possesses infinite auspicious qualities such as knowledge, blessedness and so on; who is omniscient, omnipotent, supremely merciful, from whom creation, subsistence and reabsorption of this world proceed.'[60] Or, 'The sole cause of the evolution, maintenance, dissolution and release from Samsāra, of the world of sentient and non-sentient entities, of a nature different from all things other than Himself, on account of being opposed to all evil. and being one with infinite auspiciousness, of hosts of lovely qualities, boundless and unsurpassable, who is known in the entire Veda under the various designations of soul of all,[61] the Supreme Brahma[62] Supreme Glory,[63] Supreme Principle,[64] Supreme Spirit,[65] Real Being[66] etc., all of which denote the Venerable Lord Nārāyaṇa, the Supreme Person. The śrutis are meant to set forth His manifestation, so they expound the universal dominion of the Supreme Spirit as the inner Soul of the totality of spiritual and non-spiritual entities by expressions like His power,[67] His portion,[68] His manifestation,[69] His form,[70] His body,[71] His shape,[72] etc. by sāmānādhikaraṇya constructions.[73] Notable in this connection is his introduction to the Gītā Bhāṣya. All his works abound with such descriptions.

According to Rāmānuja Brahman is metaphysically the ground of all existences, religiously their final refuge, morally their inner controller and aesthetically the beauty and bliss inhering in them. He is the 'whole' of metaphysics, the 'Holy' of religion, and the 'Abode' of all ethical and aesthetic values. That He is 'All' is described variously by Rāmānuja in the Gītā Bhāṣya as follows. 'He is the End to be attained, the Supporter, the Ruler, the immediate Witness, the Abode, the spiritual Resort, the well-wishing Friend. He is the place of origination and annihilation of whatever and whenever. He is all that can be begotten and destroyed. He is the imperishable Cause of all that'.[74]

(ii) Various attributes of Brahman

Time and again Rāmānuja emphatically writes that Brahman is a treasury of numberless qualities such as brilliance, beauty, comeliness, youthfulness, compassion, generosity, goodness, love etc. which are in accordance with His pleasure and will, and which are unimaginable, miraculous, impecable and incomparable. The traditional attributes like satyam, jñānam, anantam, ānandam etc., are also dealt with. Along with these, on the authority of the Viṣṇu Purāṇa, he mentions six other attributes of Brahman viz., jñāna, bala, aiśvarya, vīrya, śakti and tejas—which are characteristically ascribed to Lord Nārāyaṇa in the Pāñcarātra school. Rāmānuja simply enumerates these attributes and does not explain their meaning and mutual relation. Though these attributes are essentially pāñcarātric, they are employed in the Viṣṇu Puārṇa, and Rāmānuja took them from there only.[75]

Rāmānuja dwells lovingly on two attributes of Brahman as the Redeemer. They are saulabhya (easy accessibility) and sauśīlya (graciousness). The Redeemer is so condescending to His beloved devotee that He says in the Gītā, 'I reckon that when to a loving devottee I deliver my own self entirely, even that is no sufficient compensation for the love he has borne for me. I reckon, too, that even when I have given my own self to him I have done little or nothing for him.'[76] Elsewhere He declares that 'As for the jñānī I deem him as my very self.'[77]

Besides ascribing numerous attributes to the Lord, Rāmānuja is quite emphatic in maintaining that He is devoid of all evil qualities. In the Upaniṣads not only innumerable metaphysical, moral and religious attributes are ascribed to the Supreme Being, but He is also proclaimed to be free from evil.[78]

Rāmānuja frequently uses the words 'niravadya' nirvikāra' and the like to denote God's absolute freedom from all imperfection. Another equivalent expression more frequently used by him is 'samasta heya guṇa pratyanīka'. That God is full of all imaginable auspicious attributes and devoid of all evil is derived by him from the positive and negative passages of the Upaniṣads.

This ascription of a plurality of attributes to God does not make Him plural. All these attributes are co-ordinative and not contradictory. While each attribute by itself is different from the other, all the attributes belong to one single substratum, and do not divide its integrity, That is to say, they are different facets of the same Reality. Rāmānuja explains this by the law of coordination.[79]

Form and body of Brahman

Unlike the advaitin, Rāmānuja lays stress upon the concrete nature of Brahman, implying a synthesis of attributes, which lends to Him a character and personality. The advaitin denies character and personality to Brahman, who is for him mere identity. Rāmānuja disagrees with the advaitin on this point. To him Brahman is both a principle and a person. He has a personality of His own. He alone is a perfect personality. He possesses an infinite number of exalted auspicious attributes and analogously a divine form of supreme excellence suitable to His nature, peculiar to Himself, not made of the stuff of Prakṛti, nor due to Karma. His form is altogether different from all entities other than Himself.

Rāmānuja writes that just as on the authority of the scriptures he has maintained that Brahman has excellent attributes, similarly on the same authority he holds that He has a form. The scriptures deny only the Prākṛta attributes and form, but proclaim that He has aprākṛta attributes and form.[80] He writes that the Sūtrakāra has also declared that Brahman has a form.[81] Further he quotes Ṭanka and Dramiḍa who hold that Brahman possesses a supra-sensible body, not made of māyā or prakṛti, and that it is not artificial.[82] It should be made clear here tbat for whatever attributes he enumerates and for whatever discription of divine form and weapons he gives, he intensively quotes from the Vedic

Samhitās, Āraṇyakas, Upaniṣads, Rāmāyaṇa and Viṣṇu Purāṇa and therefore all this is purely Vedic and should not be traced to non-Vedic sources.

Regarding the form of Brahman he writes, 'The Highest Brahman possesses an infinite number of qualities of unimaginable excellence, and analogously a divine form suitable to His nature and intentions. i.e., adorned with infinite supremely excellent and wonderful qualities, splendour, beauty, fragrance, tenderness, loveliness, youthfulness, and so on. And in order to satisfy His devotees He individualises that form so as to render it suitable to their apprehension.[83] In the Vedārtha Saṃgraha he writes, 'There are thousands of śrutis that declare that this Supreme Brahman Nārāyaṇa has a proper form of undefinable knowledge and beatitude in the purest state...... He possesses an invariable divine form that is in accordance with His pleasure and in harmony with Himself......'[84] In a similar language he writes at other places also.[85]

In the metaphysics of Rāmānuja we have another description of the body of Brahman, which is quite irreconcilable with this vividly anthropomorphic description. He defines body as, 'Any substance which a sentient soul is capable of completely controlling and supporting for its own purposes, and which stands to the soul in an entirely subordinate relation. The world is body of the Supreme Person, for it is completely controlled and supported by Him for His own ends, and it is absolutely subordinate to Him.[86]

This concept of 'world-body' of Brahman logically follows from the organicismic ontological position of Rāmānuja, which we have discussed earlier. It is named by him as 'Śarīra-śarīrī-bhāva'. This concept is fully in the fitness of his metaphysics and raison de'tre of his philosophy. He has borrowed it from the Antaryāmī Brāhmaṇa of the Bṛhadāraṇyaka Upaniṣad which says, 'He who dwells in the self and within the self, whom the self does not know, of whom the self is the body, who rules the self from within, He is thyself, the Ruler within, the Immortal.'

Abode, Consorts and entourage of Brahman

Along with the form of Brahman Rāmānuja dwells upon the abode of Brahman. He writes that Brahman has a divine residence, the proper form and nature of which are beyond the ken of thought and the power of expression.[87] This divine residence is not made of the stuff of Prakṛti.[88] But this does not mean that Rāmānuja has advocated the idea that the divine residence is made of Śuddha Sattva, a peculiar spiritual matter, as some writers have misrepresented him.[89]

Rāmānuja further writes that Brahman has an infinite entourage of attendents and necessaries, suitable to Him. There is a class of beings perfect in knowledge, eternally free, who serve Him.[90]

Brahman is further said to have a consort Śrī, who suits His pleasure and who is in harmony with His possessing an immeasurable eminence of proper form, qualities, supernal power, ascendency and character ; and who is held dear by the Lord because of her boundless, perfect and numberless beautiful virtues such as faithfulness and the like.[91]

In this way Rāmānuja describes the form, attributes, ornaments, weapons, abode, consort, entourage etc., of Brahman in a paurāṇic way, which absolutely fall apart from his metaphysical set up.

Incarnation of Brahman

Lastly, Rāmānuja deals with the incarnations of Brahman. Dr. Radhakrishnan remarks that 'Rāmānuja's God is not an impassive absolute who looks down upon us from the height of heaven, but joins us in the experiences of our life, shares our ends, and works for the upbuilding of the world'.[92] God of Rāmānuja is not an Absolute who is rigid, motionless, totally lacking in initiative or influence, who cannot comfort in stress and suffering when weak and erring human beings call from the depths, and who does not extend His helping hand but remains indifferent to the fear and love of his worshipper. He is a God of grace and favour, love and kindness, who is always at the disposal of His devotees, and who descends from the supernatural to the natural order in order to gratify His ardent devotees.

The idea of the descent of God in the form of incarnation is by no means alien to the character of Viṣṇu who from the Vedic times is recognised as the God of grace, favour and help. There are glimmerings of the doctrine of incarnation even in the earliest Vedic literature. The Yajurveda clearly declares that 'the One unborn takes manifold births'.[93] The unique contribution of the Gītā lies in clothing the Absolute of the monistic philosophers with flesh and blood, and in illustrating that the all pervading unknowable Supreme indeed appears in a human form, speaks through human tongue and is concerned about human affairs. About the Gītā Prof. Kumarappa has rightly remarked that the revolution in the thought of the Divine can hardly be more complete.[94]

On the authority of the above scriptures Rāmānuja accepts and advocates the view that God incarnates Himself in the world. He writes that God in His infinite mercy 'assumed various forms without putting away His own essential God-like nature.'[95] 'In order to fit Himself to be a refuge for gods, men etc., the Supreme Person, without, however, putting aside His true nature, associates Himself with the shape, make, qualities and works of the different classes of beings, and thus is born in many ways.'[96] 'Never divesting myself of my essential attributes of suzerainty, that of being birthless, of being exhaustless, or being the Lord of all, etc., I go into birth...'[97] These incarnations of God 'are not special combinations of earth and the other elements.'[98] On the authority of the Viṣṇu Purāṇa Rāmānuja holds that along with Viṣṇu Lakṣmī also descends on the earth. They are ontologically one, but appear as two.'[99]

The motive behind incarnation is to uphold righteousness[100] and to be accessible to His devotees.[101] In this way in Rāmānuja's view the Infinite crystalises as finite, the Unborn becomes born, the Immortal works as mortal, all through the urge of love and surge of grace.

Pāñcarātra view of Reality—transcendental aspect

The Supreme Being, which was conceived of philosophically in the Upaniṣads, came to be thought of in religious terms in the Purāṇas. The same sort of transformation we witness in the Pāñcarātra school as well. The description of the nature of Reality in Its transcendental aspect, and the qualities predicated to It are essentially the same as those given in the Upaniṣads, a fact which suggests that here an intensely ardent religion seeks to find support in the speculations of the Upaniṣadic sages.

The Reality in its transcendental aspect is named as Parama Brahma, a term which recalls the nirguṇa upaniṣadic Brahman. Brahman is described as originally unmanifest and impersonal, but assuming a personal form.[102] In Its original nature]It is beginningless and endless, eternal and immutable, and cannot be designated either as existent or as non-existent.[103] It is timeless,[104] nameless,[105] and beyond past, present and future. It is neither before nor behind, neither below nor above, neither short nor long, neither gross nor atomic.[106] It is beyond all dualities, unique, unparallel, supreme and highest. It cannot be given any simile, and cannot be referred to as 'is'.[107] It is all-tranquil, unchanging, unpolluted, eternal, static, non-active and unruffled like a waveless sea.[108] It is self-existent and the support of all other things.[109]

Its essence is pure consciousness and pure bliss. It is devoid of all that is evil and the abode of all that is good and blissful. It is beyond all prākṛta guṇas and yet is hidden by guṇas (guṇaguhya.)[110] More often It is referred to as 'nirguṇa' and 'nirguṇātmakaḥ.'[111]

(ii) *Immanent aspect*

The Parama Brahma, who is described as 'wholly other' in the transcendental aspect, is regarded in Its immanent aspect as somehow associated with a creative power which is spoken of figuratively as Its consort Lakṣmī. She is not merely a consort of Brahman, but also a philosophical principle. In the Pāñcarātra School Brahman is not at all concerned with the creation etc. of the world. Lakṣmī practically usurps Its place in this respect. In her two aspects kriyā and bhūti—she is the material as well as the efficient cause of the world.[112]

With the association of Lakṣmī (who is said to be lying dormant in Brahman before the start of creation), Brahman passes from Its undifferentiated to differentiated form. This is called 'guṇonmeṣadaśā' wherein It gets characterised by six guṇas, viz., jñāna, aiśvarya, śakti, bala, vīrya and tejas. In this immanent aspect Brahman is referred to as 'para' or sometimes as Vāsudeva. It should be noted here that these guṇas are not associated with and hence do not in any way affect the 'being' or essence of Brahman, because they are merely concerned with Its 'becoming' or manifestation.[113]

Manifestations of Brahman in Its immanent aspect

The central dogma of the Pāñcarātra religion is that the Supreme Being manifests Itself in five-fold forms, viz., Para, Vyūha, Vibhava, Antaryāmin and Arcā.[114] Schrader suggests that this dogma is an attempt to interpret philosophically the Pāñcarātra sattra of Puruṣa Nārāyaṇa spoken of in the Śatapatha Brāhmaṇa (III.6.1).[115] It, however, seems to be an attempt to bring the supreme transcendent One into living and loving touch with the mundane world.

Para manifestation

The para form is sometimes described as the first immanent manifestation of the Supreme Being. But sometimes it is said to have sprung from a still higher, the very first form of God.[116]

This first form is referred to as 'the best of the Puruṣas' and 'the Highest Light', seen by the Brāhmaṇas in meditation.[117] This form is immanent only and should not be confused with the supreme transcendent One (perhaps this is the form which is in association with Lakṣmī, and is named as Lakṣmīnārāyaṇa or Vāsudeva). This is clear when it is said that this form has originated from that 'which has all forms and no forms, Brahman without beginning, middle or end'.

God as Para is sometimes identified with and sometimes distinguished from Vyūha Vāsudeva. When the two are distinguished the Vyūha Vāsudeva is said to have sprung from the Para Vāsudeva.[118] The Padma Tantra describes the Para Vāsudeva as dividing himself 'for some reason' and becoming with one half the Vyūha Vāsudeva and with the other Nārāyaṇa, the creator of the primeval waters. The Para is adorned with nine chief ornaments and weapons which symbolically represent the principles of the universe.[119]

Vyūha manifestation

The apparition of guṇas in Lakṣmī and Nārāyaṇa denotes the beginning of the process of Vyūha or emanation. Vāsudeva characterised by the six guṇas, is sometimes called the first Vyūha. From Vāsudeva emanates Saṃkarṣaṇa in whom jñāna and bala alone get manifested. From Saṃkarṣaṇa comes Pradyumna to whom belong aiśvarya and vīrya. From Pradyumna emanates Aniruddha to whom śakti and tejas appertain. This, however, does not mean that each Vyūha has only two guṇas, but each Vyūha is Vāsudeva himself with his six guṇas, of which, however, only two in each case become manifest.[120] In the Lakṣmī Tantra all these Vyūhas are said to proceed from Lakṣmī.[121] The Vihagendra Saṃhitā, however, maintains that they come from Vāsudeva.[122]

As we have seen, the Pāñcarātra thinkers are very much particular in safeguarding and preserving the purity and unchanged nature of the transcendent Supreme Being. From that point of view, the chief merit, and hence the primary significance of Vyūha doctrine, is that it is such a process of emanation in which the Supreme Being remains unaffected and unchanged in Its five-fold manifestations.

Avatāra manifestation

Closely connected with the doctrine of Vyūhas, is the next manifestation, named as Vibhava (manifestation) or Avatāra (descent). The only Supreme Being the Pāñcarātra philosophers know about is the transcedent One, who is not in any way directly related to the world. Therefore, they explicitly describe the avatāras either all springing from Aniruddha[123] or some from Vāsudeva and the rest from the other three Vyūhas.[124] One should not be mistaken here in assuming that the Supreme Being Itself takes avatāra. This is a Paurāṇic conception. The Pāñcarātra school no where maintains that the Supreme Being, laying aside Its transcendent, static nature assumes these finite forms. This is unpermissible by the premises of the system. The Supreme Being is merely a spectator, with an attitude of passivity and indifference. It cherishes no regard and love for the mundane world, and it is beyond Its nature to do so.[125]

Antaryāmin manifestation

The fourth manifestation is the Antaryāmin avatāra, which is Aniruddha as the 'Inner Ruler' of all souls.[126] It is a mysterious power seated in the 'lotus of the heart'. Here again it should be noted that this is not a manifestation of the Supreme Being but only of Aniruddha.

Arcā manifestation

The Pāñcarātra Samhitās, finally recognise the arcā manifestation of God. An inanimate object (i.e. image of Visnu), if duly consecrated according to the Pāñcarātra rites, acquires a miraculous power and the Śakti of Viṣṇu descends into it. It is meant for the purpose of daily worship.[127]

This arcā worship is different from the Pratika worship. In the latter the symbol is the locus, on which a devotee concentrates his thoughts. But no sooner the thought is centralised, the locus gets out of his vision and no necessity thereof is felt. But in the arcā worship, on the other hand, the devotee feels the very presence of God in it. And as such the inanimate image, soon acquires a new meaning, becomes the object of love, of heart's hankering and of eyes' rest. This we find in the religion of the Āḷvāṛs as well.

Āḷvārs' view on nature of God

The concept of God in the works of Āḷvārs bears an explicit religious influence. The predominant thought of the Āḷvārs regarding the nature of the Supreme Being is essentially religious. Though they tacitly recognise the existence of an unknown, transcendent, all-pervading Absolute, yet their main concern is only with that aspect of the Deity which is revealed in the world to the devotees. So much they busy themselves in dwelling upon God of grace, love and benevolence that they even forget the reality of the transcendent One. The Deity they describe is one who is endearing to His devotees and who takes personal interest in their welfare.

Regarding the nature of the Deity Nāmmāḷvār declares in the upaniṣadic fashion that 'He has a form; He has no form.'[128] 'He has neither beginning nor end.'[129] 'He is the highest goal of virtue and is higher than the Highest'.[130] 'Lord's nature is very deep. It is very wide and very high, and it is very sweet and it is above material existence.'[131] 'He is perfect goodness......His nature is to give wisdom and to be blissful'.[132]

Attributes of God

Like the Pāñcarātra school the Āḷvārs also attribute six guṇas to the Lord. 'In Him wisdom, strength, power, lordship, energy and splendour attain their perfection. He has innumerable good qualities.'[133]

But more than all these personal qualities, what the Āḷvārs emphasise and appreciate is the loving and gracious nature of the Deity who showers His mercy and grace even to the most down-trodden and degraded. 'To be condescending is His nature'[134] 'My Lord is of such nature that any man of any knowledge can understand that my Lord is very condescending'[135]. 'He is the Lord who does not cast out the undeserving nor does He take up only the deserving.[136] This thought that the Deity does not reject the undeserving fills the heart of the Āḷvār with infinite joy and he cries out, 'My tongue sings to me divine songs. My body dances as if it is possessed by a Deity, worships the Lord, and reverts to Him. The angels and the gods discuss about His nature and reel as if their brains were deranged. He does not take a few deserving only. He does not leave the undeserving. He is not vexed with sinners nor does He love the good only. He is unseconded nectar to those who join and love Him.'[137]

God in Arcā form

The Āḷvārs are particularly fascinated by the Lord's manifestation in arcā form. They are deeply touched by His infinite mercy in making Himself easily accessible to men in this form. They feel His immediate presence in the shrines and are moved to tears in the contemplation of His attributes. They regard the shrine at 'Śrī Rangam' as the most important and worthy shrine of the Deity. Tondarādippoḍi, for example, exclaims 'Is not Rangam the glorious shrine of Him !'[138]

The Āḷvārs are the devoted bhaktas who dress and adorn the images of God, who love to dwell on His infinite perfections, on the beautiful shapes He assumes, on the radiance of His countenance, on the brilliance of His ornaments and on the splendour of His form.

The Āḷvārs are very much enchanted by the bewitching beauty of the Lord and express their rapturous passion and ardent longings. They also experience the reciprocation of love on the part of the Lord, who is described as being infatuated with the beauty and charms of the beloved, the Āḷvār. Ṇammāḷvār, for example, writes that God is constantly trying to woo His devotees to love Him.[139]

Incarnations of God

The Aḷvārs dwell with love not only on the Deity as incarnate in images, but also as incarnate in individuals. They deal with great devotion with the various stories connected with Viṣṇu and His avatāras and also with the great acts of helpfulness done by Him. We shall deal with this aspect of the Deity in the chapter on 'Means of emancipation'.

The Deity, thus, according to the Āḷvārs, is above all gracious, and though in His transcendent form He is beyond human conception, He has manifested Himself in incarnate form, e.g. as Rāma and more especially as the heart entrancing Kṛṣṇa. In times past, as Viṣṇu, He came in diverse finite forms to help those who cried to Him in trouble. In His infinite mercy He exists in images, delighting the hearts of men and receiving their worship. What He desires from His devotees is their whole-hearted devotion, expressing itself in loving worship at the shrine uttering His name, meditating on His acts of grace etc. He Himself aids them in this by His grace, however ignorant, morally depraved, down-trodden or unworthy they may be, and entering into their hearts He wipes out their sin and ignorance, and making them morally pure He takes them to Himself.

The Āḷvārs have not dealt with the five-fold manifestations of the Deity, because their main concern was with the all-absorbing devotion for the Deity. Among all the Āḷvārs only Tirumalsai in the 'Tirucchandavirutum' mentions this Pāñcarātra doctrine.

Appraisal of Advaita :

Having given an account of the concept of Reality according to the Advaita school, Rāmānuja, Pāñcarātra school, and the Āḷvārs, we may now proceed to assess their comparative merits.

To start with the advaita school and Rāmānuja, both teach advaita, i.e., the view that there exists only one all-embracing being. But while the advaitin's advaita is a rigorous and absolute one (kevalādvait a), the advaita of Rāmānuja is qualified (viśiṣṭādvaita).

According to the advaitin whatever is, is Brahman. Brahman is absolutely homogeneous, so that all differences and plurality must be ultimately nòtreal. According to Rāmānuja also, whatever is, is Brahman, but Brahman is not of a homogeneous nature. On the contrary, it contains within Itself elements of plurality, owing to which It truly manifests Itself in a diversified world. The Brahman of the advaitin is in Itself impersonal, a homogeneous mass of pure consciousness, transcending all attributes ; a personal God It becomes only through Its association with the principle of māyā which is not real, so that, strictly speaking, advaitin's personal God is something which is not real. Rāmānuja's Brahman, on the other hand, is essentially a personal God, the omniscient and omnipotent Ruler of a real world. There is, thus, no room in his philospohy for the distinction between Para and Apara, Nirguṇa and Saguṇa, Indeterminate and Determinate, Intuitional Highest and Logical Highest etc.

The advaitin draws a distinction between transcendent Reality and empirical Reality. He lays supreme emphasis on the transcendental aspect and throws away the empirical as philosophically unsubstantial, though it has a value for exoteric purposes. The transcendent one is the Absolute which is uncognisable. The moment we try to make this ultimate Subject an object of consciousness, we miss Its essential nature. Then no longer does It remain unconditioned, but becomes conditioned as it were. This we call Iśvara or God who is the conditioned aspect of the unconditioned Brahman which alone is real. God, thus, is the highest appearance that we have.[140] Such a personal God has meaning only for the practical religious consciousness and not for the highest philosophical insight.

In this respect the position of the advaitin can be compared with that of Bradley when he writes, 'For me the Absolute is not God. God for me has no meaning outside the religious consciousness, and that essentially is practical. The Absolute for me cannot be God, because in the end the Absolute is related to nothing, and there cannot be a practical relation between It and the finite will. When you begin to worship the Absolute, or the universe and make It the object of religion, you in that moment have transformed It.'[141] 'A personal God is not the ultimate truth about the universe'. 'The

Highest Reality, so far as I see, must be super-personal.'[142] 'If you identify the Absolute with God, that is not the God of religion. If you separate them, God becomes a finite factor in the whole........ short of the Absolute, God cannot rest, and having reached that goal, He is lost and religion with Him ....we may say that God is not God till He has become all in all, and that a God which is all in all is not the God of religion. God is but an aspect, and that must mean an appearance of the Absolute'.[143]

Like Bradley the advaitin points out a contradiction in religious consciousness. If we regard God's nature as perfect, it cannot be so, as long as man's imperfect nature stands over against it; if it is not perfect, then it is not the nature of God.

The advaitin denies self-revelation to Brahman. The Absolute is timeless and has in Itself no history or progress. Bradley also holds the same view. For him 'nothing perfect, nothing genuinely real can move. The Absolute has no seasons, but all at once bears Its leaves, fruits, and blossoms.[144] The Advaitin feels that it is only the personal God who can reveal Himself. The demand for a Godhead is a demand of practical reason, but the satisfaction of such a demand is a descent in māyā. Accordingly all impulses and feelings of religion, however lofty and noble, are relegated to the lower plane of empirical consciousness. and have no place in the transcendental consciousness.

In spite of the marvellous subtlity, great speculative daring, austere intelligence and remorseless logic of Śankara,[145] the foremost advaitin, it is not possible either for philosophy or religion to rest satisfied with the unpleasant position he has arrived at. He posits a God of religion who has no reality of His own, who has no ultimate existence, who in the end is to be vanished in the Absolute and whose omniscience is in a way an ignorance at a cosmic scale.[146] It is a God who is beset with inner contradictions and who is merely a false projection of the empirical mind. Śankara, as it has been said, gives us an Absolute, 'rigid and motionless' staring at us with frozen eyes regardless of our selfless devotion and silent suffering. It is like 'a bloodless Absolute dark with the excess of light', 'a blank which has every perfection except one small defect of being dead'.[147]

There surely cannot be this incurable contradiction between the higher religion and the higher philosophy. Both are but the theoretical and practical aspects of one and the same attempt at realising the highest end of life, and therefore the Absolute of philosophy and the God of religion cannot be different. Our religious as well as intellectual needs must ultimately find their satisfaction at one and the same source. Religion cannot be content with worshipping a Supreme Being who is discovered not to be supreme at all, but to be an appearance of a more ultimate Being. The truth of religion cannot be essentially different from the truth of philosophy. Truth is one and indivisible. Whatever is true in religion cannot be false in philosophy and vice-versa. We cannot bifurcate it into two, otherwise it would be like a house divided against itself which cannot stand. As a matter of fact in their ultimate interpretation the two must converge into one.

The other difficulty with the advaita system, which is pointed out by Deussen, is 'How does Brahman become joined with avidyā ?' In reality (paramārthataḥ) there is nothing else besides Brahman. If we imagine, we perceive a transformation (vikāra) of It into the world, a division of It into a plurality of individual souls, this depends on avidyā. But how does this happen ? How do we manage to decieve ourselves into seeing transformation and a plurality, where in reality Brahman alone is ?'[148]

Lastly, we are faced with the problem of the ontological status of the God of religion. Does He really exist anywhere in the universe? If so, has He a being for Himself as well as an appearance for us ? The advaitin holds that He is the Lord of māyā and is more real than any other finite being, yet He is regarded to be a product of māyā—product because He is conceived under the association of māyā—something unsubstantial which may at any moment be withdrawn into or lost in the Absolute. The advaitin points out the fundamental inconsistency of religion and of other forms of human consciousness, but in an effort to remove this inconsistency he leaves us with an unbridgable chasm at the summit of things, and gives us in turn an empty, abstract and inscrutable Absolute which has no content continuous with anything we can identify in human experience, which has no history, no life, no movement, which has no quality that we can know except that of barren self-consistency.

Here an admirer of Śankara may say, 'Again to say that Śankara has no place for religious feeling is, to say the least, to make a mischieveous statement. It is to miss the depth of his soul-inspiring hymns-a great and rich contribution to Sanskrit poetry-in which the words almost burst forth due to the pressure of intense emotional devotion with which they are packed.'[149] To this we reply that we are well aware of those sublime and lofty elements, but Śankara gives us those richer and more positive results only when his insight breaks through the limits of his own logic. His thought is more satisfying when he surpasses the formal limitations of his monistic logic and follows the higher intuitions. Reality is too rich and complex to be imprisoned within the narrow walls of monistic logic, and consequently the solution that he offers on its basis is too concise and meagre to do justice to all the facts.

It will not be irrelevant to end this review of the advaitic concept of Brahman with a consideration of the question as to whether Bādarāyaṇa's Brahma-sūtras afford any evidence for this sort of two-fold distinction of Brahman into lower and higher. In the very first sūtra Bādarāyaṇa declares that the task of the work is an enquiry into the nature of Brahman. The second sūtra defines Brahman as that 'whence the origination and so on of this world proceed.' Śankara in his Bhāṣya maintains that this definition pertains to lower Brahman only, who is associated with māyā. If Śankara's interpretation were true, it is quite startling that at the very outset Bādarāyaṇa should have given a definition of that Brahman which is not real and which is of a lower order only. If the object of the text is to know the natuıe of Brahman, it is quite improbable that the Sūtrakāra should start with a definition of lower Brahman only, whose knowledge accrues no permanent benefit. In the Upaniṣads also Brahman is sometimes described as personal and sometimes as impersonal, but it is nowhere said that thereon rests a distinction of two-fold Brahman.

Appraisal of Rāmānuja's view

Let us now turn ʈo Rāmānuja. Rāmānuja's Absolute has been called a concrete individual, an identity in and through difference, or an identity impregnated with differences. It is like the Absolute of Hegel or the personal God of Pringle-Pettison. Rāmānuja identifies God with the Absolute. God is a concrete whole of which matter and souls form the body. He is the concrete unity which consists of the inter-related and interdependent subordinate elements which are called 'viśeṣaṇas'. God, further, is an individual, a person with a divine body and a divine abode. He is in need of the universe which is a necessary phase of His self-realisation. In this respect Rāmānuja seems to be similar to Hegel who treats the universe as an eternal differentiation of the all-inclusive Absolute. Like Rāmānuja Hegel also identifies Absolute and God. Philosophy is to him the rational explanation of the true content of religious faith and the only difference between the Absolute and God is that the former is Ultimate Reality interpreted in terms of pure thought, whereas the latter is the same Reality represented in terms of imagination and èmotion. But in Hegel we find another line of thought in which he reduces everything finite into something illusory. And here he completely breaks away from Rāmānuja.

It is truly remarked about Rāmānuja that he has given us 'the best type of monotheism conceivable.'[150] No one can deny the greatness of his philosophy, specially his concept of God as an organic whole which does not deny its parts but harmonises them in its own being, though it transcends them. In Rāmānuja we find a sincere attempt to reconcile the demands of the religious feeling with the claims of logical thinking. 'Much more remarkable is the deep earnestness and hard logic with which he conceived the problem and laboured to bridge the yawning gulf between the apparently conflicting claims of religion and philosophy'.[151] His religious feeling seizes on the concrete idea of God as a person and his philosophic spirit enables him to conceive the finite things and beings as moments in the life of God.

In spite of the sincere attempt of Rāmānuja to reconcile the truth of philosophy and the truth of religion, the personal and the impersonal aspects of God, we some time find his mind oscillating between personal and anthropomorphic concepts of God. This becomes clear from his two different irreconcilable descriptions of the body of God. So long as he regards matter and souls as body of God, he is true to his basic ontological standpoint, and merits our appreciation. But when he starts giving the account of the anthropomorphic body, form, abode, consorts, retinue etc. of God we feel perplexed. Such an attempt is certainly a concession to the figurative and mythological tendency and to the habit of the religious consciousness to embody its description of God in an anthropomorphic way. In this adulteration of anthropomorphism in the metaphysical truth Rāmānuja loses the severity of his metaphysical contemplation and gives vent to mythological fancy.

To call God a person is not a sign of anthropomorphism. God is a person not in the sense of having a physical body, but in the sense that He is a self-existent and self-conscious Being having perfect freedom of will. He is also person in the sense that He is love-incarnate. As Royce has put it, 'The divine love is not a thing of God, it is God Himself'.[152] McTaggart writes, 'It is in love and in nothing else that we find not only the Supreme value of life, but also the supreme reality of life and indeed of the universe.'[153]

So there is nothing wrong in interpreting Brahman as personal and determinate, but to do so on the basis of superstition and a very wide extrapolation of the constitution of human being is quite irrelevant to and out of place in his metaphysics. Sentimental expressions like these fall short of the highest expressions of truth. Śankara is rightly criticised for elevating Absolute to such a height from which there is no path to lead down to the low lands of humanity. But against Rāmānuja also it must be said that his facinating description of the body etc. of God based on some scriptural sayings and on arbitrary fancy incapable of verification, carries no conviction, and gives rise to a genuine doubt as to whether there is a corresponding reality. Here a question demands our attention. Does the ontological position of Rāmānuja justify these anthropomorphic accretions based on popular imagination and figurative consciousness ? One must frankly admit that such sentimental expressions are quite superfluous and unwarranted in his ontological set up. We appreciate his attempt to reconcile the demands of religious feeling with the claims of logical thinking, but to subdue intellectual penetration before mythological fancy is quite deplorable. He should have kept himself aloof from narrow orthodoxy and sentimentalism and should have exercised discriminative faculty proper to a true philosopher. It is true that a thinker who is reaching forward to a larger conception of truth should not break entirely from the common beliefs of his age, but this does not mean that he should justify all forms of superstitions which become associated with religion. It is certainly expected of him not to incorporate them in their crudest form. His attitude should be sympathetic and critical. He may not attack old dogmas violently and thereby injure popular hearts, but he can quietly reject them suggesting something more reasonable which is at the same time more spiritual too.

In this respect we appreciate Śankara's repugnance to all anthropomorphism. He could successfully refuse to lower down his philosophical standards to accommodate common mythological feelings.

However, this much must be said in favour of Rāmānuja that his views are based on Vedic scriptures. The fault of Rāmānuja lies in his blind acceptance of these texts literally on the authority of the Bhāṣyakāra who maintains that 'yathā bhūtavādi hi śāstram', i.e., scriptures assert things so as they are. On the basis of this fact J.A.B. Van Buitenen has tried to defend Rāmānuja against the criticism of Dr. Radhakrishnan.[154] He writes that other worldly stories never sound convincing to unbelieving ears. These descriptions of Rāmānuja are based on scriptures and their validity depends on faith and not on proof. He argues that if these texts, the authority of which is the very foundation of orthodox metaphysical thought, happen to speak about the golden splendour of God, about the supreme immaterial heaven, about angelic beings eternally absorbed in the contemplation of God's essence, and if Rāmānuja accepts them in their literal sense, he should not be made responsible for that.[155] We do not agree with Buitenen in this defence of Rāmānuja. As regards the contents of these descriptions we cannot throw any blame on Rāmānuja nevertheless we cannot give him a clean chit with regard to his accepting and borrowing these descriptions uncritically on the basis of blind faith.

Rāmānuja and Pāñcarātra school - a study in contrast

It has been generally maintained by many scholars that Rāmānuja's concept of God is very much influenced by the Pāñcarātra view, and that he has made a bold attempt to give a Vedāntic basis to the non-vedic Pāñcarātra theology. We, therefore, propose to see how far this contention is true and justified.[156]

The Pāñcarātra thinkers, like the advaitin, tend to make a distinction between the Absolute of philosophy and God of Religion. Originally there is only one Supreme Reality which is unambiguously declared to be nirguṇa etc. It has been ascribed almost all those negative epithets with which the Upaniṣads describe the Ultimate Reality. This Impersonal Brahman, One and the only Reality, appears as personal God due to māyā or śakti. In the Nārāyaṇīya the personal form is said to be assumed only for the purpose of devotion and worship. This means the personal form has meaning and value for the purposes of worship only, and is ultimately not-real. In the Samhitās Brahman is said to have appeared as personal, due to Its Śakti, for the purpose of creation, but this personal God is, in all respects, less than the Absolute. Because after all it is not the whole, but a mere aspect, and therefore mere appearance, so that He and with Him religion, must suffer the transforming plunge into the Ultimate. This conclusion seems to be quite inevitable in the Pāñcarātra philosophy. After declaring God of religion (i.e. Vāsudeva) as a later appearance and hence a reality of lower order, the Pāñcarātra school has no choice but to accept its ultimate unreality. Religion then becomes merely a practical affair, its images and concepts, being wholly concerned with the fulfilment of practical ends. Though this conclusion would be unpalatable to the modern viśiṣṭādvaitins, we cannot legitimately draw any conclusion other than this.

The Pāñcarātra thinkers do not emphasise the Māyāvāda of the Advaita Vedānta, but their predominantly transcendent Absolute seems to be a denial of the plurality of the immanent being and consciousness. From some of the extremely advaitic utterances of the Samhitās, one can only be led to think that the Absolute is the only reality, the immanent expression is not the reality and in so far as it has any reality it is non-different from the Absolute. In fact such a conclusion is against the spirit of the practical Pāñcarātra school but this alone is its legitimate theoretical position. From the above it will not be wrong to maintain with Prof. P. T. Srinivasa Aiengar that the teachings of the Pāñcarātra Samhitās tend towards advaitism.[157]

The Pāñcarātra thinkers not only emphasise the absolute and the transcendent nature of Brahman, but also regard It as a

Being self-centered and self-contented, so much so that it is not in the least concerned with the world. In their eagerness to preserve and emphasise the purity, perfection and transcendent nature of Brahman, they give rise to the view that it is not Brahman who is responsible for creation, sustenance and absorption of the universe. It Itself does not create the universe, and remains quite unaffected by the changes which are necessary to bring about the universe. It is the unchanging One who though unchanging is the basis of all changes. In order to preserve Its transcendence and perfection which seem incompatible with Its being an active agent in relation to the universe, attempts are made by these thinkers to introduce mediating principles like Śakti, Vyūhas, creator-Brahmā etc. to relate the Brahman to the universe.

In this respect Brahman of the Pāñcarātra school comes nearer to the concept of advaitic Brahman. It has been aptly described in the Saṃhitās as 'windless atmosphere' or 'motionless sea' which is 'darkness' and 'emptiness' everywhere. To speak of such waveless stage and a quietness in the Absolute and also of its transcendent changeless nature which remains intact even in the process of creation resembles the absolutistic position of the advaitins.

Like the advaitins the Pāñcarātra thinkers so much emphasise the transcendence of Brahman that they forget entirely Its immanent aspect. Consequently they have to posit a series of emanations of Deity and other intermediaries to relate it to the world. This necessitated the cardinal Pāñcarātra dogma of five-fold manifestations of Deity. The Pāñcarātra thinkers never equated Brahman with all these five forms individually or taken together. It is not Brahman Itself who appears in these forms. These forms rather emanate from It and the speciality of the process of emanation is that in it while bringing the product into existence the source of the product remains unchanged. Since Brahman alone is ultimately real, these manifestations are only phenomenal and they do not enjoy the same ontological status which Brahman does.

The very transcendence of Brahman in the Pāñcarātra signifies an artificial relation with the world. But such a Real, 'wholly other', is as good or bad as the Absolute of the advaitin, with whom we can maintain no relation, from whom we can cherish no hopes, and to whom we can offer no oblations. To be wholly other is for us to be nothing at all. We recognise the uniqueness and perfection, transcendence and supra-mundane existence of Brahman but in being sheer transcendent It hopelessly falls short of our expectations. Neither religious experience nor a true philosophy can rest contented with such an Absolute, conceived negatively who has no unfulfilled purposes, unsolved problems and who needs not wait upon us. The concept of the Absolute as a self-contained Being who cannot function dynamically in time and cannot enter into reciprocal intercourse with the finite spirits, cannot be intellectually satisfying. It leaves unanswered a fundamental problem, why the Absolute who is eternally perfect, to whom there is nothing unaccomplished, should instruct the 'Śakti or Brahmā' to create the universe. Further, how can the unrelated Absolute be related to the universe ? Are both the perfect Absolute and the imperfect universe real ? Strictly speaking both cannot be so, otherwise, we will have to give some place to the imperfect world in the perfect Absolute, which is manifestly a contradiction. So in order to preserve the perfection of Brahman the Pāñcarātra thinkers will have to regard the world as something not real. Then we seem to get an Absolute in which all is lost, though the Pāñcarātrins may explain that everything is found. The fundamental defect with both Śankara and the Pāñcarātra thinkers is that they draw a distinction between the Absolute who is wholly beyond and God who works and creates.

They start with a static and empty Absolute arrived at negatively, and through It they try to explain the world. The more fruitful method is to start from the concrete world and to transfer to the Absolute the most significant and revealing features of our experience. The Absolute then comes to be a system of relations, a system in which every element of experience has a place and meaning not in its coarse form, but in a transmuted form.

Rāmānuja, on the contrary, repudiates the distinction between the transcendent and the immanent Being, the Impersonal Absolute and the Personal God. The double aspect of the Pāñcarātra philosophy presents us with a two-fold reality transcendental and empirical. Rāmānuja, on the other hand, consistently refuses to be drawn into this division. For him the Ultimate Reality is one and one only, which is at once both transcendent and immanent. To him the categories of transcendence and immanence are not contradictory and incompatible. Therefore, he resents advaitic (and thereby of the Pāñcarātra as well) bifurcation of Reality into transcendent and immanent. Rāmānuja, unlike the Pāñcarātra school and Advaita, does not understand transcendence of God in the sense that He is alien to, or apart from, or unrelated to, the universe. God transcends the world of things and spirits, for He is not limited to them either individually or collectively. He is beyond them in the sense that while they intimately depend on Him and He acts on them, His self-consciousness does not depend on them. God's transcendence lies in the fact that the spatial and temporal world is a manifestation of the Divine will, but He Himself is beyond the spatial and temporal order. He is the transcendent Ground of the whole world and invests it with the order which comes of its constant dependence on Him. Further God is transcendent in the sense that He is a perfect personality with a unique character of His own, which is untouched by the mutation of matter and limitations of finite spirits.

Unlike the Pāñcarātra, Rāmānuja does not fight shy of the immanence of God. By being immanent God does not become imperfect or impure. To Rāmānuja immanence means something different from pantheistic identification. God is immanent in the sense that He is the Inner soul of the universe and the universe constitutes His body. That means all sentient beings and non-sentient things are completely controlled and supported by God for His own ends, and are absolutely subordinate to Him. That is, God brings the world into being as an expression of Himself and continually sustains it by the energy of His will.

Thus the position of Rāmānuja is fundamentally opposed to that of the Pāñcarātra. In his pantheistic system both transcendence and immanence are reconciled and are given their due places. Rāmānuja never bothers to preserve the bare transcendence of God by introducing the intermediaries like Śakti, Vyūhas etc. in the creation of the world, because according to him God in spite of being immanent in the world, can remain unaffected by the changes etc. of the world, in the same way as the soul is not touched by the pains, miseries and imperfections of the body. Therefore, as against the Pāñcarātra, Rāmānuja emphasises the intimate and inseparable organic relation with which God stands related to the universe.

The fundamental difference between Rāmānuja and the Pāñcarātra starts with the dynamic and static concepts of Reality. Rāmānuja upholds the dynamic character of Being, in which he finds the possibility of inner self-revelation and unfoldment. This basic conception naturally leads him to build up a synthesis of Being and attributes, and to unite the extremes of abstraction, either of substance without attributes or of attributes without substance. The Pāñcarātra, however, favours the static concept, as a result of which it could only conceive the Supreme Being as a bare identity and not a unity. But the Pāñcarātra thinkers could not remain for long satisfied with this unhappy position, for it did not gratify fully the religious fervour. So they had to bring in the dynamic concept through some other way. In Advaita this necessitated the concept of māyā, and in the Pāñcarātra the Śakti, Vyūhas and creator Brahmā. It is this necessity which is responsible for the queer combination of Deism and Pantheism in the Pāñcarātra philosophy.

Examination of arguments regarding the Pāñcarātra impact on Rāmānuja

Having reviewed the fundamental position of the Pāñcarātra school and Rāmānuja, we may now proceed to examine the view that Rāmānuja in formulating his concept of God, has borrowed substantially from the Pāñcarātra. So far as the ontological position of the two is concerned, as we have seen, they fundamentally differ. Now it remains to be seen whether they share any theological beliefs. This we shall do by pointing out the extent to which the two agree and also by tracing out the source of such ideas and beliefs which Rāmānuja holds in common with the Pāñcarātra.

In repudiating the idea of Brahman as a substance devoid of all attributes Rāmānuja maintains that It is the Highest Person whose essential nature is knowledge characterised by bliss and who is possessed of unlimited number of auspicious attributes. Very frequently he dwells with great emotion on the attributes of God, such as knowledge, bliss, brilliance, beauty, comeliness, compassion, generosity, goodness, love etc. and along with these he also quotes six attributes from the Viṣṇu Purāṇa, viz., glory, strength, dominion, wisdom, energy and power, which are characteristically ascribed to Para Vāsudeva (not the Supreme Being) in the Pāñcarātra. He simply enumerates these attributes and does not dwell upon them.

It is said that the concept of God as a person full of all imaginable auspicious attributes, devoid of all evils and as possessing six attributes, was borrowed by Rāmānuja from the Pāñcarātra and Śrīvaiṣṇavism. Prof. Kumarappa, for example, holds that the idea of God as having excellent attributes, has been obtained by him from his religious sect. Only that part of his teaching, he opines, is based on the Upaniṣads which describes thought and bliss as constituting the essential nature of Brahman.[158] Kumarappa writes, 'But it may be asked where did Rāmānuja obtain this doctrine ? He claims that Scripture (i.e. in this case, the Upaniṣads) teaches it. But our own account of the Upaniṣads has already shown that no such clearly formulated doctrine is to be found in them.'[159]

It seems to be rather injudicious on the part of Kumarappa to opine that Rāmānuja makes a false claim for the Upaniṣadic basis of his views. He himself accepts that 'the conception of Brahman as an all-perfect Being characterised by grace is not altogether absent even in the Upaniṣads'[160] and while dealing with the philosophy of the Upaniṣads[161] he elaborately explains this point, yet quite inconsistently he remarks that this doctrine of Rāmānuja has no basis in the Upaniṣads. He writes that 'the Upaniṣadic passages which he (Rāmānuja) cites as teaching his view of the nature of Brahman are so few and uncertain in meaning that we may be sure that he did not derive his doctrine from them.'[162] This argument seems to be baseless mainly because Upaniṣadic passages teaching personal aspect of the Ultimate Reality are not few in number and as regards their uncertainty many of the Upaniṣadic utterances bear such character. If the accounts of the Upaniṣads were quite clear and consistent, what was the need to write commentaries to systematise them ?

Further Kumarappa writes, 'Besides, his (Rāmānuja's) very eagerness to claim support for his view from Scripture seems to reveal the fact that he obtained his doctrine from other sources.'[163] This argument is quite inconsistent with the immediately preceding sen.ences in which he states that Rāmānuja was aware of the fact that in the scripture no clearly formulated basis is found for his view. Kumarappa appears to be wrong in saying that there is no such basis in the Scripture. Secondly, if there was no such basis in the Scripture and if Rāmānuja was aware of it, why was he eager to claim support from the Scripture ? As a matter of fact, the attempt of Prof. Kumarappa to falsify the account of Rāmānuja himself and to impute to him what he does not own seems to be quite unwarranted.

Another argument which Kumarappa puts forth in suppport of his thesis is that 'after showing that his doctrine regarding the nature of Brahman is taught by Scripture, Rāmānuja proceeds to show that it is also taught by the Viṣṇu Purāṇa, and the passages which he cites so fully reflect the view which he advocates throughout the Śrī Bhāṣya, that Brahman is the highest person, characterised by the most blessed attributes, and free from all evil qualities, that it is not by any means improbable that it is to the Viṣṇu Purāṇa in particular and Vaiṣṇavism in general, that Rāmānuja turned for his doctrine regarding the nature of the Deity.[164] Here we reiterate that Rāmānuja's conception of God is not at all absent in the Upaniṣads and that it is wrong to trace its source to the Pāñcarātra school. As regards the Viṣṇu Purāṇa Rāmānuja has clearly declared it as an authority as good as the Gītā and the Mahābhārata. He also regards it as corroborating the Upaniṣads.[165] Not only Rāmānuja but Śankara also quotes the Viṣṇu Purāṇa as an authority, in his Bhāṣya on the Brahmasūtra. Kumarappa is mistaken in regarding the Viṣṇu Purāṇa as a sectarian work of Vaiṣṇavism.

Rāmānuja's view of God as free from evil-not Pāñcarātric

Similarly Kumarappa holds that Rāmānuja has derived the idea of God devoid of all evils from the Vaiṣṇavism. He writes, 'Another point is also noticeable, though it cannot be said to be peculiarly Vaiṣṇava, for as we have seen, it is not lacking entirely even in the Upaniṣads—the view, namely, that the Deity is a perfect being, in whom there is no evil. But while in the Upaniṣads this doctrine is never clearly or consistently formulated, the Śrī Bhāṣya passages we have cited show Rāmānuja consistently maintaining that Brahman has only auspicious qualities, and that He is entirely free from evil qualities.[166]

Here Kumarappa does not do justice to the Upaniṣads. He himself writes that, 'In this way Rāmānuja brings to full fruition the tendency of some of the Upaniṣads to ascribe numerous perfections to the Supreme Being.'[167] And elsewhere he writes, 'When, however, we turn to the later Upaniṣads, it seems likely that Brahman was regarded as free from evil, understood also in its moral sense.'[168] In great details he deals with how in the Upaniṣads Brahman is conceived as possessing many transcendent qualities and perfections including the moral ones.[169] If this idea is already there clearly formulated in the Upaniṣads, there seems no reason why Kumarappa should try to trace to Vaiṣṇavism the inspiration for Rāmānuja to make his idea central in his view of the Deity. Not only Upanisads but the Viṣṇu Purāṇa also makes it very clear that Brahman is free from all defects, and that nothing but auspicious qualities constitute His Nature.

Six attributes of God mentioned by Rāmānuja not based on Pāñcarātra

In a similar manner Kumarappa smells sectarianism in Rāmānuja's reference to the six qualities of God, which are characteristic in the Pāñcarātra school. He writes, 'He (Rāmānuja) at any rate found in the Viṣṇu Purāṇa a description of the blessed qualities of the Deity, which description he failed to find except in a very meagre form in the Upaniṣads.'[170] Then he reproduces passages of the Viṣṇu Purāṇa which Rāmānuja has cited in the Śrī Bhāṣya and remarks, 'There are two points worthy of note in connection with the qualities above enumerated, for they reveal ideas not to be found in the Upaniṣads, and hence are to be regarded as distinctly sectarian. Rāmānuja accepts them, though there is no warrant for them in the Upaniṣads, and they form a fundamental part of his view regarding the Deity. One of them is the enumeration of six qualities-glory, strength, dominion, wisdom, energy and power as belonging to Brahman'.[171]

Here Kumarappa overlooks that for Rāmānuja the Viṣṇu Purāṇa is an authority and that it has not been regarded as a sectarian work. These six qualities, it is true play an important part in the Pāñcarātra philosophy but they form no less important part of the nature of Deity in the Viṣṇu Purāṇa. These qualities in the Pāñcarātra are associated, not with the Supreme Being, but with Para Vāsudeva, whereas in the Viṣṇu Purāṇa they are mentioned as the qualities of the Supreme Being. In Rāmānuja also these qualities are associated with the Supreme Being. Any way there can be no doubt about it that he has borrowed this idea from the Viṣṇu Purāṇa only, and it is significant that in the few citations given by him from the Viṣṇu Purāṇa these qualities are repeated as many as three times. If he accepts these qualities on the authority of the Viṣṇu Purāṇa, there seems to be no basis to trace them to the Pāñcarātra.

Loving nature of God accepted by Rāmānuja not non-Vedic

Another point that Rāmānuja seems to share with the Pāñcarātra and Śrī Vaiṣṇavism is that God is characterised by abiding love for His devotees. This idea, according to Kumarappa, has been borrowed by Rāmānuja from the religious sect to which he belonged.[172] But Kumarappa forgets the fact that right from Ṛgvedic period Viṣṇu has come down to be a God of grace and that the burden of the teachings of the Śvetāśvatara and some other minor Upaniṣads and the Gītā is that the Deity is eminently loving. In holding any particular idea, doctrine or belief there is no exclusiveness of any particular school, and if one idea is held by two schools together it should not lead one to a hasty conclusion that one of them has borrowed it from the other. Further Kumarappa has failed to discern a point of subtle difference. In Rāmānuja it is the Supreme Being who out of love manifests Himself by assuming numerous forms so as to delight the hearts of the devotees. This is perfectly in accordance with the Gītā and with the scriptural saying viz., 'ajāyamāno bahudhā vijāyate'. But in the Pāñcarātra the Supreme Being being unmoved, transcendent and wholly other, He Himself cannot have any feeling of love towards individual souls and, therefore, cannot manifest Himself. It is only the phenomenal God, the God of religious aspiration, who is endowed with this quality.

Dogma of five-fold manifestations of Deity not in Rāmānuja

Another element that Rāmānuja is alleged to have borrowed is the cardinal Pāñcarātra dogma of five-fold menifestations of the Deity.[173] Though the only Supreme Being the Pāñcarātra thinkers conceived of was the one transcendent Brahman, they could no longer remain satisfied with It and soon recognised the Deity in five-fold forms, viz., Para, Vyūha, Vibhava, Antaryāmin and Arcā. Brahman Itself does not assume all these forms, since It is unable to do so on account of Its transcendent and changeless nature. Therefore, strictly speaking, all these are not manifestations of but only emanations from Brahman. These five forms are purely in relation to the world. They have meaning for the world only and exist so long as the world exists.

In the works of Rāmānuja we do not come across this dogma. From his treatment of the Pāñcarātra school under the Brahma-sūtras II-2-39 to 42, which is the only reference to the Pāñcarātra school in all his works, it appears as if he was not aware of this five-fold dogma. There he refers to the Pauṣkara Samhitā in which four-fold forms are taught, but he enumerates only three, viz., Sukṣma (which perhaps means Para), Vyūha and Vibhava. Not only he does not mention all the five forms, but he also does not expound the three forms that he enumerates. He simply mentions them as doctrines accepted and advocated by the Pāñcarātra school, and further upholds their non-contradiction to the scriptures, and the favourable attitude of the Sūtrakāra towards them. How far Rāmānuja is justified in doing so, we shall deal with elsewhere.[174] But the point that interests us here is that he has shown no inclination for incorporating them. It is therefore a misgiving of the scholars to write that he has incorporated in his theology this Pāñcarātra dogma. Prof. Kumarappa confesses that 'The doctrine being sectarian Rāmānuja does not systematically expound it' and yet maintains that Rāmānuja 'recognised all these forms.'[175]

Prof. Kumarappa identifies the 'Para' form of the Pāñcarātra with Rāmānuja's Deity which exists in the heavenly world with Śrī and a host of eternal beings.[176] But he overlooks the ontological status of the 'Para' of Pāñcarātra and God of Rāmānuja. In the

Pāñcarātra 'Para' is not Supreme Being but merely an emanation from Him, phenomenal in nature but in Rāmānuja it is the Supreme Being Himself who resides in the heavenly world with Śrī, and He is not a manifestation of, or emanation from, any one else. Thus there is no point in saying that the two are identical.

We agree with Prof. Kumarappa that Rāmānuja speaks with approval of the doctrine of Vyūhas in establishing that the Vedānta Sūtras do not mean to reject the Pāñcarātra school. Rāmānuja does so on the authority of the Mahābhārata. But this does not mean that Rāmānuja himself has accepted and incorporated this doctrine. The doctrine of Vyūha, which is essentially a cosmological principle, finds no place in the cosmology of Rāmānuja. Except under the Vedānta Sūtras II.2.39-42 nowhere does this doctrine appear in his works.

Rāmānuja deals with the doctrine of incarnation. But this doctrine is not peculiar to the Pāñcarātra. The idea of avatāra is by no means alien to the character of Viṣṇu who from the Vedic times was recognised as a God of grace and as saviour of the world. The fundamental difference between the Pāñcarātra and Rāmānuja with regard to this doctrine is that in the Pāñcarātra the Supreme Being Himself does not incarnate. This task is assigned there to the Vyūhas. But in Rāmānuja it is Brahman Itself who incarnates, without putting away Its God-like nature. Secondly, unlike the Pāñcarātra Rāmānuja does not dwell on the forms, goddesses, activities etc. of various avatāras and the mythological fancies connected with them.

According to Rāmānuja there are two motives for incarnation. The first motive which is propounded in the Gītā is to uphold righteousness. The second one is to gratify Its devotees. This motive is peculiar to the Pāñcarātra and the Ālvārs. On this basis Prof. Kumarappa holds that Rāmānuja has borrowed this idea from them.[177] But this inference may not be legitimate, because the Viṣṇu Purāṇa (VI.6.47ff) also teaches the same view and it is most likely that Rāmānuja has derived it from there.

Rāmānuja delares Brahman as Antaryāmin, i.e., Inner Ruler. He declares that Brahman resides within the world and controls it from within. This view claims a long descent of which there is abundant evidence in the Upaniṣads. It goes back at least to a time as remote as that of the Antaryāmin Brāhmaṇa of the Bṛhadāraṇyaka Upaniṣad. (III. 7.3 to 22) where we find its classical formulation. The same view appears also in the later Upaniṣads. (e.g., Iśa 1, Katha V. 9-13, Śve. I. 16. VI. 2, VI. 34, Mundaka 11.4, 9). This is the view taught in the Gītā (X. 19, 20) as well. On these as well as on the authority of the Chāndogya Upaniṣad (VIII.I.I.) Rāmānuja declares that Brahman abides as the Inner Ruler in the heart of the devotee for the purpose of meditation.[178]

This idea of God as Antaryāmin is not the same as the Pāñcarātra idea of Antaryāmin manifestation of God, as Prof. Kumarappa has wrongly thought it to be.[179] In the Pāñcarātra the Inner Ruler is not the Supreme Being, but Aniruddha. Further, Aniruddha is Inner Ruler of the souls only and not of the material world. But in Rāmānuja the whole world constitutes the body of God and, therefore, God is the Inner Ruler of the material world as well as of the individual souls. Thirdly, in Rāmānuja God resides permanently in the world as its Inner Soul whereas in the Pāñcarātra Aniruddha takes a special descent for this purpose.[180]. Lastly, the concept of Antaryāmin as a form of the Deity is different from the concept of Antaryāmin as the soul of the world.

The Pāñcarātra school is very much given to the worship of arcās, which is the last of the five-fold manifestations of the Deity. Like other forms this arcā form is also for the purposes of worship. We may say that the Pāñcarātra thinkers have accepted it as a concession to the religious consciousness.

Rāmānuja does not mention at all this form of the Deity, and to argue that Rāmānuja must have favoured it because the Śrīvaiṣṇava tradition mentions him to be a worshipper at the shrine of the great Śrī Rangam temple[181], is not sound mainly because the Śrīvaiṣṇava tradition is not quite historical and whatever the sectarian followers say need not be true and acceptable.

Form, abode, consort etc. of God in Rāmānuja different from those of Pāñcarātra

Rāmānuja lays emphasis on the concrete nature of God and begins his commentary on the Gītā with a mythological description of the form and abode of the Deity in a Paurāṇic way which has no philosophical significance, and such descriptions are found in the Vedārtha Samgraha as well. These accounts at places have striking similarity with the Pāñcarātra accounts. This has prompted Prof. Kumarappa to attribute sectarian motive to Rāmānuja. But on the basis of the citations given by Rāmānuja from the Ṛgveda etc. we can be sure that Rāmānuja has a purely Vedic basis for this belief. This can be substantiated from the differences prevailing between Rāmānuja's belief and the Pāñcarātra belief. The fundamental difference between the two is that this form and abode in Rāmānuja pertains to the Ultimate Reality, whereas in the Pāñcarātra the Ultimate Reality being formless, it is only Para Vāsudeva, the Personal Deity, who is associated with this form and abode. Further, in the Pāñcarātra the form and abode of the Deity come into existence only in the process of pure creation, but in Rāmānuja these are not the outcome of any process of creation. In the Pāñcarātra this abode of the Deity is said to be made of some special stuff called Śuddha Sattva. Some scholars have wrongly thought that Rāmānuja has accepted the Pāñcarātra view that the abode of God is made of 'Śuddha Sattva'. Under this impression Prof. Sirkar writes,[182] 'We confess we cannot understand what kind of substance Rāmānuja's Śuddha Sattva is'. But we should make it quite clear that Rāmānuja nowhere mentions this element. He has not said anything about the stuff out of which the abode of God is made. He only says this much that it is not physical. Similarly Rāmānuja mentions Śrī as the consort of God and quotes Vedic authority in support of it. The concept of Śrī plays an important part in the Pāñcarātra philosophy as well, but there she is essentially a creative principle and a mediator between the Deity and devotee. This aspect of Śrī is not present in Rāmānuja.

On the basis of the above examination the conclusion we arrive at is that Rāmānuja and the Pāñcarātra school differ fundamentally. Those ideas that seem common in them have an apparent similarity only, and they differ widely in details. The similarity in respect of such ideas and inspirations need not by any means necessarily imply borrowing on either side. Secondly, this circumstance can also be explained by the fact that both have a common source of information. The philosophy of Rāmānuja is mainly Upaniṣadic, being supported by the Gītā and the Viṣṇu Purāṇa. There is no doubt about it that Pāñcarātra has borrowed a lot from the Upaniṣads. The conclusion that Rāmānuja has not borrowed these ideas from the Pāñcarātra is evinced from this that whenever Rāmānuja expresses such ideas he seeks support from the Upaniṣads etc. and not from the Pāñcarātra works. Both Rāmānuja and the Pāñcarātra school have repeated and reasserted some common theological principles which have been furnished to them by the Upaniṣads, and hence one is likely to find some similarity between them.

Rāmānuja and Āḷvārs-a study in contrast

Some scholars are of the opinion that Rāmānuja was a follower of the Aḷvārs and gave an intellectual championship to their intense religious experiece. Through the Śrīvaiṣṇava ācāryas he is regarded to have inherited the Āḷvār religion of passionate devotion. Dr. Radhakrishnan writes, 'His study of the Āḷvārs and his training by the ācāryas helped him to develop elements which otherwise would have remained latent in the Upaniṣads and the Brahmasūtras'.

In the previous section we have observed that these scholars had alleged the impact of the Pāñcarātra on Rāmānuja but there was no ground for this allegation. Let us see how far the alleged impact of the Āḷvārs on Rāmānuja is justified. It will not be superfluous to repeat here what we have said in the introduction that there are some scholars who opine that the Āḷvārs were rather the disciples of Rāmānuja. If this were true the very basis of the above allegation crumbles down.

It is really a very difficult task to undertake a comparative study of the Āḷvārs and Rāmānuja mainly because the Āḷvārs are purely religious whereas Rāmānuja is essentially philosophical. The Āḷvārs move in the wonderlands of myths and legends and leave their imagination free to roam at large in the realm of faith. No distinction is drawn between mythological fancy and religious truth, fiction and fact. Rāmānuja although gives undue recognition to such mythological fancies, he does not remain entangled in them and steers away to the realm of logic and reflection. Under the impact of scriptures, he sometimes mixes up mythology with philosophy and religion, but this does not affect his philosophy. Intrusions of mythical elements in his philosophy certainly does not have any rational basis, but they have their basis in the scriptures.

Like the Āḷvārs, Rāmānuja also dwells on the beauty of the form of God, but he does so with no touch of eroticism. For him God is not an eros-producing mate but the soul of the world. He does not describe the form of God in an amorous language. But the Āḷvārs feel and describe the Lord as a lover, who has stolen their heart. They not only express their rapturous passions and ardent amorous longings, but also describe the raciprocation of love on the part of the Lord who is described as being infatuated with the beauty and charm of the beloved, the Āḷvārs. Such an experience of a constant company of the Lord in a delirious state and such rapturous reciprocation of ravishing love and enticement on the part of God, are altogether absent in Rāmānuja.

The Āḷvārs are very much given to the worship of God in the form of arcās. They are so much engrossed in this form that they completely forget His transcendent aspect. The idea of a personal God satisfies the deepest yearning of all religious people all over the world. No religion can therefore escape from symbolism and icons employed to focus its faith. The emotional nature and finitude of man requires some definite object of worship and adoration, help and protection. The idol of God brings to man, what Brahman can never give him, a present and accessible God. Brahman being beyond thought and speech can never be that what an idol is for many. God alone can hold the human heart to whom man turns in prayer at any moment and receives help from Him.

But the image is not God. It is only a repesentation of God and not a presentation of Him. It is merely a means to enable the worshipper to visualise God and to give him something concrete on which to fix his attention, and to convince him of the reality of the transcendental. Therefore, the image should not be regarded as God Himself, something final. The religious thought should seek to pass beyond the limits of mere symbolism in its endeavour to relate the symbol to the transcendental. To be content with symbolism without raising any question about the truth of that which it symbolises, is to be satisfied with mere subjectivity. This gives rise to slender idolatry and the belief that some idols are the actual incarnations of God and not mere symbols, and that there are many gods residing in separate places each one to be worshipped with particular articles of worship etc. This sort of idolatry we find in the Pāñcarātra and the Āḷvārs, but it is absent in Rāmānuja.

All the doctrines of the religion of the Āḷvārs are, thus, conspicuously absent in Rāmānuja, except one, viz., the concept of grace and devotion. But as we have seen in connection with the comparative study of Rāmānuja and Pāñcarātra school, this idea is found in a fully developed form in the Vedāntic scriptures.

From the above it seems to be evident that there seems to be no ground for the contention that Rāmānuja was influenced by the Āḷvārs.

References and footnotes :

1. Bṛhadāraṇyaka, III. 4.2.; III. 7.2, 3.; Mundaka, III. 1.8; Kena, 3; Katha, VI. 12, II. 6, 9.
2. Sārīraka Bhāṣya of Śankara, III. 2.23.
3. Śrī Bhāṣya of Rāmānuja, I.1.3. See S. N. Das Gupta—A History of Indian Philosophy, Vol. III, pp. 189-192 for Rāmānuja's refutation of rational proofs.
4. Śrī Bhāṣya, I.1.3, II.1.12.
5. Katha, II.6.8, Kena, I.3ff.
6. Śvetāśvatara. IV.15 ff.
7. Mundaka, II.3.2.
8. XI.8.
9. I. 1.1., III.2.23, III. 2.26.
10. Śrī Bhāṣya, I.2.23. By scripture Rāmānuja means only the Vedas, Upaniṣads, Vedānta Sūtras, Smṛtis like Gīṭā, Viṣṇu Purāṇa and some portions of the Mahābhārata (Śrī Bhāṣya, I.1.1. II.1.1), He does not include the Pāñcarātra Samhitās in the scriptures.
11. Nārāyaṇīya, 339.4. Jayākhya, V.29.
12. Nārāyaṇīya, 340.21.
13. Jayākhya, IV.76.
14. Ibid, IV.50.
15. Nārāyaṇīya, 340.44, 45.
16. Ibid, 337.19
17. Ibid, 340.1.
18. Ibid, 337.12.
19. Ibid, 337.19
20. Ibid, 337.53
21. Śārīraka Bhāṣya, I.2.14

22. Tiruvaymoli, C.I. 1.1.
23. Ibid, C.I. 1.8.
24. Ibid, C.I. 1.6
25. Ibid, C.I. 2.1.
26. Ibid.
27. C.I. 1.3.
28. Śrī Bhāṣya, I. 1.1.
29. The Philosophy of Rāmānuja in this respect may be compared to that of Bradley when the latter writes, 'The parts are members. The whole is an organic unity in which they function.' (Mind, P. 32. Jan. 1925) 'What we discover rather is a whole in which distinctions can be made, but in which divisions do not exist.' (Appearance and Reality. p. 128). But this comparison cannot be carried too far, because Bradley's Absolute is neither a self-conscious spirit, nor a person, and also because for him God and Absolute are not one and the same.
30. Essentials of Indian Philosophy, p. 177.
31. Comparative Studies in Vedantism, p. 26.
32. Outlines of Indian Philosophy, p. 399.
33. The Naiyāyikas distinguish between samavāya and samyoga. A relation is samyoga (conjunctive) when the relata are separable (yutasiddha). It is samavāya (inherent) when they are inseparable (ayutasiddha).
34. Radhakrishnan, Indian Philosophy Vol II. p. 217.
35. Outlines of Indian Philosophy, p. 230.
36. Proceedings of Indian Philosophical Congress, 1927, p. 162.
37. Appearance and Reality, p. 527.
38. Śrī Bhāṣya, I.I.1. p. 80, Vedārtha Samgraha, p. 23-26 (Buitenen).
39. Ibid.
40. Padyabhāga, II.18.183.
41. See his edition, p. 236.
42. Rāmānuja's Vedārtha Samgraha, Introduction p. 63, F. N. 174.
43. Śrī Bhāṣya., I.1.1. p. 130.
44. The word 'attribute' here is not to be understood in the ordinary sense of the term. It denotes an object which depends upon something else for its existence etc.

45. Gītā Bhāṣya, VII. 7.
46. 'Whenever we cognise the relation of distinguishing attribute and the thing distinguished thereby, the two clearly present themselves to our mind as absolutely different.' Śrī Bhāṣya, I.1.1., I.1.13.
47. Sacred Books of the East Series vol. XXXIV, pp. XXIV-V.
48. Śrī Bhāṣya, I.1.1.
49. Śrī Bhāṣya, I. 1.1.
50. Ibid. The last argument of Rāmānuja does not appear to be a sound one, unless it is interpreted in the Jaina sense of anekāntavāda, for which there is no basis here.
51. Ibid, I. 1.1.
52. Ibid, I. 1.1 see Kumarappa—The Hindu Conception of the Deity' pp. 167-172 and Das Gupta, Loc. cit. p. 167 for detailed analysis.
53. Ibid, I. 1.1.
54. Ibid, I. 1.1.
55. Ibid, I. 1.1. see Kumarappa Loc. cit, pp. 179-185 for details.
56. Ibid, I. 1.1.
57. Rāmānuja summarises advaitin's position as follows : The advaitin puts forth two grounds for his contention :

    (i) While all other things are seen to exist in relation to consciousness, which thus explains and illuminates all, consciousness alone is not explained in relation to anything other than itself, for consciousness is self-illumined. It therefore proves itself as well as all other kinds of beings, and hence is supremely real.

    (ii) Secondly, since difference is ultimately unreal, all things other than pure undifferentiated consciousness are ultimately unreal. Ibid, I. 1.1,
58. Ibid, I. 1.1. See Das Gupta Loc. cit., pp. 168ff. for details.
59. Idid, I. 1.1. I. 1.12, See Kumarappa, Loc. cit. pp. 177-78.
60. Ibid, I. 1.2.
61. Sarvātma-Śve. Up., III. 21.
62. Parama Brahma-Taitt. Up., II. 12.
63. Parama Jyotiḥ-Chānd. Up. VIII. 3.4.
64. Parama Tattvam—Ibid, VI. 2.1.
65. ParamātmāBṛh. Up. III. 1.1.

66. Sat-Chānd Up. VI. 2.1.
67. Śve. Up., VI. 8
68. Gītā, XV. 7; cf. Maitr. Up., V. 2.
69. Gītā, X. 7., Praśna Up., V. 4.
70. Katha Up., V. 12.
71. Bṛh. Up., III.7.3-22.
72. Katha. Up., II.23.
73. Rāmānuja's Vedārtha Samgraha, 6.
74. IX. 18.
75. See Rāmānuja's introduction to the Gītā Bhāṣya: also Śrī Bhāṣya, I.1.1.; For the Six guṇas, see our account of the Pāñcarātra infra. Rāmānuja borrowed them from the Viṣṇu Purāṇa. He quotes the latter extensively to that effect. (I.2.10-14; I.22. 53; VI.5.72, 82-87) In these quotations these qualities are repeated as many as three times.
76. IX. 2.
77. VII. 18.
78. Kumarappa, Loc. cit. pp. 21-25.
79. Śrī Bhāṣya, I.1.1. See the details about the attributes of God in K. D. Bharadwaja — The Philosophy of Rāmānuja, pp. 118ff.
80. Ibid, I.1.21.
81. I.1.21 which refers to Chānd. Up. VII-1.8.
82. Vedārtha Samgraha, 133, 135.
83. Śrī Bhāṣya, I.1.21.
84. Vedārtha Samgraha, 127; cf. 81, 128ff; Introduction to the Gītā Bhāṣya. In all these Rāmānuja profusely quotes from the scriptures for his support.
85. Vedārtha Samgraha, 134; cf. 81,127; and the Introduction to the Gītā Bhāṣya. This description is inspired by the Chāndogya Upaniṣad, I.6. and is elaborated on the basis of the Viṣṇu Purāṇa, VI. 76.80ff. and I.22 (Aṣṭrābhūṣanādhyāya). There is no non-Vedic element in it. cf. Śve. III. 7. Taitt. I.6.1; Tait. Āry. VI. 1.6., Bṛh. II. 3.6. IV.4.22, Rāmāyaṇa 6.1.4, 14.14.7. Chānd, VIII. I, 2, Mundaka, 3.1.8.
86. Śrī Bhāṣya, I.1.1., I.1.9, I.4. 26,27 etc.; Vedārtha Samgraha, 6,80 etc.

87. Vedārtha Samgraha, 127, 128, 131. Introduction to the Gītā Bhāṣya.
88. Rāmānuja quotes Ṛgveda, X.129.7, Tait. S.II.2.12., Mahānā. Up.1.5, Subala. Up,6, Śve U.p.,III.8; Tait. Up,II.I; Mahābhā; XII. 5.27; Viṣṇu Purāṇa, IV.1.84.
89. M. N Sirkar—Comparative Studies in Vedantism, p. 33.
90. Vedārtha Samgraha, 127,128,131 etc. Introduction to the Gītā Bhāṣya. Rāmānuja quotes for his support Ṛgveda, X.90.16; VII.110.13, Subāla. Up.6, etc.
91. Vedārtha Samgraha, 127, etc. Introduction to the Gītā Bhāṣya. Here Rāmānuja quotes Tait. S , IV.4.12.5; Tait. Āry, III.13.1, Rāmāyaṇa, VI.1.15; Viṣṇu Purāṇa, I.9.145.
92. Indian Philosophy, Vol. II. 689-90.
93. 31.19; also Tait. Āry, III. 13.3.
94. Kumarappa, Loc. cit., p. 58.
95. Introduction to the Gītā Bhāṣya.
96. Śrī Bhāṣya, I.3.I.
97. Gītā Bhāṣya, III.6.
98. Śrī Bhāṣya, II.1.9. cf.I.1.21 where Rāmānuja refers to the Mahābhārata for his support.
99. Vedārtha Samgraha, 133; quotes Viṣṇu Purāṇa, I.9.143-5 and Rāmāyaṇa, VII. 2. 13.
100. This is based on the Gītā, IV 7-8.
101. This is based on the Viṣṇu Purāṇa — 'Subhāśraya Prakaraṇa' III. 6.47 ff.
102. Jayākhya, IV. 20.
103. Ibid, IV. 63; Ahirbudhnya. II. 50.
104. Ahirbudhnya, II, 47, Lakṣmī Tantra, II.8, Parama Prakāṣa, I.3.43.
105. Ahirbudhnya, II.6.
106. Ibid, II.47., II.49.
107. Ibid, II 53; Jayākhya, IV.61, V.29.
108. Lakṣmī Tantra, II.8. II.10, Ahirbudhnya, II.23.
109. Lakṣmī Tantra IV. 61 Ahirbudhnya. II.53; Jayākhya, V.30.
110. Ahirbudhnya, II.62, Laksmī Tantra, I.1, Jayākhya, IV 60, IV. 65.
111. Mahābhārata, 339.3; 340.28; 348.13, 352.18 of the Nārāyaṇīya Parvan.
112. Ref. The Philosophy of Pāñcarātra

113. See ibid for details.
114. Viśvakṣena, p.122.
115. See Schrader, Loc. cit; p. 25 for details.
116. I.I. ff., Viṣṇu Tilaka, I.10, Ahirbudhnya; XLIII. 7.
117. Padma Tantra, I.316 ff.
118. Parama Prakāśa, I.2.3., cf. Padma Tantra, I.2.
119. Viṣṇu Tilaka, II. 29ff. See the forms, colours, ornaments and weapons of Para in Schrader, Loc. cit, p. 52,
120. See supra footnote 44 and infra-chapter on Cosmology.
121. II. 27-35.
122. II. 15.
123. Lakṣmī Tantra, II. 55.
124. Padma Tantra, I.2.81 ff.
125. The Ahirbudhnya Samhitā mentions thirty-nine principal avatāras (V. 50 ff, of Sāttvata Samhitā, V.57ff).) See forms, Saktis, colours and kinds of avatāras in Sāttvata Samhitā, chapters III, VI and V, and Schrader, Loc. cit; pp. 42-48.
126. Viśvakṣena Samhitā, p. 122.
127. This form is exhaustively treated in Viśvakṣena Samhitā. The major portion of the Samhitā literature concerns with the treatment of this topic.
128. C.I. 1.3.
129. C.I· 2.5.
130. C.I. 2.3.
131. C.I. 2.6.
132. C.I. 2.2.
133. C.I. 2.5.
134. C.I. 2.2.
135. C.I. 2.3.
136. C.I. 6.3.
137. C.I. 6.5.
138. Tirumalai, 16.
139. See Das Gupta, Loc. cit, p. 78.
140. C.D. Sharma, 'A Critical Survey of Indian Philosophy,' p. 280.
141. Truth and Reality, p. 428.
142. Ibid, p. 432 ff.
143. Appearance and Reality, p. 447.

144. Ibid, p. 500
145. See Radhakrishnan, 'Indian Philosophy', Vol II. pp. 445-46.
146. Śārīraka Bhāṣya, II. 1.14.
147. Radhakrishnan, Loc. cit, pp. 659-683.
148. System of Vedanta, p. 302
149. C.D. Sharma, Indian Philsophy, p. 524.
150. Radhakrishnan, Loc. cit, p. 721.
151. Ibid, p. 720
152. Two sources of Morality and Religion, p. 216.
153. Quoted by T.M. Forsyth-God and the World, p. 146.
154. Indian Philosophy, Vol.II, p. 720.
155. Rāmānuja's Vedārtha Samgraha-Introduction, p. 36.
156. The Hindu Conception of the Deity, p. 193 N., p.149, cf. pp. 185-8; 250, 311ff.

    S.B.E. Series, vol. XXXIV. Introduction, p. XXIII. Collected works, Vol IV. p. 80
157. Outlines of Indian Philosophy, pp. 184-85.
158. Loc. cit, p. 193 N.
159. Ibid, p. 185.
160. Ibid, p. 193 N.
161. Ibid, p. 22-25.
162. Ibid, p. 185
163. Ibid, p. 186
164. Ibid, p. 186
165. Vedārtha Samgraha, section 110, 111, 141, 145 etc.
166. Loc. cit, p. 118
167. Ibid, p. 190
168. Ibid, p. 23.
169. Ibid, p. 22-25
170. Ibid, p. 186.
171. Ibid, p. 187-88
172. Ibid, p. 328.
173. Ibid, p. 188, 322 ff; also Thibaut, loc. cit, introduction, p. XXIII.
174: See my paper 'Does Bādarāyaṇa favour Pāñcarātra ?
175, Loc. cit, p. 311

176. Ibid, p. 313
177. Ibid, p. 313.
178. Śrī Bhāṣya. I. 3.13
179. Loc. cit. p. 315
180. Schrader, loc cit., p. 49.
181. This is contended by Prof. Kumarappa, p. 316.
182. Studies in Vedāntism, p. 45,

CHAPTER II

NATURE OF THE WORLD

One of the perennial problems of cosmology is, 'How the world has come to exist ?'[1] The earliest philosophical view with regard to the Ultimate Reality appears to have arisen out of an attempt to answer the question, 'whence this universe ?' This problem attracted the attention of Rāmānuja and the Pāñcarātra thinkers. In the Āḷvārs, however, we do not find any specific cosmogonical speculation. Cosmology did not interest them, perhaps, because of their all-absorbing concentration on the Deity.

Both Rāmānuja and the Pāñcarātra thinkers maintain a realistic attitude towards the universe, but their realism differs fundamentally. In the account of the creative order both betray the impact of Sāmkhya thought. However, both deny the dualism of Sāmkhya and institute in its place monism by accepting the subordination of the creative potency and characterising it as inherent in Brahman. But this monism of the Pāñcarātra, unlike the thoroughgoing monism of Rāmānuja, is a half-hearted assertion, because it, like the Puruṣa of the Sāmkhya, regards Brahman as pure, transcendent, and leaves the cosmic evolution severely alone to the Śakti, which answers to the Prakṛti of the Sāmkhya. Rāmānuja on, the contary, gives place to the creative aspect in the very being of Brahman. In the Pāñcarātra the cosmic evolution, issuing out of Śakti, lacks the character of a līlā. Anything unconscious has existence, a law of growth, but no character. Rāmānuja, on the other hand, characterises the evolution as a līlā of Brahman, and this characterisation brings into the creative evolution a meaning and a purpose which it acquires in close touch with Brahman.

Rāmānuja's view contrasted with that of Advaita.

The system of Rāmānuja has come into existence with a conscious motive to oppose the māyāvāda of the Advaita. Both these systems of Vedāntic thought draw their source from the Prasthāna-trayī. Both of them have always put implicit faith on the supremacy and infallibility of the revelations of the above scriptures. Neither of the two has advanced any theory of his own, but both have mainly followed the traditional account. Both were driven to the same problems, their texts were the same, their methods were based on the same assumptions, and yet their results showed striking differences. They have divergent explanations of the Śruti texts, to conform their ideas of creation to their epistemological and metaphysical settings. Both agree that the cosmic evolution should be traced to some sort of creative effort, and that this creative effort must have a place in our conception of the Absolute. Both regard the becoming as the expression of the Supreme Being, and the creative order as issuing out of It. But the basic distinction of static and dynamic conception of Being immediately introduces a difference in the cosmic conception. The advaitin regards the creative effort of Brahman as an apparent expression of the Absolute under the conditions of māyā. Rāmānuja, on the other hand, accepts it as a self-transformation of Brahman. For the advaitin the world is a vivarta (illusory transformation). The difference between these two positions is very well explained by Sadānanda. He observes that when a thing actually appears as another, it is called vikāra, when it falsely appears as another it is called vivarta.[2]

The static concept of Being leads the advaitin to deny ultimate reality to the cosmic process, for the dynamic concept of life and experience has been over-shadowed by the extreme transcendentalism of the static Absolute. The static and eternally complete Absolute admits of no change or transformation. Therefore, according to him, the universe is empirical (vyavahārika) or phenomenal (prātibhāsika) or intrinsically not real (mithyā) from the point of view of the Absolute, which is the only reality, andwhich is identity par excellence.

Doctrine of māyā as inevitable correlate of monism of Advaita

The theory of reality advocated by the Advaita school presents a crucial problem. If Brahman alone be real, how the plurality of the universe which we experience is to be accounted for ? How can the world of manifold multiplicity arise from one unitary self-same Being ? This is the vexed prolem of 'one and many'. The solution of this problem offered by the advaitin is that Brahman alone is real and the varying world is an illusory manifestation of Brahman caused by māyā or avidyā which is positive and beginningless but an indescribable phenomenon.

But this principle of māyā is more a dialectical mystification than a genuine solution. It is a 'third position' or 'middle position' between being and non-being, sat and asat, which aims at doing away with the contradiction with which conjunction of sat and asat is supposed to be riddled. But instead it looks like an evasive device which itself harbours the very contradiction it aims at resolving. Further the existence and reality of the world is a perceived fact and in denying it complete reality the Advaita seems to be giving a go-by to the verdict of the normal experience.

Rāmānuja's refutation of doctrine of māyā.

This doctrine of māyā has evoked great protest from all other schools of Vedānta founded by Rāmānuja, Madva, Nimbārka, Vallabha etc. and from other thinkers like Jñānadeva and Aurobindo. All these thinkers almost followed the same line of criticism which was adopted by Rāmānuja.

Rāmānuja outrightly rejects the advaitic two-fold account of Reality as transcendental and empirical, and the consequent phenomenality of the world of experience. For him the unity of Brahman is in no way incompatible with the reality of the world. Since the Advaita school tries to explain the phenomenality of the world by means of the theory of māyā or avidyā, Rāmānuja advances a vigorous polemic against this theory and tries to refute it by raising certain ontological, epistemological and logical objections, which may be summarised as follows.[3]

Āśrayānupapatti

One cannot determine the locus of avidyā which is nothing

but a mere baseless fabrication of imagination. Its substrate can be either the individual soul (the position of Vācaspati) or Brahman, (the position of Sarvajñātmamuni) but neither of the two can be so conceived. It cannot be the individual soul, 'for the individual soul itself exists in so far only as it is fictitiously imagined through avidyā,' nor can it be Brahman, 'for Brahman is nothing but self-luminous intelligence, and hence contradictory in nature to avidyā, which is avowedly sublated by knowledge.'

Nor can avidyā be admitted as a second principle, having itself as its substrate, because this would be contradictory to the advaita hypothesis of 'non-duality'.[4]

Tirodhānānupapatti

The advaitin maintains that avidyā conceals the essential nature of Brahman and thereafter projects cosmic appearance. But Rāmānuja points out that there can be no obscuration of the essential nature of Brahman by avidyā because Brahman is by nature consciousness. If it is said that such a Brahman can be hidden by avidyā, this would mean destruction of Brahman's essential nature.

Svarūpānupapatti

Rāmānuja further points out that even if we admit the existence of avidyā, as an existence it escapes all determination. Because the problem, then, would be, 'is it something real or something unreal ?' The former alternative is excluded as not being admitted by the advaitin himself. The latter one is not acceptable to Rāmānuja because, 'if the imperfection inhering in consciousness is itself of the nature of consciousness, and at the same time unreal, we should have to distinguish two kinds of consciousness—which is contrary to the fundamental doctrine of the oneness of consciousness. And if, on the other hand, we should say that the consciousness in which the imperfection inheres is of the same nature as the latter, i.e., unreal, we are landed in the view of universal unreality.'

Further the theory leads to an infinite regress, because according to the advaitin avidyā is the cause of the unreal world and this avidyā in itself is also unreal. If so, another avaidyā would have to be postulated in order to account for this avidyā and so on ad infinitum. 'To avoid this difficulty it might now be said that real consciousness itself, which constitutes Brahman's nature, is that avidyā. But if Brahman itself constitutes the avidyā, then Brahman is the basis of the appearance of a world, and it is gratuitous to assume an additional avidyā to account for the world. Moreover, as Brahman is eternal, it would follow from this hypothesis that no release could ever take place. Unless, therefore, you admit a real avidyā apart from Brahman, you are unable to account for the great world error.'[5]

Anirvacanīyānupapatti

Rāmānuja further argues that the concept of avidyā is itself unintelligible and hence incapable of being used as a principle of explanation. The advaitin himself describes it as inexplicable (anirvacanīya), but he holds that though inexplicable, it must be admitted as a fact, a positive entity 'which affects the obscuration of the real, which is the material cause of the erroneous superimposition on the real, of manifold eternal things.' This avidyā is said to have been attested in experience and is apprehended through perception as well as inference.

To this Rāmānuja replies that neither perception alone, nor perception aided by reasoning reveals to us this avidyā. Even in erroneous perception when a man mistakes a shell for silver, there is an apprehension of the qualities which a shell has in common with silver. The apprehension is regarded as erroneous, not because it is a case of non-apprehension or nescience, but because though it apprehends some qualities of the shell, it does not apprehend all; and the mistake is terminated, not by substituting knowledge in the place of nescience but by perfecting the former knowledge. Avidyā, therefore, is not only inexplicable in theory, but is also not vouched for as a fact of experience.

Pramāṇānupapatti

Rāmānuja contends that the theory of avidyā is not supported by scriptures, smṛtis or purāṇas. It is true that Prakṛti is in some texts declared to be māyā, and māyā may mean mithyā. But māyā does not in all places refer to what is mithyā. We see it applied for example, to such things as the weapons of asuras which are not mithyā but real. Māyā in such passages denotes that power which produces various wonderful effects, and it is in this sense that Prakṛti is called māyā. This is clear from Śvetāśvatara Upaniṣad (IV. 9).

Again, when in certain texts it is said that, 'Then there was neither non-Being, nor Being.' (Ṛg. Samhitā. X. 129.1) the terms 'being' and 'non-being' denote intelligent and non-intelligent beings in their distributive state, and there is no reference whatever to something 'not definable either as being or non-being.'

Nivartakānupapatti

There is no remover of Avidyā. The advaitin believes that knowledge of the unqualified attributeless Brahman removes avidyā. But such knowledge is impossible. Discrimination and determination are absolutely essential to knowledge. Pure identity is a mere abstraction. Identity is always qualified by difference and distinction. Hence there can be no knowledge of an undifferentiated attributeless thing. And in the absence of such a knowledge nothing can remove avidyā.

Nivṛtyānupapatti

In the preceding point it was argued that there is no remover of avidyā. Here it is said that there is no removal of avidyā. Avidyā is said to be positive (bhāvarūpa) by the advaitin. How, then, can a positive thing be removed ? A thing which positively exists cannot be removed from existence by knowledge. The bondage of the soul is due to karma which is a concrete reality, and cannot be removed by abstract knowledge.

These arguments of Rāmānuja have been further elaborated in great detail by Vedānta Deśika in his 'Śataduṣaṇī'. These criticisms are more or less beside the point if we keep Śankara's exposition in view but if we take into consideration the Advaita system in general, these arguments hold good. These days appreciable attempts have been made to reinterprete māyā doctrine in a scientific manner as a doctrine teaching relativity, and such an interpretation seems satisfying, but the māyā doctrine in its traditional garb does not seem to be so.

Rāmānuja's repudiation of phenomenality of world

Rāmānuja further repudiates the advaitic contention that the world is phenomenal. He argues that to hold that the objects are not real simply because they do not persist, is rather strange. The material world is changeable and perishable and may be called 'non-being' in so far as it is observed at a certain moment in a certain form and at some other moment in a different form. But there is no contradiction between the two different conditions of a thing which are perceived at different times, and hence there is no reason to call it mithyā.

Rāmānuja makes a distinction between 'sublation' and 'non-persistence' and contends that it is the failure on the part of the advaitin to make this distinction that is responsible for his view that the world of plurality is not-real. By sublation we mean one experience being contradicted by another and is thus proved to be false. An object may be non-persistent, i.e., may exist for only a brief period of time, nevertheless it is real. That an object exists only for a short time does not condemn it as not-real.

He further remarks that it would be ridiculous for the scriptures to teach that Brahman became many if they believed at the same time that the many did not exist. Accordingly even those scriptural texts which appear to deny the existence of plurality do not really mean to do so. 'What all these texts deny is only plurality in so far as contradicting that unity of the world which has its being entirely as an effect of Brahman, and has Brahman for its inward ruling principle and its true self'.

Thus, Rāmānuja concludes that the advaitin's device of relating pure non-differenced Brahman to a world of plurality by declaring the world to be unreal product of beginningless avidyā is void of reason and scriptural authority.

World as real manifestation of God

Rāmānuja holds that the world with all its change and multiplicity is real. In the world there is a real development presided over by Brahman. The cosmic evolution is an effect of self-transformation of Brahman. The creative impulse is inherent in Its nature which is a result of inherent necessity. Brahman creates and sustains this whole world from Its own Being without losing Its purity and perfection. Rāmānuja does not accept the transcendence of consciousness and immanence of will in the creative effort of Brahman. The Reality cannot be so bifurcated. It is one and the same Brahman who is immanent in the world as its inner Contoller and who is transcendent to it as its Ground and Support. Rāmānuja is quite clear in saying that Brahman Itself is not the world, but It is the soul of the world. The Ultimate Reality is a triad consisting of Brahman, the material world and the individual souls, where the distinction of each is maintained and at the same time Brahman is regarded as containing matter and souls within Itself. In this view the reality of the world is recognised, the supremacy of Brahman is taught, and yet both are brought together into a unity.

Upaniṣadic basis for Rāmānuja's view

The general frame-work of the above view has been derived by Rāmānuja from the Upaniṣads and the Gītā. The Upaniṣads abundantly testify realistic attitude towards the world. They do not recognise a second principle side by side with Brahman to provide It with the materials necessary for creation. Accordingly they picture world process as an emanation rather than a creation. 'As a spider comes out with its thread, as small sparks come forth from fire, even so from this Soul come forth all vital energies, all worlds, all gods, all beings'. (Bṛh. II.1.20) 'I, indeed, am this world for I emitted it all from myself.' (Bṛh. I. 4. 5). World is said to be the result of what originally was undifferentiated becoming differentiated by nāma and rūpa (Bṛh. I.4.7., Chānd. VI. 2). Creation therefore is the sending forth by Brahman of the world out of Itself. The world with all its diversity depends on It for its matter as well as form.

Though the world emanates out of Brahman, it does not fall apart from It. Brahman is said to be immanent in it through and through. The Upaniṣads repeatedly declare that after creating the world Brahman entered into it 'even to the finger-nail tips' (Bṛh. 1.4.7) There are innumberable passages in the Upaniṣads where the thoroughness of this immanence is emphatically declared.[6]

It is true that there are many passages in the Upaniṣads which seem to identify Brahman with the world, but they are not to be understood literally in a pantheistic way. One must always seek to understand them in the light of their context. For example, when the Mundaka exclaims, 'The puruṣa Himself is everything here' (II.1.10), it means only to say in a forceful way that everything is completely dependent on Brahman, not that Brahman is Itself everything, for the passage occurs at the end of nine stanzas which portray dramatically how everything in the world comes from Brahman as its supreme source. The general trend of the Śvetāśvatara and the Katha is to distinguish clearly between the Brahman and the World.[7] In the Śvetāśvatara so completely the world is regarded as dependent on Brahman that it speaks of Brahman poetically as Itself the various objects of the world (IV. 2, 3); but this does not mean that Brahman is identical with them, for in the next stanza it declares that Brahman is 'immanent' in these all.

Thus it appears that by means of such exaggerated statements the Upaniṣads merely teach in a striking manner the great truth they had discovered that Brahman is in all things as that which makes them what they are.

Lest these utterances declaring Brahman as completely pervading the world be mistaken as pantheistic, the Upaniṣads clearly maintain that the Ultimate Reality is a triad (Śve. I.7, 12). Symbolically the wheel which holds together the diverse parts within its unity, or a river composed of several tributaries, best represents the nature of Brahman in relation to the world. (Śve. I.4, 5; VI.1.)

This idea that Brahman in relation to the diversity of the world must be conceived as a unity-in-diversity, or the One which holds together the many is not by any means peculiar to the Śvetāśvatara. On the other hand, the conception which we have indicated as predominant in the Upaniṣads, that Brahman is the all-pervading soul of the world, is only another way of stating the truth that multiplicity of this world is held together in, and energised by, Brahman. Even the thought that Brahman as pervading principle remains hidden in all things, and that It is ultimately to be conceived as a triad, is not unknown in early Upaniṣadic philosophy.[8] Thus in the Bṛhadāraṇyaka (II.6) it is declared that the world is a triad of name, form and work, and it is said, 'Although it is that triad, this ātman is one. Although it is one, it is that triad. That is the Immortal, veiled by the real (satya). Life (prāṇa) verily is the Immortal. Name and form are the real. By them this life is veiled.' The 'real' by which the 'Immortal' is veiled is obviously the world of multiplicity (or 'name and form' as the passage explains).

Thus the instinctive realism of the early upaniṣadic thinkers and possibly the Sāmkhya tendencies of later philosophers prevented them in the main from reducing the diversity of the world to the characterless unity of distinctionless Brahman. But it would be too much to claim that always this was done. The thought that Brahman is the Supreme Real could easily lead to the thought that It is the only Real. Nevertheless we may conclude that the predominant thought of the Upaniṣads regarding the relation of Brahman to world is that the latter in all its diversity is real and exists in Brahman. Brahman is its soul, it is Brahman's body.

The Gītā also like most of the Upaniṣads teaches that the world forms a part of the Supreme, being created, supported and dissolved by Him.[9] While accepting this general position of the Upaniṣads the Gītā goes a step further in describing the process of creation and dissolution, and enumerating the various elements involved in it.

In these two sources Rāmānuja could get not only the basis of his system, but also sufficient material to fill in the required details. From the Gītā he derived the doctrine of repeated creation,[10] which is taught also in the Śvetāśvatara Upaniṣad,[11] and the view that the creation proceeds in the main according to the stages enumerated in the Sāmkhya philosophy. From the Gītā he also derived the idea that in creating the world Brahman is not prompted by a desire to overcome any lack or imperfection in Its nature.

Brahman as cause and world as effect

The entire universe, according to Rāmānuja, has sprung into being from Brahman, is sustained by It and will ultimately return to It. It stands combining in Itself all the three kinds of causes, material, operative and accessory. Rudiments of creation which are real and which differentiate Its character, reside in It in the shape of Its power. Brahman is not static but essentially dynamic, and here alone lies the roots of creation. It is the immanent ground of all existence, the source of all life and the home of all eternal values. It is the first and the final cause, the root and the fruit, the whole and sole explanation of the world. It is above all, in all and through all. All things are out of It, in It, and unto It.

The fact that Brahman creates the world establishes that Brahman stands in causal relation to the world. Unlike Sāmkhya, Rāmānuja maintains that Brahman is both the operative as well as the material cause. This is the basic view of the Upaniṣads also which often describe the emanation of the world from Brahman on the analogy of the sparks which proceed from fire, or the threads which are emitted by the spider. Rāmānuja writes that this view is in harmony with the promissory declaration and the illustrative instances. The promissory declaration is the one referring to the knowledge of all things through the knowledge of one (Chānd. VI. 1.3.) And the illustrative instances are those which set forth the knowledge of the effect as resulting from the knowledge of the cause. (Chānd. VI.1.4)[12] There are some passages which declare Prakṛti to be eternal and the material cause of the world, but Prakṛti, writes Rāmānuja, in such passages denotes Brahman in Its causal phase when names and forms are not yet distinguished, for a principle independent of Brahman does not exist.[13] In addition, scriptures directly state that Brahman alone is the material as well as the operative cause of the world. For example, 'Brahman was the wood, Brahman the tree, from which they shaped heaven and earth.'[14]

If Brahman were the cause both of the form and matter of the world, the problem that arises is that how the perfect Brahman can be the cause of an imperfect world ? How the perfect One differentiates Itself into finite things and beings may be a riddle or mystery, but It does so is a fact for Rāmānuja. It may be argued that the general rule is that an effect is non-different in character from its cause, and therefore the world cannot be an effect of Brahman from which it differs in character. To this Rāmānuja replies that Brahman and the world cannot have complete sameness of all attributes, because in that case the causal relation—which requires some difference—cannot be established. There should be some similarity in cause and effect and Rāmānuja points out that such is actually the case with regard to Brahman and the world, both of which have attributes of 'existence' etc. in common. It may be objected that the essential distinguishing characteristics of a causal substance persist in its effect also, but the world has the opposite of Brahman's essential nature of being antagonistic to all evil etc. To this Rāmānuja replies that even things of different nature stand to each other in causal relation. For example, sentient worms etc. are produced from the non-sentient honey; and hence it is not unreasonable to assume that the world also although differing in character from Brahman may originate from the latter.[15]

Rāmānuja further writes that though the world differs in nature from Brahman, this does not mean that the two are altogether different and separate. They possess some elements of similarity as well. But the point here is, in what sense we may say that the world is one with Brahman. Rāmānuja is aware of this difficulty and therefore analyses the causal relationship. He examines the causal theories propounded by various schools of thought and concludes with a statement of his own view, which is that the effect is nothing but the causal substance which has passed from one state of existence to another. Thus, for example, the jar, which is an effect, has the causal substance clay, which has assumed another configuration and name. It is one in substance with clay, and yet it has attributes which are different from those of clay in its causal state. The effect is one with the cause in the sense that it is potentially contained in the causal substance as a state which this substance is capable of assuming.[16]

Rāmānuja here introduces into the idea of cause the concept of growth borrowed from the organic world. This is mainly to avoid the idea of external agency which we find, for example, in the case of a jar being produced out of clay by the potter. He accordingly writes, 'The case of the cause and effect is thus analogous to that of the child and youth. The word 'effect' denotes nothing else but the causal substance which has passed over into a different condition.[17] In this way Brahman as the cause must be thought to be one in substance with the world in the sense that It holds the world within Itself in a potential form, and that creation is only the passing over of Brahman from one state of existence, where the world exists potentially, into another state of existence, where the world exists actually. Brahman is regarded as existing in two periodically alternating states which are referred to as Kāraṇāvasthā (causal state) and Kāryāvasthā (effect state). Brahman in the first state is the causal substance of the world. The second state of Brahman is the actual manifestation of the world. So the creation of the world means only the actualisation of that which is potential. What exists as a real possibility in the causal state turns out to be an actuality in the effect state.

The individual souls and matter, which are the modes of Brahman, are also regarded as existing in two different conditions. One is a state of absolute quiescence when the intelligence of the individual souls gets contracted, the matter becomes unevolved, and the two exist in Brahman as Its potentiality in a dormant state. It is this state which is referred to in the Upaniṣads when they describe, 'Being alone was there in the beginning, one without a second'. The other is the evolved state when creation takes place, matter becomes evolved, souls get associated with bodies and their intelligence becomes expanded according to their deeds.

The evolution and the involution thus signify two states of the same substance, viz., God qualified by matter and souls. The Ultimate Reality is a triune unity which in one state is differentiated into names and forms, and in another state is not so differentiated. So all the time unity is there, but sometimes in a homogeneous state and sometimes in a heterogeneous state. Both these states are equally real and none is false or unreal. When the Upaniṣads (Tait. II. 7) declare that 'Non-being was there in the beginning, from it being came into existence' what they mean by 'non-being, is not 'non-existence' but only the latent or causal state, as the Bṛhadāraṇyka (I.4.7) makes it clear, 'verily, at that time the world was undifferentiated. It became differentiated just by name and form'.

Before concluding this section it will not be out of place here to undertake a review of the doctrine of causality propounded by

Śankara and Rāmānuja, for it is this doctrine which is the basis of Rāmānuja's view enunciated in this section.

Transcendentally speaking, causation has no value in Śankara's philosophy, because for him identity is the only truth. Yet for phenomenal purposes he accepts its value and makes a synthesis of causation with identity, the result of which is the doctrine of Vivartavāda, which simultaneously accepts and denies causation. In fact, it is a denial rather than an acceptance of causation. In it first we posit a world through the law of causation, and then deny it to indicate the illusoriness of position and the reality of identity.[18] The doctrine of Vivartavāda is fully in conformity with the logic of identity and transcendent oneness. Śankara finds it difficult to reconcile causation with identity, for causation is a relational concept whereas identity denies relation. Brahman does not stand in causal relation with any one, because it is the only Reality; causation is the necessity of thought, but identity transcends thought. Being unable to reconcile the claims of identity and causation at the transcendental level, Śankara retains the former and sacrifices the latter and with it the reality of the immanent existence as well.

Rāmānuja, on the other hand, does not surrender the law of causation to the logic of identity. Like the Sāmkhya, he accepts the dynamic view of causation, though this dynamism is spirituo-material and not mere material as it is in the Sāmkhya. In the place of static identity of Śankara, Rāmānuja establishes a dynamic unity in which identity and difference (causation) are reconciled. Causation makes explicit what is implicit in identity. The cause persists in the effect and the effect is latent in the cause. Causation is nothing but a manifestation, a manifestation from latent to patent and again from patent to latent. It is not that sort of transformation which obtains between milk and curd wherein there is no possibility of retransformation, but it is that transformation in which the effect appears out of and again disappears into the cause. It is nothing but a change of state in one substance. Cause and effect are only different successive stages that a substance undergoes. Being alone becomes and is the cause of becoming: One alone becomes many and is the cause of manifold. Therefore, none of the entities of the world have popped up at one particular point of time. All things are eternal and form a part of Brahman, who is the abode of all and abides in all. All things are really eternal and real, even though they are subject to change from subtle to gross and gross to subtle state.

Brahman as soul and world as body

Rāmānuja speaks of Brahman as undergoing a change in effecting the world. In order to make clear what exactly this change implies, he makes a distinction between two aspects of Brahman, viz., body and soul, the soul representing Its own perfect nature and the body that part of It which is the world. Rāmānuja explains the relation of the world to Brahman as that which obtains between body and soul. The idea of Brahman as the Śārīrin or Embodied Soul may be regarded as the raison de' tre of his philosophy.

This designation of Brahman is quite in agreement with the emphasis the Upaniṣads place upon the immanence of Brahman in the world. There is abundant evidence in the Upaniṣads for the view that Brahman pervades the world as soul pervades the body. The classical formulation of this view is to be found in the Antaryāmin Brāhmaṇa of the Bṛhadāraṇyaka Upaniṣad. This is the view taught in the Mundaka (II. 1, 4, 9) and Śvetāśvatara (VI. 11.)

This modification of Brahman in the world does not introduce any imperfection in Its nature.[19] Because this change occurs only in the body of Brahman and not in the soul of Brahman. Rāmānuja writes, 'While the Highest Self thus undergoes a change in the form of world comprising the whole aggregate of sentient and non-sentient beings—all imperfections and suffering are limited to the sentient beings constituting part of His body, and all change is restricted to the non-sentient things which constitute another part. The Highest Self is affected in that sense only that He is the ruling principle, and hence the Self, of matter and souls in their gross or evolved state; but just on account of being this, viz., their Inner Ruler and Self, He is in no way touched by their imperfections and changes.'[20]

When the world is regarded as a body of God it may be asked, in what sense can it be so? Rāmānuja first of all rejects the common sense definitions of body, which have physical reference, and then defines it as 'Any substance which a sentient soul is capable of completely controlling and supporting for its own purposes, and which stands to the soul in an entirely subordinate relation, is the body of that soul....In this sense, then, all sentient and non-sentient beings together constitute the body of the Supreme Person, for they are completely controlled and supported by Him for His own ends, and are absolutely subordinate to Him.'[21]

Thus God is in the world but not as the world. All sentient beings and non-sentient things live, move and have their beings in Him, and depend on Him for their form and functions. He is the first and the final cause of all things, the root of life as well as its fruit. He is the ground of existence and the goal of experience, the summum genus and the summum bonum. He is the immanent ground and inner sustaining life. This concept of God as the Inner Soul shows that the finite is not only rooted in but is also controlled by the Infinite. Though the finite has its source and sustenance in the Infinite, the Infinite is not wholly in the finite. The chief value of this concept lies in the fact that it emphasises the Divine sovereignty without in any way endangering the reality and existence of the finite world.

Brahman as Substance and world as attribute

The relation of Brahman to the world is further explained by Rāmānuja in terms of substance-attribute relationship. This conception is a logical conclusion of his epistemological position. As we have seen, by empirical reasoning as well as by an appeal to Scripture Rāmānuja establishes that Brahman cannot be regarded as Pure Being, but must be thought of as a unity which includes differences within itself. This conception of Brahman is an important foundational tenet of his philosophy. While criticising the Śankarite view of Reality he prepares the ground for his view that the substance-attribute relationship holds good not only in case of objects and their generic qualities, but also in case of two distinct objects, one of which may be an attribute of the other. For example, in the judgement, 'He is a staff-bearer', the predicate 'staff-bearer' is what is called a separable accidens, for the staff can exist by itself apart from the staff-bearer. But in the judgement 'Man is rational' the predicate 'rational' is a differentia of the subject. Both these sorts of attributes hold the same relationship with a substance, irrespective of the above difference.

If one grants that Brahman is a substance qualified by attributes, and that attributes need not necessarily be only generic such as satyam, jñanam etc. then there can be no objection to saying that the world is an attribute or a mode of Brahman, though it, even like a staff, is in a sense substantive and not merely attributive. In this way the world with all its plurality may be accepted as real, and yet at the same time it may be regarded as not endangering the unity of Brahman, for it stands to the latter in the relation of attribute to substance. The difference of the world from Brahman, and at the same time its complete dependence on Brahman, will thus be explicable.

Rāmānuja explains the causal relation in terms of substance-attribute relationship. According to him an effect is nothing other than a mode of the causal substance. A cause producing an effect means only that a substance now characterised by a certain attribute, state or mode of existence, assumes another attribute, state or mode of existence, which it always had potentially within itself.[22]

Rāmānuja similarly reduces the soul-body relationship to substance-attribute relationship. The body is so completely dependent on the soul that it ceases to exist when separated from the soul, even as an attribute or mode ceases to exist except when supported by the substance to which it belongs. It thus is nothing but a mode or an attribute of the soul. He writes that whenever we see body the soul is also apprehended but we cannot perceive it as it is formless.[23]

But, it may now be asked, 'if the world is a mode of Brahman, how can imperfection exist in the world without effecting the nature of Brahman ?' Rāmānuja provides its answer in his definition of an attribute. 'Whenever we cognise the relation of distinguishing attribute and thing distinguished thereby, the two clearly present themselves to our mind as absolutely different.'[24] The difference in characteristics of the mode from the substance therefore need not alarm us, for that, Rāmānuja assures us, is quite the usual characteristic of the modes. What makes a thing a mode is not sameness of character with the substance to which it belongs, but complete dependence.

From the foregoing consideration Rāmānuja concludes that the whole world is, 'predicative to, or mode of, Parama Puruṣa; hence Parama Puruṣa alone exists adjectivated by everything else. All terms are thus connotations of Him by the rule of sāmānādhikaraṇya, or the rule which expresses the inseparable relation existing between substance and attribute, or the invariable co-existence of subject and predicate.'[25] Further the whole world, though different from Brahman, derives its substantial being and living from Brahman only, as it constitutes Brahman's body.[26]

Process of creation

Prior to creation, the world with its distinction of matter and souls, remains latent within Brahman in a 'form so extremely subtle that it hardly deserves to be called something separate from Brahman'. When the time for creation draws near Brahman 'broods', i.e. forms the resolve 'May I again possess a world-body constituted by all sentient and non-sentient beings, distinguished by names and forms as in the previous aeon.'[27] 'Brahman swells through brooding'; 'brooding consists of thought'—Brahman swells, through thought in the form of an intention, viz., 'May I become many'. Thus Brahman becomes ready for creation.'[28] This brooding, which consists of thought and intention, signifies that Brahman creates out of free choice, there being no external force constraining It to create. It also signifies that the creation is not arbitrary and irrational but intelligent and rational. This brooding denotes knowing, viz., reflection on the shape and character of the previous world which Brahman is about to reproduce,[29] because it is necessary that souls should in the new creation have a nature in accordance with their deeds in a previous creation.[30]

The creative process starts from Prakṛti which remains dormant in Brahman prior to evolution.[31] The creation from

Prakṛti onwards proceeds much as in the Sāmkhya system by the mutual influence of matter and soul, but animated and controlled at every stage by Brahman. Regarding his acceptance of the evolutionary scheme of the Sāmkhya Rāmānuja writes, 'The Śārīraka Śāstra (i.e. the Vedānta) does not disprove the principles assumed by tbe Sāmkhyas, but merely the view of their not having Brahman for their Self.'[32] He elsewhere writes, 'We by no means wish to deny unevolved matter and all its effects in themselves but in so far only as they are maintained not to have their self in the Supreme Person. It is just on the ground of this dependence on the Lord not being acknowledged by the Sāmkhyas that their system is disproved by us'[33].

This opinion of Rāmānuja has ample support from the Upaniṣads and the Gītā. The later Upaniṣads, notably the Śvetāśvatara, envisage the material universe in the Sāmkhya fashion as composed of matter and its qualities. There is no explicit reference in the earlier Upaniṣads, to any such material principle. The Chāndogya IV. 4 explains all objects as composed of three elements, a procedure suggestive of the Sāmkhya account of all material objects as composed of the three guṇas. In the Katha III. 10-13; VI. 7-8 and Praśna IV. 8 we meet with an enumeration of principles similar to those found in the Sāmkhya. The Śvetāśvatara makes use of the doctrine of three guṇas and the Maitri refers to the three guṇas by name, and enumerates their effects, as in the Sāmkhya philosophy. But this Sāmkhya which finds expression in the Upaniṣads is theistic, and not atheistic and dualistic which appears in Iśvara Kṛṣṇa.

In the Gītā (VII.4, XIII. 5) creation proceeds much as in the Sāmkhya philosophy. But unlike the classical Sāmkhya Prakṛti here is not an independent principle which exists outside of, or side by side with, God. It is regarded as the part of God and as controlled by Him in all its developments.[34] From Prakṛti come forth numerous elements. The Gītā, being uninterested in cosmological details, does not mention each of these elements individually, nor does it observe any consistent order in enumerating them. Much less does it seek to trace them step by step through the evolutionary process.

Along with this Sāmkhya process of evolution of the world, Rāmānuja also brings in the idea of Cosmic Egg in which all the elements of matter and souls after they have been evolved are combined together, and in which is born the creator Brahmā, who brings about the world. Rāmānuja bases this idea on the Śvetāśvatara (VI. 18) and quotes several passages from the Manu Smṛti and the Purāṇas.[35] The reason why the various elements when once evolved need to combine into an egg, he borrows from a Smṛti text which says, 'Possessing various powers these (elements), separate from one another, were unable to produce creatures without combining. But having entered into mutual conjunction they from the Mahat down to the individual beings, produce the Brahmānda.'[36]

With regard to the relation of Brahman to the creator Brahmā, Rāmānuja makes it quite plain that Hiraṇyagarbha, the creator Brahmā, is only as it were the instrument of Brahman who dwells within him and uses him even as the soul uses the body.[37] So, ultimately it is Brahman who creates and not Brahmā.[38]

Brahman's relation to Prakṛti

Prakṛti is the principle which Brahman employs in creation. It is that which produces manifold and wonderful effects under the supervision of Brahman. It possesses two chief characteristics. First, it is essentially a principle of change and differentiation.[39] Secondly, it is a principle of pleasure and pain meted out to a soul bound to worldly existence as a result of its acts.[40] Rāmānuja bases this view on the Śvetāśvatara (I. 9), Mundaka (III. 1.1.) and the Gītā (XIII. 20-21).[41]

Though Prakṛti is associated with these two characteristics and also forms a part of Brahman, Rāmānuja is quite emphatic in maintaining that Brahman does not share these characteristics, Prakṛti forms only the body of Brahman and these changes etc. in the body of Brahman do not affect Its soul or essence.[42] The three qualities of Prakṛti are not manifested in the causal state when Prakṛti is absorbed in Brahman.[43] Though the ultimate Reality comprises non-sentient matter, sentient beings and the Lord, this does not in the least imply any confusion of their respective essential characteristics.[44]

Motive for creation

The last cosmological problem that faces Rāmānuja is that, if Brahman is quite distinct from Prakṛti and shares none of its characteristics, and yet maintains it as Its mode, for what purpose, if any, does It keep it in existence ? Prakṛti, being a principle of change, seems to exist to effect the manifoldness of the world. But it may be asked, why is the manifoldness of the world necessary? If Brahman is a perfect Being, eternally complete, who has no objects to achieve, no desires to fulfil, then why does It divide Itself into multiplicity ? The very idea of a perfect Being indulging in creation to fulfil some purpose appears as self-contradictory, for it implies a lack or imperfection in It which It is seeking to overcome. This also cannot be said that in creation Brahman has no personal motive, but is motivated entirely by desire for the welfare of finite souls, because pain and suffering of souls in the world disprove this.[45] Rāmānuja is aware of these difficulties and therefore following the Sūtrakāra he holds līlā (sport) as the main purpose of creation.[46] Thus the world is līlā, a purposeless purpose, which implies disinterestedness, joyousness, free will and superabundance of energy on the part of Brahman, and it must be distinguished from conscious volitional effort. The creation follows the mere will, or free choice, of Brahman. It is to preserve the superme perfection of Brahman that the Sūtrakāra has given līlā as the motive for creation.

Though the creative act gives an expression to the Divine sport, this sport is not meaningless like a child's play, as it involves 'brooding' or thinking on the part of Brahman. This brooding, as we have seen, is for meting out to souls the fruits of their acts. This not only explains the pains and suffering of souls as due to their own previous deeds, but also suggests that the purpose of creation is concerned with the deeds of the souls as well. It may be argued that before the first creation there was no accumulated karma, then how can there be any consideration and consequent discrimination ? To this Rāmānuja replies that the flow of karma is beginningless. At the time of dissolution the past deeds of the individual are not annihilated since there is no unmerited suffering (akṛtābhyāgama) or annihilation of karma (kṛtavipraṇāśa).[47]

Brahman, therefore, maintains Prakṛti, for the sake of individual souls.

We may conclude, then, that according to Rāmānuja the world is a mode or an attribute of the Divine Being. It is both its material and the operative cause, for Prakṛti and souls form one part or body of It and It pervades them as their Inner Soul. The world is quite distinct from It, and their distinctness is never lost. It is the only true substance of which the world is an eternally distinct mode. Though It is perfect and the word is imperfect and though the world completely depends on It, nevertheless Its perfect nature is not affected to the slightest extent, and the distinct reality of the world is not in any way destroyed.

Pāñcarātra Account of Cosmology

Of all the philosophical problems that attracted the attention of the Pāñcarātra thinkers, it is the cosmology that interested them most. To indulge in cosmological speculations and to promulgate elaborate cosmological doctrines seem to be a favourite topic with them. Dr. Schrader has rightly remarked that their theoretical philosophy is inseparably bound up with the story of creation.[48] All the Pāñcarātra doctrines, theological as well as eschatological, are stated only in their cosmogonical contexts. They were much concerned with pointing out the various stages through which the world passed before it arrived at its present state. In formulating the details regarding the process of creation they are much influenced by the Sāmkhya philosophy, but in facing the problems which arise in connection with the relation of the transcendent and perfect Brahman to the imperfect and the changing world, they show great skill, depth and originality of thought. The main feature of the Pāñcarātra cosmology is that it assumes a pseudo-realistic attitude towards the world. In some of the Samhitās the advaitic doctrine of māyā finds a distinct expression.[49] But most of the Samhitās are apparently indifferent to this doctrine.

The only Ultimate Reality the Pāñcarātra thinkers recognise is the transcendent Brahman. But It is so far removed in character from this changing imperfect world that not only It is regarded as the cause of the world, but It is also regarded as incapable of being actively or directly related to the world. Consequently, great care is taken in showing how the changing world springs from the unchanging Brahman. In order to account for this the Pāñcarātra thinkers postulate various intermediaries between Brahman and the world, and also various intermediate stages in the process of the emanation of the latter from the former. It is only because of this reason that they regard the world as springing not from Brahman but from Lakṣmī, who, described as an aspect of Brahman, is so eternally distinct from It that though engaged in creation etc., she leaves Brahman quite unaffected. The introduction of the theory of Vyūha, which while bringing the world into existence from Brahman leaves the latter unaffected, is also motivated with the same consideration. Similarly, the cardinal Pāñcarātra dogma of the five-fold manifestation of the Deity, the three stages and the five Kośas through which the evolution of the world passes, and the Brahmāṇda theory etc. are all the various devices employed by these thinkers for saving Brahman from being polluted by directly giving rise to the world. However, this way of overcoming the difficulty, though seemingly satisfactory, is really no solution to the problem at all. In so far as these mediating principles were regarded as distinct from Brahman they served to bridge the gulf between Brahman and the world; but when it was recognised that they could not be regarded as really distinct, for then the problem arose of explaining their relation to Brahman, they were immediately declared as none other than Brahman Itself in one or the other of Its aspects.

Process of Evolution

The evolution of the world is described as consisting of three stages which are named as Śuddha sarga, Prādhānika sarga and Sthūla sarga respectively. The first stage comprises guṇonmeṣadaśā (i.e., manifestation of Vāsudeva and Lakṣmī with six guṇas), emanation of the three Vyūhas and the appearance of the subtle elements from the Vyūhas. The creation at the second stage consists of the development of the Kūṭastha puruṣa and Māyā Śakti (primordial matter consisting of niyati, kāla and guṇa). The evolution at the third stage is creation of the gross world. The account of this stage is similar to the Sāmkhya account with some important differences. The most striking difference is that whereas the Classical Sāmkhya has two principles only, to start with, the Pāñcarātra school holds that the evolution at this stage results from the combined activity of the three principal agents, viz., Prakṛti, Puruṣa and Kāla. The first two exist in the same relation as in the Sāmkhya, but both are regarded as being cooked by Kāla. Secondly, in the Sāmkhya the Prakṛti is regarded as independent, but, in the Pāñcarātra it is subordinate to Brahman, strictly speaking to Its Śakti. Thirdly, at this stage there are not many puruṣas in the Pāñcarātra as there are in the Sāmkhya. Fourthly, unlike the Sāmkhya, the Pāñcarātra school introduces the mythological account of njāñabramśa (fall from knowledge), of the origin of Brahmānda and of commissioning Brahmā to create and superintend the gross world. Lastly, in some of the Samhitās we find the creation of the world out of a tāntric process, whereas in the Sāmkhya tāntrism is altogether absent.

Samhitā account compared with Advaitic account

The Pāñcarātra account of the world is very much similar to the advaitic account. In both the schools the Ultimate Reality which is perfect, unchanging and static is not directly related to the world. The Iśvara in the Advaita and the Vāsudeva in the Pāñcarātra who is as phenomenal as the Iśvara of the Advaita, are the cause of the world. The only difference between the two is that the Iśvara of the Advaita is associated with māyā whereas the Vāsudeva of the Pāñcarātra is associated with Lakṣmī. The Lakṣmī of the Pāñcarātra is conceived in a more positive and determinate way than the māyā of the Advaita.

Secondly, in both the schools intermediaries (like Hiraṇyagarbha, Virāt etc. in the Advaita and Vyūhas, Brahmā etc. in the Pāñcarātra) between the transcendent Supreme and the immanent world are postulated so that the perfect nature of the Supreme Being may remain unpolluted.

Lastly, the advaitic doctrine of Vivartavāda and the Pāñcarātra doctrine of Vyūhavāda have this element in common that in both the Supreme Being though regarded as the basis of the world, is not affected by the mutations of the world. It is not clear as to whether all the Pāñcarātra thinkers believe in the Satkāraṇavāda or not, and the consequent view of the illusory manifestation of the phenomenal world, but from the premises of the sehool one must legitimately expect them to believe in it. And, as we have said above, some of the Samhitās do uphold this view.

Rāmānuja's concept of avidyā contrasted with Advaitic concept

In order to account for the phenomenon of bondage Rāmānuja also takes the help of the concept of avidyā, but avidyā has different meanings in the Advaita and in Rāmānuja. Avidyā in the Advaita lies at the root of the cosmic experience. In the system of Rāmānuja avidyā can produce ignorance but cannot create experience. Cosmic experience here is never subject to avidyā. In the Advaita māyā or avidyā spins out a universe under the control of Iśvara, in Rāmānuja's system, māyā, in the sense of ignorance, cannot do so, since the universe is ever-existent.

Do Upaniṣads teach māyāvāda ?

There has been a great controversy as to whether the doctrine of māyā in relation to the Upaniṣads is a graft or a growth, but this much is quite certain that the advaitic theory of adhyāsa is not present in the Upaniṣads. As a matter of fact the 'how' of creation, the question of the relation of the timeless perfection of pure Being to the perpetual becoming of the world, is exactly what the Upaniṣads leave unexplained. The candid admission of the author of Vivaraṇaprameya Samgraha that 'Sruti is indifferent with regard to the reality or unreality of bondage' shows that the advaitins were themselves sceptical as to the presence of māyāvāda in the Upaniṣads.

The word 'māyā' occurs but rarely in the Upaniṣads, and whenever it occurs, it admits of being construed either as mysterious power or as a 'moral defect'. The word which occurs more frequently in the Upaniṣads is avidyā (Mund. II. 1.10) but it has no metaphysical implication. To argue from the presence of the word māyā the advocacy of māyāvāda in the Upaniṣads is quite unwarranted, for it amounts to finding that doctrine in words rather than in ideas. In fact the māyā doctrine is suggested more by those passages which do not contain the word māyā or avidyā, e.g., 'Mṛtyossamṛtyumāpnoti yaḥ nānevātra paśyati.' This passage contains the seed of the māyā doctrine, but not its metaphysical fruits.

Though there are such other passages which contain the germ of the later developed māyā doctrine, this does not afford any valid reason for interpreting māyā into other texts which clearly yield a realistic sense. For example, there is no reason to assume that the teachings of Uddālaka in the Chāndogya upaniṣad were meant to represent vivarta rather than pariṇāma, or that the 'sending forth' of the elements from the primitive 'sat' is to be conceived as anything else but a real manifestation of real powers hidden in the primeval Self. When it is said that the whole world has Brahman for its causal substance just as clay is the causal matter of every earthen pot, it is not in the least implied that the process through which the causal substance becomes an effect is an unreal one. We may very well hold that all earthen pots are in reality nothing but earth — the earthen pot being merely a special modification (vikāra) of clay which has a name of its own — without thereby committing ourselves to the view that this change of form is not real. It is true that this material world is unsubstantial in the Spinozistic sense of the word 'substance' for it has no independent existence apart from Brahman, but this unsubstantiality does not constitute its unreality.

Does Bādarāyaṇa favour māyāvada ?

Bādarāyaṇa also in his Brahma-sūtras does not seem to uphold the doctrine of māyā. Śankara has tried to maintain that the Sūtrakāra in the Sūtra II. 1.14 has declared the phenomenality of the world. But this does not seem to be plausible. This sūtra is based on the Chāndogya passage where Uddālaka wants to teach his son 'the knowledge of all by the knowledge of One'. Now the knowledge of 'all' is possible only when 'all' has existence and is ananya (not-different) from 'one'. To explain this Uddālaka gives three instances through all of which it is suggested that Brahman and the world stand in causal relation. From these instances it is wrong to conclude that Brahman as cause alone is existent and the world as an effect is not so. Instead of using these instances only to explain the nature of the world, Śankara uses more often the instances of snake and rope, conch-shell and silver, mirage etc. This suggests a strong inference against Śankara that neither the Upaniṣads nor Bādarāyaṇa have in mind the doctrine of vivarta. It is true that the Sūtrakāra regards the dream-creation as illusory (III. 2.3.) but he also clearly distinguishes it from the real creation (II. 2.29). The Sūtrakāra is quite clear in maintaining Brahman's material causality and reality of the creation.

Rāmānuja and Pāñcarātra school — A Study in Contrast

A comparative study of the cosmology of Rāmānuja and of the Pāñcarātra school would bring out the fact that there are striking and far reaching differences between them, and that there is nothing significant that can be said to be common to them.[50] The contrast is so strong that it leaves no ground for the Pāñcarātra impact on Rāmānuja. As a matter of fact, Rāmānuja shows little interest in cosmological speculation, and is contented to borrow cosmological ideas ready-made from the Sāmkhya school. He has given no new thoughts of his own, nor did he worry himself with the 'how' and 'why' of the world. This is, perhaps, because of the fact that his interest is too definitely centred round Brahman to trouble him much about the problems of why the Infinite and Perfect changes into finite and imperfect, and of the various stages through which the world passed before it arrived at its present state. He is merely concerned with pointing out that whatever order evolution follows it is Brahman who underlies it, and creates it from Itself as Its līlā. In this respect Rāmānuja contrasts very strikingly with the Pāñcarātra philosophers who, as we saw, were deeply interested in, and concerned with, cosmological problems, who propounded elaborate cosmological theories and doctrines, and in whom all metaphysical problems are set in cosmogonical context. It will not be too much to say that in the Pāñcarātra thinkers philosophy begins with the story of creation. The problem that worried them most was how the changing world is to be related to the unchanging Brahman, who is its source.

Though both Rāmānuja and the Pāñcarātra thinkers seem to assume a realistic attitude towards the world, the realism of Rāmānuja is thorough-going, but the realism of the Pāñcarātra, strictly speaking, can be said to be apparent only. According to Rāmānuja the world constitutes the body, mode or attribute of Brahman. Brahman is a triad or an organic whole containing matter and soul within Itself. It is immanent in the world as its Inner Controller or Soul. Brahman of Rāmānuja need not completely transcend the world, because for him even if Brahman is regarded as the author of the world and as immanent in it, Its supreme perfection and transcendence can be preserved. By creating and containing the world Its perfect nature does not get polluted. Therefore, Rāmānuja regards the world as a part and parcel of Brahman, and as real as Brahman Itself.

For the Pāñcarātra thinkers, on the other hand, the purity and perfection, transcendence and unchanged nature of Brahman is incompatible with the changing and imperfect world, and this gives rise to the Samhitā view that the Supreme Being Himself is not responsible for creation etc. of the world, but only Its Śakti. They feel shy of the idea of Brahman being an active agent in relation to the world. Śakti, therefore, in the Samhitās practically usurps the place of the Supreme Being in relation to the world. If Brahman were the only reality and if Brahman does not stand related to the changing world, the only conclusion logically follows is that Brahman alone is real and the universe is not real but phenomenal. But this is quite a precarious and unsatisfying position for them and in order to avoid from falling into it, they tried to maintain that the Śakti is an aspect of the Supreme and is subordinate to It. But this position would have again affected the transcendent and unchanged character of Brahman, for the universe being an expression of Śakti and Śakti being an aspect of Brahman, the world with all its imperfections would have been an aspect of Brahman. So in order to preserve the transcendent and perfect nature of Brahman — which is their main concern—they again had to shift their position and regard Śakti as a principle eternally distinct from the former. Thus with regard to the relation of Śakti to Brahman they oscillate between the two positions. The two cannot be regarded as identical, nor can they be regarded as distinct.

In this respect the position of the Pāñcarātra thinkers does not differ much from that of Śankara, who also from his static standpoint maintains that the unity and multiplicity cannot be organically related and be equally real. Śankara ushers in the concept of māyā with the only purpose of relating the static Brahman with the changing world, and the principle of Śakti is also introduced by the Pāñcarātra thinkers manifestly with the same purpose. Both these principles are taken resort to in order to supply the missing link between the transcendent Brahman and the immanent world. Śankara and the Pāñcarātra thinkers are so much eager to maintain the purity, perfection and unchanged nature of Brahman that they emphasised Its transcendence at the cost of the reality of the world. It is this eagerness which refrained them from regarding Brahman as immanent in the world. Therefore, they took resort to the view that it is only Its manifestations which are related to the world.

Though the logical position of the Pāñcarātra thinkers is thus non-dualistic, they did not rest content with it — rather they had a dislike for it — and, therefore, they tried to maintain the reality of the world as well, in spite of the fact that their premises, as we have seen, did not warrant them to do so. Consequently, we find in them a juxtaposition of non-dualism and realism, and they oscillate in between advaitic and non-advaitic tendencies. The failure on their part to be consistent in their views resulted in serious ambiguities, an instance of which can be seen from how the same passages which were used by Schrader to prove that 'illusionism is altogether absent from them' were utilised by P.T.S. Aiyangar to establish advaitism as 'the view towards which the Samhitās incline'. Consistent thinking requires that either we must deny creation and the creative manifold as Śankara did or we must accept the creative manifold to be the expression of the Absolute; but it is difficult to accept the creative manifold along with a static Absolute which can admit of no expression, though the Pāñcarātra thinkers have not refrained from doing so. With the help of the principle of Śakti they tried to reconcile the two positions, but at no moment could they find escape either in realism or in transcendentalism. They could easily bring in Śakti to bridge the gulf between Brahman and the world, but when it was realised that Brahman and Śakti could not be regarded as really distinct for that would affect Brahman's supremacy — they immediately tried to identify them. But thereby they placed themselves in an unhappy dilemma. Either they should regard Śakti as identical with Brahman and thus sacrifice Its unchanged and transcendent nature, or else, they should declare that the two are distinct and thereby barter Its supremacy. In neither of the positions they could have been comfortable. Consequently they left the matter unsolved and tried to escape in a 'half-way house'.

Apart from the problem of the ontological status of the world another basic problem before Rāmānuja and the Pāñcarātra thinkers is, how can the world of imperfections arise out of a perfect Being.

This much is quite indisputable that the world is full of imperfections, that the Supreme Being is perfect, and that the world issues out of the Supreme Being. But the point in dispute is, can the Supreme Being be regarded an active agent in relation to the world, and yet be conceived as unaffected by the changes which are necessary to bring about the world ? Can the unchanging One, though unchanging, be the explanation of the changing world ? Will Its perfect nature be not polluted if It is conceived to be directly related to the world ?

The answer to this problem was given differently by Rāmānuja and the Pāñcarātra thinkers. Śankara also faced the same problem. Bādarāyaṇa in the Vedānta Sūtras had maintained that Brahman and the world are 'ananya' (non-different) but this non-difference does not mean absence of difference or change. Both Śankara and Rāmānuja agree that some change in Brahman is necessary in order to have the world, but the ontological position of this change is explained differently by them. For Śankara the change is 'vivarta', i.e. apparent only. In other words, the change undergone by Brahman to create the appearance of the world is not real. For the explanation of this apparent change Śankara postulated the principle of avidyā or māyā. As a matter of fact Brahman does not undergo any change but it falsely appears as if It has undergone the change. Similarly the world also is not real. It exists only for those who are under the influence of avidyā, even as the imagined serpent exists only for those who have the wrong view of the rope.

Rāmānuja, on the other hand, believes this change to be real. The world is real as a mode or determination of Brahman. The statement that Brahman is the material cause of the world suggests that the world is a modification of the substance of Brahman.

Rāmānuja believes that the power of creation etc., belongs to Brahman Itself. Brahman does not need the help of any tertium quid, a third entity like māyā or Śakti in between Itself and the world. Out of Its own līlā it developes Itself into the world without undergoing the least change. On the analogies of the relationships of cause and effect, body and soul, substance and attribute Rāmānuja explains how this can happen. He further says that

Brahman has wonderful powers by which even the inconceivable can be achieved. Śankara's difficulty that from Brahman who is absolute perfection the world of imperfection cannot be said to take its rise in a real manner does not trouble Rāmānuja, since he is willing to accept on the authority of the Śruti that the finite springs from the Infinite. What the Śruti says must be capable of being logically determined. From a philosophical point of view, however, this position is unsatisfactory. Further, it is difficult to conceive how Brahman could be supposed to be unchangeable in view of the changing conditions of Its attributes, matter and souls. Rāmānuja was aware of this difficulty and was obliged to concede that this does not affect the soul or essence of Brahman, but is limited to Its body, i.e., the world only.

The Pāñcarātra thinkers, like Śankara, denied the possibility of Brahman being an active agent in relation to the world, but, unlike Śankara, hesitated to brand the manifold world as not real in an explicit language. Here it must be remembered that no effort is made in the Pāñcarātra school to refute the doctrine of māyā, but Rāmānuja, as we have seen, fights tooth and nail with this doctrine and makes it as the main target of his criticism. In some of the Samhitās, on the contrary, the world is regarded as unreal and illusory which is quite in consonance with their advaitic tendency. Unlike Rāmānuja, they maintain that Brahman does not change Itself in the world. The world is not a modification of Brahman but an emanation from Its Sakti, which is considered to be Its aspect. It is in no way concerned with the world but only with Śakti which It is said to subordinate. The Pāñcarātra thinkers were of the view that the imperfect world cannot arise directly from the perfect Brahman. Consequently they had to postulate various intermediaries and mediating principles like Śakti, Vyūhas, Creator Brahmā, and the various stages like śuddha sarga, miśra sarga and aśuddhasarga, to bridge the gulf between Brahman and the world and to make less difficult the transition from Brahman to a world so different from It in character. They made a constant effort to preserve the reality of the world without thereby detracting from the transcendence and perfection of Brahman, but logically it resulted in a fiasco; because if the world is real it must have a place in Brahman, but the very transcendent nature of Brahman denies any such place to it. A Supreme Being who is a creator ceases to be merely transcendent.

The various intermediaries that the Pāñcarātra thinkers postulate between Brahman and the world to account for the transition from one to the other, do not find acceptance in the philosophy of Rāmānuja. The main feature of the Pāñcarātra cosmology may be said to be the concept of Śakti or Śri or Lakṣmī (which is the first intermediary) as the creative principle. This concept is altogether absent in Rāmānuja and in the Vedāntic scriptures. Rāmānuja refers to her as the beloved consort of Viṣṇu but never as a creative or philosophical principle. This doctrine of Śri as the creative aspect of Brahman is peculiar to the Pāñcarātra school. In the Viṣṇu Purāṇa (I. 9) she is invoked as 'the mother of all things' and as 'the bestower of the fruit of emancipation' but not as the creative principle.

It is true that the ideas of the Cosmic Egg and Creator Brahmā are present in Rāmānuja's cosmology, but they do not function there as intermediaries. These ideas are not at all peculiar to the Pāñcarātra, and are given a prominent place in the Ṛgveda, Upaniṣads and Purāṇas. These ideas have little philosophical significance in Rāmānuja but in the Pāñcarātra cosmology they play an important role. In the Pāñcarātra the gross creation proceeds from the Cosmic Egg, but in Rāmānuja the Cosmic Egg, Brahmā and Hiraṇyagarbha do not function independently. It is Brahmā who creates through them and therefore they can easily be dispensed with. Further the various details and elaborate complexities associated with these ideas in the Pāñcarātra are altogether absent in Rāmānuja.

Similarly the process of creation in Rāmānuja and in the Pāñcarātra is altogether different. In the Pāñcarātra there are two processes of creation intermingled. One is the Vyūha process which is a tenet distinctive of this school. The other is similar to the Sāmkhya enumeration of principles. Rāmānuja accepts only the Sāmkhya account of the evolution of the world. He did not incorporate the Pāñcarātra doctrine of three or four Vyūhas. Though in his treatment of the Pāñcarātra school he mentions the four Vyūhas as forms assumed by the Deity out of tenderness to His devotees for the purposes of worship, he makes no use of this doctrine as principles through which evolution of the world proceeds. On the contrary, it seems as if he is aware of the theological aspect of this doctrine only and is unaware of its cosmological application. It is, therefore, purely a misgiving of the scholars to say that Rāmānuja has utilised this doctrine in his cosmology.

The elaborate and complicated account of the process of evolution in the Pāñcarātra school with its characteristic doctrine of three stages and six Kośas of creation is altogether unknown to Rāmānuja. Rāmānuja gives a very simple and straight forward account of the process of evolution borrowed readymade from the Sāmkhya.

All the cosmological details which are original to and distinctive of the Pāñcarātra school are not available in Rāmānuja. Here we must remove some other misapprehensions of the scholars. The Pāñcarātra concept of Śuddha Sattva—a supra-physical substance out of which the forms and abode of the Deity are made, is not found in the works of Rāmānuja, though many scholars under wrong impression hold that Rāmānuja has accepted and incorporated this idea in his ontology. Similarly the concept of time is treated in the Pāñcarātra school in great details and it occupies a prominent place in Pāñcarātra cosmology but it is not present in the philosophy of Rāmānuja, though it is also wrongly ascribed to him.

Another point with regard to the process of creation in the Pāñcarātra is the prevalence of tāntrism. Almost all the Samhitās are replete with the tāntric elements, occultism and ritualistic details. A notable feature of these Samhitās is the account of the process of creation through mantras. But no such account of tāntric elements is found in Rāmānuja.

With regard to the purpose of creation, i.e., why should the Infinite appear as the finite, Rāmānuja holds that the world is a līlā of Brahman and is an instrument for meting out the deeds of the individual souls. The creation of the universe requires thought as well as intention on the part of Brahman. In the Pāñcarātra no specific purpose for the creation is mentioned. There a distinction is drawn between the transcendence of consciousness and immanence of will. The Ultimate Reality — The supreme Consciouess — Itself does not descend in the universe. It simply expresses a will and

Śakti — Its creative aspect—starts the process of creation. It is said to have suddenly stirred up with an independent resolve to create the world and orders Śakti accordingly. But why It gets stirred up and so resolves is not answered.

Lastly, the theory of causation in Rāmānuja and in the Pāñcarātra is widely different. Rāmānuja accepts pariṇāmavāda under which the cause undergoes a real change in order to bring out the effect. Pāñcarātra, on the contrary, propounds Vyūhavāda according to which the effect though emanates out of cause, leaves the cause entirely untouched. In Rāmānuja Brahman Itself gets transformed into the world. Brahman of Rāmānuja is Itself both the material and the efficient cause of the world. It is not only the creator but also the sustainer. It takes active interest in the affairs of the world. But Brahman of Pāñcarātra is not at all the cause of the world. It is Its Śākti which is entrusted with this task. She alone is the creative principle and not Brahman, who in Its transcendental aloofness remains unconcerned with the world. Thus Brahman of Pāñcarātra school is as if not only an absentee Deity but also a slumbering Deity, who once motivating Śakti to create the world, is no longer interested in it.

From the foregoing considerations it appears conclusive that Rāmānuja and the Pāñcarātra have no significant cosmological idea in common. The cosmological accounts are so divergent in them that there can be no basis for any meeting point. They bear only two elements in common which are quite insignificant. The first one is the incorporation of the Sāmkhya account of evolution and the second is acceptance of the ideas of Cosmic Egg and Brahmā. But from the account given by Rāmānuja it is quite evident that his basis for these elements is not Pāñcarātric but purely Vedāntic. Therefore, these do not in any way suggest the impact of the Pāñcarātra.

References and foot-notes :—

1. The same problem found expression in the Viśvakarmā hymns (Ṛgveda, X.81.4) .The intricasy and insolubility of the problem led the author of the Nāsadīya sūkta to admit his defeat when he said, 'who can know the origin of this world. It is also

doubtful whether the very supervisor of this world in the highest heaven knows it or not ?'

2. 'Vedānta Sāra' edited by M. Hiriyanna p. 8 (text) p. 54 (tra.). On p.36 Hiriyanna quotes the following verse, 'Samasattākaḥ pariṇāmaḥ viṣama sattākaḥ vivartaḥ', i.e., when the effect is a real transformation of its material cause (which is its essence) it is called vikāra or pariṇāma, but when it is an apparent transformation it is called vivarta.
3. Śrī Bhāṣya, I.1.1. See Thibaut's translation pp. 102ff.
4. See M.N. Sirkar, loc. cit, pp. 65-66 for the criticism of the argument.
5. See Thibaut's translation of Śrī Bhāṣya, p. 106.
6. Bṛh; I.4.16; II.1, II.5, III.7, III.9, IV.4.13, Chād., V.18.1.2, Tait., II.6; Kauś., 4; Iśa, I,6; Katha, V.9.13; Mund, II.1.4.9, Śve, I.16, VI.11; VI.34 etc.
7. Śve. I.7-12, III.1-2, 10,14,17,18; IV.1.etc; Katha, II.22; IV.9,12, 13; V.9,11,13; VI.2,3.
8. Bṛh., I.5.15; II,5.15; Kauś; III.8; Praśna, II.6; VI.6.
9. VII.6; IX.7,8,10,17; X.39; XIV.3. etc.
10. IX.7,9.
11. III.2, IV.1, V.3.
12. Śrī Bhāṣya, I.4.23.
13. Ibid, I.4.23.
14. Ibid, 1.4.25
15. Ibid, II.1.4
16. Ibid, II.1.15
17. Ibid, II.1.16
18. As Sarvajñātma Muni has put it :—
    Vivartavādasya hi pūrva bhūmiḥ Vedāntavāde pariṇāmavādaḥ.
    vyavasthitesmin pariṇāmavāde svayam samāyāti vivartavādaḥ
    Samkṣepa Śāriraka, p.40, Benaras edition.
19. Śrī Bhāṣya, I.4.27.
20. Ibid, I.4.27
21. Ibid, II.1.9.
22. Ibid, II.1.15.
23. Ibid, I.1.1.
24. Gītā Bhāṣya, VII.7.
25. Śrī Bhāṣya, I.1.1.

26. Ibid, I.1.1.
27. Ibid, I.4.27.
28. Ibid, I.2.23
29. Ibid, I.4.27
30. Ibid, I.1.1.
31. Ibid, I.4.10
32. Ibid, II.2.43
33. Ibid, I.4.3.
34. IX.7-8; XIV.3; VII.4.
35. Śrī Bhāṣya, 1.3.29.
36. Ibid, IV.2.6
37. Ibid, I.1.1
38. Ibid, II.4.17
39. Ibid, I.1.1.
40. Ibid, I.3.6
41. Ibid, I.4.8.
42. Ibid, I.1.1
43. Ibid, I.4.10.
44. Ibid, I.1.1.
45. Ibid, II.1.32
46. Ibid, II.1.33
47. Ibid, II.1.35
48. Introduction to the Pāñcarātra and the Ahirbudhnya Samhitā P.27.
49. Nārda Pāñcarātra. II.2.100; Jayākhya IV.85; Parama 1.80.
50. For details, see my work on Pāñcarātra philosophy.

CHAPTER III

NATURE AND DESTINY OF INDIVIDUAL SELF

Introduction

Metaphysics is the consideration of what is involved in the facts of experience. One of the most striking phenomena revealed in experience is the existence of individual spiritual entities named as finite selves. Though we know that the self is, we do not know what its nature is. Its nature has been an occasion of much speculation and sometimes scepticism. Here we are led to such questions as : What is the status of the individual selves within the system of the universe ? Are they real individuals existing in their own rights; or are they real modes of a single absolute Reality having finite but inalienable individuality; or are they mere figments of imagination or the vanishing appearances of the Absolute, the only true individual there is or can be ?

All these questions were discussed at length by the Vedāntic and the Pāñcarātra thinkers. In the Āḷvārs, however, we do not find any such speculations mainly because their interest is too all-absorbingly centred round God to spare them for other matters. They are out and out devotees rather than philosophers, and therefore, nature of self, as also world process, has no interest for them. Little interested as they are in speculations about self, they remain satisfied with the thought that the individual self is a wonderful entity indescribable, eternal and essentially characterised by intelligence. Nāmmāḷvār declares that the individual self is a mode of God. It is different from body, vital breaths, senses etc. It is very subtle. In its essential nature it is beyond good and bad.[1] From the way in which they describe their relation to God it appears that they regarded the individual self as bride or beloved of God.[2]

Advaitic view of individual self

According to the Advaita Vedānta Brahman alone is the Supreme Reality. All the finite selves are nothing but the appearances of Brahman. The relation between the individual self and Brahman can, therefore, be that of absolute identity. Strictly speaking we cannot talk of any such relation, because in reality they are not different. All the individual selves are one and the same indivisible Brahman, but owing to the particular adjuncts caused by avidyā the one unitary Brahman appears, as it were, to be broken up into multiplicity of individual selves. What is real in each self is the universal Brahman. The whole aggregate of individualising bodily organs and mental functions, which is our ordinary experience separates and distinguishes one self from the other, is the off-spring of māyā, and as such is unreal.

The individual self which is manifestly in bondage is unable to look through and beyond māyā which like a veil hides from it its true nature. Instead of recognising itself to be Brahman, it blindly identifies itself with its adjuncts which are the fictitious off-springs of māyā. The self which in reality is pure intelligence, non-active, infinite etc. thus becomes as it were limited in extent, knowledge and power. It further becomes an agent and an enjoyer. It is only when the adjuncts are removed by the right knowledge of its true nature, which consists of the fact that it is in no way different from the Highest Self, that final emancipation takes place. Then it shines in its original nature which amounts to annihilation of its finite existence and finite nature.

Rāmānuja's refutation of Advaitic view

Rāmānuja directs a severe criticism against this advaitic view,[3] and declares that the individual self is the most palpable and concrete entity. Its reality is given in the facts of consciousness, for consciousness which is ever-changing requires a substratum.

It is also given in the facts of memory and recognition, for recognition implies a conscious subject persisting from the earlier to the later moment.[4] It is also implicit in inference, for it presupposes the ascertainment and remembrance of general propositions.[5]

Rāmānuja supplements these empirical arguments by the testimony of the scriptures. He quotes Bṛhadāraṇyaka III. 7.22, Śvetāśvatara I.6, I.9, VI. 9, VI. 16, VI. 13 etc. in all of which the plurality of self is explicitly recognised and taught.[6] He further derives support from the Gītā (II. 12) which clearly teaches the reality of individual self and its eternal distinction from Brahman.

It is said that the texts like 'Thou art that' teach the absolute identity of the individual self and the Supreme Self but Rāmānuja replies that these texts are not meant to convey the idea of the absolute unity of a non-differentiated substance. On the contrary, they denote a Brahman distinguished by difference. The word 'that' refers to Brahman and the word 'thou' which stands in coordination to 'that' conveys the idea of Brahman in so far as having for Its body the individual selves.[7]

Rāmānuja's view of individual self

In the philosophy of Rāmānuja the absoluteness of God is so qualified as to admit the existence of real finite selves within His concrete unity. From the fundamental ontological position of Rāmānuja that God is a unity inclusive of infinite determinations, there logically follows the existence of real finite selves, which are individual centres of thought and action. They are entities in themselves, though they derive their substantiality and entire being from God. Being the eternal differentiations of God, they are called His modes, parts, body etc., yet they have their own individual nature and features. Rāmānuja thus advocates the model dependence of the type of Spinoza as well as the monadic individuality of the type of Leibnitz. Rāmānuja is quite emphatic and insistent in holding that the individual selves, being eternal differentiations of God, are as real as God Himself. They are real entities, and cannot be dismissed as illusory, or false and fictitious being due to some innate nescience associated with the nature of God. Therefore, he criticises those who regard individual selves as 'vain variations of the self-same Absolute'.

Individual self as knower

According to Rāmānuja each individual self is a real self-identical being. It is a spiritual being different from the material elements like mind, body, vital breathes, senses etc. He holds that the essential nature of the individual self is to be a knowing subject. It is not pure consciousness as the advaitin maintains, but it is the substratum of consciousness. It is not mere knowlege but an individual who possesses knowledge as its essential characteristic. That the self is a conscious principle and not mere consciousness, is emphasised by him in order to safeguard the individuality of the self against the advaitic tendency of overlooking all distinctions between the finite self and Brahman.[8]

Individual self as doer

Rāmānuja further maintains that the individual self is not only a knower, but also a doer and is thus a true self characterised by thought and activity. He declares that the agency of the self is implied in the Upaniṣadic doctrine of Karma according to which each self reaps the fruits of its deeds. The agency of the self is denied by the Advaita and the Sāmkhya. In the scriptures also at places agency is denied to the self.[9] There it is maintained as though the self is inactive all activity being due to the guṇas of the body. Rāmānuja explains this circumstance by saying that the self is an agent by virtue of its being associated with the kārmic body, in an embodied state. But, it is the self only which is an agent and not the guṇas.[10] Though the self is an agent, this does not mean that it is always active. It is provided with the capacity to act but it may act or may not act, as it pleases.[11]

Individual self as atomic

Rāmānuja further declares that the individual self is atomic. It is not all-pervading because the scriptures speak of it as passing out of the body, going and returning, all these movements on the part of the self would clearly be meaningless if it were omnipresent.[12] Rāmānuja bases this view on Śvetāśvatara V. 8-9, and Mundaka III.1.9.

The logical basis for Rāmānuja's rejection of the omnipresence of the self is that if it were so there would be everywhere and at all times simultaneously consciousness and non-consciousness, but this never is the case. He writes, 'On our view, on the other hand, the actually perceived distribution of consciousness and non-consciousness explains itself, since we hold the self to abide within bodies only, so that naturally consciousness takes place there only, not anywhere else.' Moreover, he points out against the Vaiśeṣikas that if the self were omnipresent all the selves would be in permanent conjunction with all organs, and besides, the adṛṣṭas due to the actions of the different bodies would be entirely confused, for all selves would then be in contact with all bodies.[14]

Rāmānuja further maintains that though the individual self is atomic and dwells in one part of the body, it is conscious of the sensations taking place in any part of the body. Thus it extends through the whole body by means of its quality, namely, consciousness.[15] When the scripture describes the self as all-pervasive it refers to its consciousness only. It, however, may be referred to as all-pervasive in the sense that being infinitely small it can penetrate all unconscious material substances. It has uniqueness like a monad, but is not exclusive and windowless because of its all-pervasive consciousness. So although the self is atomic it has knowledge as its invariable accompaniment, which can stream forth to any distance and is able to comprehend things, even though they are far off.

This concept of the individual self as atomic, indicates the eagerness of Rāmānuja to emphasise the individuality of the finite self, as against the advaitic tendency of all-pervasiveness which virtually would imply a denial of individuality. Further, Rāmānuja's insistence that each individual self has its own distinctive centre of experience avoids the confusion between one self and another.

Individual self as eternal and immutable

Rāmānuja further maintains that the individual self is eternal and immutable in the sense that it is sui generis and has its own intrinsic value. It is unborn and immortal. It is real, and the real, as the Gītā declares, never ceases to be. Therefore no dissipation of the individuality of the self can be admitted. When the scriptures speak of origination and destruction of the self they only point out the association with and dissociation from the body of the embodied self. But in all these births and deaths and rebirths which continue upto release, there is no addition to or diminution of its essence and existence. Those texts which deny origination mean to say that the self does not undergo changes of essential nature.

In the Gītā Bhāṣya Rāmānuja gives three arguments to prove the eternity and immortality of the individual self. The first argument is on the authority of God Himself who declares in unequivocal terms that the individual self is immortal in no way less than God Himself.[16] The second argument is that the individual self is a spiritual being and pervades the non-spiritual entity which is different from it. From this it follows that it is subtler than all non-spiritual entities which necessarily must be grosser if the individual self is to pervade them. Now the thing that destroys is subtler than the thing which is destroyed, for it can only destroy by pervading a thing and thereby decomposing it. Nothing, however, is subtle enough to pervade the individual self, so the self is indestructible. Lastly, the individual self is not destructible because it is a unity by itself, and as such cannot increase or decrease.[17]

Individual self in relation to Brahman.

The real nature of the individual self cannot be known apart from that of God, since the two are inseparably united and indissolubly related to each other. Regarding the relation of the individual self to God Rāmānuja repudiates various views which hold that (i) the individual self is absolutely different from Brahman (God), or (ii) it is nothing else but Brahman under a delusion, or, (iii) it is Brahman determined by a limiting adjunct. Against all these he holds that the individual self is a part of Brahman.[18] For this he finds support in the Chāndogya Upaniṣad III.12.6. He also quotes the Gītā (XV.7) in which the Lord declares, 'An eternal part of myself becomes the individual self in the world of life.'

When the individual self is said to be a part of Brahman it does not mean that it constitutes a part of the extention of Brahman, since Brahman is partless. Further it would also imply that all the imperfections of the individual self would belong to Brahman. The word 'part' should be understood in its qualitative sense only. That is, it is a part of Brahman in the sense that it is a mode or an attribute of Brahman.

Though Rāmānuja regards the individual self as an attribute or mode of Brahman this does not mean that it has a mere adjectival existence with no individuality of its own. As we have seen before, according to Rāmānuja the substance-attribute relationship holds not only in case of objects and their generic qualities, but also in case of two different objects, one of which may be an attribute of the other. Accordingly the individual self may be an attribute of Brahman and at the same time may have an individuality of its own. The individual self is an attribute of Brahman only in the sense that it belongs to Brahman and is completely dependent on It. In this way it has a substantive as well as an adjectival existence. This relation of individual self to Brahman can be considered under three heads.

Individual self in relation to Brahman prior to world creation

The Ultimate Reality in Rāmānuja's philosophy is a triune unity consisting of Brahman, matter and the individual selves. The latter two, which are the constituent elements of the world exist in Brahman as Its eternal part in a subtle form before It makes the world manifest. In that state of perfect homogeneity the individual selves with their intelligence in a contracted form exist in Brahman in a latent state. But this state does not involve complete suppression of their essential nature.[19]

Though the self exists in Brahman in a latent state or in a state of intimate union amounting to homogeneity, nevertheless it is not a state of coalescence. It does retain its separate existence and distinct individuality. Not only this, its past karmas are also preserved and at the start of creation Brahman makes it to be connected with the kind of body merited by its karmas.[20]

Individual self in relation to Brahman in worldly existence.

The self, prior to world creation, exists in a state of intimate union with Brahman but when creation begins, it becomes differentiated from Brahman. Now it acquires a particular body in accordance with its karmas so that it may be requited for what it has done. This, however, should not mean that the sole purpose of creation is mere retribution or stern adherence to the moral law. It is more for the ultimate good or final release of the individual self.[21]

When the individual self thus acquires its body, Brahman enters into it, and remains within it as its Inner Self. This concept of Brahman as Inner Self is inherited by Rāmānuja from the philosophers of the Upaniṣads. This is clearly stated in the Bṛhadāraṇyaka III.7.3.-22, and the Tattirīya II.6. But unlike the philosophers of the Upaniṣads, Rāmānuja is quite clear and consistent in maintaining that the 'entering into' of Brahman in the individual self and abiding there as the Inner Self does not tell upon the perfect nature of Brahman on the one hand and the individuality of the individual self on the other. In the Upaniṣads the abiding of Brahman in the individual self is very often taught, but at many places they have used such an ambiguous language that they tended often to mean that Brahman Itself is the self in the body. Therefore, Rāmānuja is very much eager to point out that Brahman exists there only as an Inner Self and not as the individual self.[22]

Brahman thus stands to the individual self in the same relation as the soul stands to the body. Rāmānuja's definition of a body in relation to the soul is as follows, 'Any substance which a sentient self is capable of completely controlling and supporting for its own purposes, and which stands to the self in an entirely subordinate relation, is the body of that self'.[23] Thus in the state of worldly existence of the individual self Brahman abides within it as its soul, not as one who robs away its individuality, but as one who supports and rules over it, without in any way being involved into it.

Individual self in relation to Brahman in the state of release.

The fundamental thesis of Rāmānuja, as we have repeatedly seen, is to uphold the supreme and perfect personality of God and the inalienable individuality of the finite selves. Both these tenets Rāmānuja tries to maintain in his account of the relation in which Brahman stands related to the finite self in the state of release.

There are clear and abundant traces in the Upaniṣads of the view that the individual self continues to exist in release, enjoys perfection and bliss, and becomes like Brahman. But the advaitin maintains that in release the finite self merges in or becomes unified without difference with Brahman, a view quite opposed to Rāmānuja's basic position. He, therefore, sets himself in sharp opposition to the advaita view and argues that if release meant 'a mere return into the substance of Brahman', it would not be anything beneficial or desirable to man, for to be refunded into Brahman means nothing but complete annihilation, which none would like.'[24]

Rāmānuja confronts the advaitin with a dilemma and declares that the advaitin's view cannot stand the test of being submitted to definite alternatives. He argues, 'Is the individual self's not being such, i.e., not being Brahman prior to its departure from the body, due to its own essential nature or to a limiting adjunct, and is it in the latter case real or unreal ? In the first case the individual self can never become one with Brahman, for if its separation from Brahman is due to its own essential nature, that separation can never vanish as long as the essential nature persists. Should it be said that its essential nature comes to an end together with its distinction from Brahman, we reply that in that case it perishes utterly and does not therefore become Brahman.'[25]

On the basis of the above reasons Rāmānuja rejects the view that the individual self merges in Brahman on attaining release. On the other hand, he urges that since the individual self is by its very nature a distinct individual, it must persist as a self-conscious being in the state of release.[26] The released individual self instead of forfeiting its individuality, rather attains its essential nature. It does not cease to be, but deepens its selfhood and effaces all stains of sins. The essential nature of the individual self obscured so far by avidyā becomes manifested, even as a mirror stained by dust shines brilliantly when it has been cleansed. Rāmānuja derives this view from the Chāndogya Upaniṣad (VIII. 12.3) which declares, 'Thus does that serene being, having risen from the body and having approached the highest Light, manifests itself in its own form.'[27] This 'cleansing' means freedom from karma and the consequent imperfection.[28]

Further Rāmānuja writes that the released individual self obtains whatever it wishes by its mere will.[29] It enters as many bodies as it pleases, not being impelled by karma, but entirely by its own will.[30] It enjoys all the worlds eternally.[31] It finds itself on an equality with all other freed selves for all distinctions of rank, caste, and the like are entirely due to the body.[32] And, more than all this, it enjoys that beatific vision of Brahman for which it longed in the worldly life.[33] This intuition of Brahman is possible only when the individual self realises its natural state.[34] Therefore, Rāmānuja writes, 'The highest Brahman which is free from all change and of an absolutely perfect and blessed nature this, together with the manifestations of Its glory, is what forms the object of consciousness for the released self.'[35] Thus the released self attains its natural character.[36] It reclaims all its attributes like knowledge which become manifest only when it attains release.[37]

Though the individual self persists as a self-conscious being in the state of release and perfects its individuality, this does not in any way annul the supremacy of Brahman and reduce It to one among a number of equally independent selves. The released self becomes like Brahman in nature in that it is characterised by uncontracted intelligence, and in that it is free from all evil.[38] Nevertheless it always remains only a mode of Brahman and never as an independent substance like Brahman.[39] The exalted qualities of the individual self no doubt belong to its essential nature but they depend upon Brahman only.[40] Therefore, the individual self can never usurp the place of Brahman.

The released self differs from Brahman in two important respects. First, it is atomic and hence strictly finite, while Brahman is universal and all-pervading.[41] Secondly, it does not have creative and ruling power over the world which belongs exclusively to Brahman.[42].

The individual selves, then, we may conclude, are real and eternal entities having knowledge, bliss and freedom from evil as their essential nature. Though they are similar in nature with Brahman, there is no conflict between their individuality and the universality and supremacy of Brahman, because they form the body or mode of Brahman, while Brahman is their Inner Self on whom they completely depend.

Pāñcarātra view of individual self

The Pāñcarātra school, because of its predominantly religious character, concentrated much of its thought on the theological considerations like the nature of Brahman, emanation of the world out of Brahman and the means of attaining release from bondage. It was very little interested in speculations irrelevant to its theological purposes. Therefore it seldom took into consideration the problem of the nature of the individual self. It was satisfied with the thought that individual self owes its existence to the Supreme Self. It considers, though not clearly and consistently, the relation of the individual self to the Supreme Self.

In consonance with its advaitic tendency the Pāñcarātra school describes the nature and destiny of the individual self in an advaitic manner. But it is not always consistent in doing so. Under the advaitic influence the selfhood of the individual self as distinct from the Supreme Self does not get recognition; but when it is guided by religious feelings it appears to recognise a self distinct from the Supreme Self.[43] However the dominant note of the Pāñcarātra thought in this regard is undoubtedly advaitic.

Advaita school and Rāmānuja—A Study in Contrast

Having discussed the views of the Advaita school, Rāmānuja and the Pāñcarātra school regarding the nature of the individual self and its relation to the Supreme Self, we may now turn to their comparative and critical analysis.

To start with the Advaita school and Rāmānuja, we find that they are poles apart on this topic. According to Śaṅkara the individual self is nothing but Brahman limited by the unreal adjuncts caused by māyā. Rāmānuja, on the other hand, maintains that it is an effect or part of Brahman, it has sprung from Brahman, and it is never outside Brahman, nevertheless it enjoys a separate personal existence and will, and remains an inalienable personality for ever.

For Śaṅkara, to whom non-duality is the ultimate truth of philosophy, the true self is one only and cannot be many. The true self is not a separate and distinct entity from Brahman, but is identical with It. The plurality of selves, thus, is unreal, caused by avidyā, and has no metaphysical value. Rāmānuja, on the contrary, maintains that every individual self is an eternal spiritual entity and thus there are many such selves each with its own individuality.

Rāmānuja maintains that the individual self is an entity denoted by the notion of 'I' (ahamārtha). Śankara does not admit that the notion of 'I' is the true self, in so far as it is only a product of avidyā. The plurality of 'I' has no metaphysical value, for it dissolves in the unity of Brahman, the only Being that is or can be. The 'I' has psychological or epistemological ideality but no metaphysical reality. It is only a reflection, or limitation of Brahman in, or by, avidyā.

The issue as to whether the individual self is pure consciousness or a conscious being has sharply divided Śankara and Rāmānuja. Śankara insists that the self is consciousness only and not a knowing subject, because knowership, for him, involves change, while the true self must be immutable. Rāmānuja refutes this theory taking his stand on experience and also on the ground that knowership does not involve change in the strict sense of the term. The Sūtrakāra has defined the nature of the individual self as 'jña' which Śankara interprets in the sense that knowledge does not constitute a mere attribute of the self but is the very essence of the self. The self is not a knower but knowledge, not intelligent but intelligence. Rāmānuja, on the other hand, explains 'jña' as 'jñātṛ', i.e., knower and regards this sūtra as directed not only against the Vaiśeṣikas but also against those philosophers who like the Sāmkhyas and Vedāntins of Śankara's type maintain that the self is not a knowing agent but pure caitanya. The wording of the sūtra certainly seems to favour the interpretation of Rāmānuja, because the most obvious meaning of the word 'jña' is jñātṛ and not jñānam.

Another point of difference between Śankara and Rāmānuja is with regard to the agency of the individual self. Śankara maintains that the self is essentially non-active, and all actions belong to the world of upādhis. The self is an agent only when it is connected with the instruments of action, viz., buddhi etc. and ceases to be so when dissociated from them. Thus when Bādarāyaṇa establishes the ageney of the self, he thereby does not mean inherent agency of the self, but only the accidental one caused by adjuncts. The arguments that Śankara has put forth in support of his thesis are that if self's agency is inherent or natural then as fire cannot be free from heat so also the self cannot be free from agency, and consequently there is no possibility of its getting release, and secondly, all agency is leading to misery. The first argument may be met by saying that though the self may be endowed with the capacity of acting it may or may not indulge in activity. To the second argument it can be replied that all actions do not lead to pain. Pain is not due to agency, but due to the attachment to fruits. One should perform disinterested actions as directed in the Gītā. Rāmānuja, whose interpretations of the sūtras is more natural and satisfactory, maintains that activity is indeed an essential attribute of the self, but therefrom it does not follow that it is always actually active, just as a carpenter, even when furnished with requisite instruments may either work or may not work as he pleases. Thus Rāmānuja holds that the agency belongs to the self by nature as inherent attribute, and is not attributed to it by superimposition. Here it must be mentioned in favour of Rāmānuja that Bādarāyaṇa in another sūtra, viz. Parāttu tacchṛuteḥ, in the same adhikaraṇa, declares that the self derives its kartṛtva from Brahman. Now if it were the position that the self was not an agent at all and that its kartṛtva was only superimposed on it, how could the question arise whether the self was an independent agent or a dependent one ? Further, if the agency were due to the limiting adjuncts of nescience how could Bādarāyaṇa have declared that this agency followed from Brahman. Undoubtedly, Śankara is right in rejecting bodily activities superimposed on the self, but he is wrong in his absolute rejection of the self's kartṛtva.

Another debatable point between Śankara and Rāmānuja is with regard to the size of the individual self. According to Śankara the individual self being in reality Brahman only, is omnipresent and all-pervading and not atomic (aṇu). When the scripture declares the individual self as atomic it refers to the individual self in the condition of the worldly existence. In the worldly existence the individual self consists essentially in its being limited by, and possessing the qualities of the buddhi, and so the atomic size of the buddhi is only metaphorically predicated to the individual self. This connection of the individual self with buddhi lasts as long as the individual continues to exist in bondage. Rāmānuja, on the other hand, regards the individual self as of atomic size only. He argues that the individual self is atomic because gati and āgati etc. are ascribed to it. Vedic passages do teach and suggest atomicity of the individual self. The objection that the consciousness of the individual self, if it is atomic, cannot be pervading the whole body, does not stand because though seated in the heart it can spread its consciousness throughout the body on the analogy of sandal, lamp or diamond.

Śankara, in support of his doctrine of all-pervasiveness of the individual self, has put forth three arguments none of which, as a matter of fact, finds any direct support from the sūtras of Bādarāyaṇa. The three arguments are (i) Utpattyaśvṛavaṇa (denial of origination), (ii) Parasyaiva Brahmaṇaḥ praveśaḥ (Brahman's entrance), and tādātmyopadeśa (teaching of identity). The first argument used by Bādarāyaṇa to establish the eternity of the individual self, does not conclusively prove that the individual self is vibhu (all-pervasive). Śankara argues that since individual self's origination is denied, it is Brahman only and hence vibhu. But on the same basis it can also be argued that since avidyā has no origination it is also Brahman. The second argument is based on Chāndogya 'Anena jīvena ātmanā anupraviśya nāma rūpe vyākaravāni'. This passage teaches Brahman's entrance into the individual self and therefore Śankara holds that the individual self is the same as Brahman, i.e., all-pervasive. But according to the reasoning of Śankara there can be no Brahma-praveśa, because Brahman is all-pervasive. The third argument is stronger than anyone of the preceding arguments, but even here one cannot say that this statement of identity is in the sense held by Śankara. Rāmānuja gives an altogther different and more convincing interpretation of the statement of identity by taking the individual self as a part of Brahman.

We now turn to the question of the relation of the individual self to Brahman, which is one of the most crucial problems of metaphysics and on which Śankara and Rāmānuja are sharply divided. According to Śankara the individual self is in reality identical with Brahman, and separated from It only due to avidyā. Rāmānuja, on the contrary, maintains that the individual self although springs from Brahman and constitutes an element of Its nature, yet it enjoys a kind of individual existence apart from It.

Another aspect of this problem is the issue as to whether the individual self in the state of release becomes identical with Brahman or simply becomes united with It without losing its individuality. The former view is held by Śankara and the latter by Rāmānuja. Both agree that in liberation the sense of separateness is disparaged and the result is infinite knowledge, being and bliss. Further both declare that it connotes transcendence from finitude; but while in Śankara it means identity in Rāmānuja it means unitive consciousness. Śankara denies relativistic consciousness, Rāmānuja accepts its assimilation in unitive consciousness. According to Śankara release from Śamsāra means absoulte merging of the so-called individual self in Brahman due to the dismissal of the erroneous notion that the individual self is distinct from Brahman. For Rāmānuja it means passing of the individual self from the troubles of earthly life into a kind of divine life where it will remain forever in undisturbed personal bliss. Śankara takes his stand on the scriptural texts like 'Brahmavid Brahmaiva bhavati' (Mundaka III. 1.2.). This text is interpreted to imply identity of individual self and Brahman. Rāmānuja on the contrary maintains that the text in question does not refer to identity (tādātmya) but to equality (sādharmya) as is taught in the same text in the statement, 'Nirañjanaḥ paramam sāmyamupaiti'.

As a matter of fact in the Upaniṣads we find texts which entail the doctrines of Śankara as well as Rāmānuja. At many places the upaniṣadic sages tend to identify Brahman with the individual self in the body. Their monistic vision does not allow them to think of plurality of the selves beyond the one Brahman. Accordingly they believe that Brahman though very different in nature from the embodied self, nevertheless It alone is undergoing experiences in the body. Though the monistic bias thus leads them to declare the final absolute identification of the individual self with Brahman, their realism also inclines them to believe in the plurality of the individual selves and their eternal distinctness from Brahman. The monistic tendency is more dominant in the earlier Upaniṣads and the realistic tendency in the later ones.

In the Gītā as well at some places the selfhood of the individual self as distinct from Brahman does not gain recognition, but at other places the individual self is clearly recognised as distinct from It. Although the Gītā often speaks as though Brahman is one without difference with the individual self, its own distinctive position, as indicated by its predominantly theistic character, is that It is distinct from the individual self whom It pervades and controls.

Thus both Śankara and Rāmānuja could claim full support from the Upaniṣads and the Gītā for their respective view-points, but so far as the Brahma Sūtras are concerned they seem to lend very little support to the views of Śankara. There is a very large number of sūtras which distinctly affirm the difference between Brahman and the individual self. Śankara himself conscious of the difficulty of finding his view in the sūtras thinks it necessary to add an explanation in several cases to the effect that all such sūtras refer to the differences between Brahman and the individual self which are saupādhika i.e., due to māyā, and that in such cases the Sūtrakāra has regard only for the popular conception which is mentioned only to be ultimately rejected.

The sūtras clearly declare that the individual se'f is a part of Brahman, a view which is expressed in the Vedic mantra 'Pādo asya sarva bhūtāni' and in the Gītā passage 'Mamaivāmśo jīvaloke jīvabhūtaḥ sanātanaḥ'. Śankara altogether arbitrarily takes the word 'amśa' as 'amśa iva' and holds that the sūtra propounds avacchedavāda, but for this there is no justification whatsoever. There are passages, it is true, which declare Brahman to be 'niṣkala' and 'niravayava' (without parts), but that does not justify one to reject all texts teaching amśatva of the individual self, because both are scriptural texts and hence equally authoritative. What is needed is not to reject the one or the cther but to reconcile the two. Whenever there is an opposition like this between passages asserting difference and those asserting non-difference, Śankara always tries to escape by saying that the passages asserting non-difference declare the truth and are to be understood literally; whereas those asserting difference only refer to the popular notions which are to be rejected.

On the other hand, the sūtras go very well with the doctrine of Rāmānuja. Both the types of passages, those declaring difference and those declaring non-difference, must be understood to be true and to represent the reality, and for this it must be admitted that the individual self is a part of Brahman, i.e., it is dependent on Brahman, but at the same time it is individually distinct in nature.

Undoubtedly there is a sūtra, viz., 'ābhāsa eva ca,' which Śankara interprets as propounding the reflection theory (pratibimbavāda) and apparently this interpretation seems to be quite natural and more convincing than Rāmānuja's interpretation, yet on the basis of the general drift and spirit of the work this much is quite evident that the Sūtrakāra by no means favours reflection theory. Further, there are sūtras which describe Brahman as 'adhika' or 'itara', i.e., additional to, or different from, the individual self. Śankara's attempt to explain them as pointing out aupādhika bheda is quite unconvincing. Had Śankara's interpretation been true, it remains quite unintelligible why Sūtrakāra should never hint at what Śankara is anxious again and again to point out and why should the Sūtrakāra devote the greater part of the work for exoteric doctrine and very little to esoteric teaching, which may however mislead the mumukṣu if he does not keep in view the exact purport of the Sūtrakāra.

If we consider the views of Śankara and Rāmānuja independent of the Prasthāna Trayī, we again find that Śankara's doctrine does not seem to be more convincing. No one should deny the compactness and impressiveness of Śankara's system and the subtle logicality with which he has worked out his case, yet one finds it too sweeping to retain individual existence and initiative, which a man of experience values the most. Such a theory which declares obliteration of the individual self as the ultimate goal of life, paralyses our energies at their very source. It provides no satisfactory status for the individuals who shrink into the position of a helpless prey of māyā, rather than being active cooperators with God in the spiritual enterprise. It is not only morally enervating and discouraging but also speculatively dissatisfying. It is quite perplexing and unintelligible why the Absolute to which there is nothing unaccomplished should come under the sway of māyā and thereby result into a plurality of illusory finite existences. By bringing the doctrine of māyā into service, Śankara could explain with a remarkable success how the unity breaks up into multiplicity. Though he could explain the 'how' of it, he failed to explain the 'why' of it. The more crucial part of this problem is why should the unity appear in the guise of multiplicity by creating the whole world appearance which is destined to be destroyed ? Why should the Absolute or for that matter māyā, lavish its energy in evolving and maintaining the world-appearance which is not to last ultimately ? If the multiplicity is nothing but a vanishing appearance there is no good reason for spending in vain a stupendous amount of energy for its creation and maintenance. Further under this view all human and personal values are regarded as fragmentary experiences to be transcended. If these values do not have any place in the Ultimate Reality, why should human beings strive hard to attain and retain them. In a true system of philosophy instead of being annulled these values should be accepted as one of the available clues to the Ultimate Reality.

It is of course a sound principle that the individual can find its meaning within the context of the Absolute. But this does not mean depriving the individual of its uniqueness and permanent value. They are, on the contrary, the very conditions on which the individual can attain fulness and abundance of life. The universe respects the individual life and lavishes its energy in its production and development. There is indeed a force in the universe working for an ever richer and more inclusive unity, integration and coordination, but side by side with that there is another tendency in the universe working for greater and greater individuation, shaping fuller and better personalities. The highest kind of unity is not the static unity of a solitary, self-centred, self-determined Absolute, but a dynamic unity of a society of souls realising their highest perfection in love and in mutually enriching fellowship. This is only possible where each has a unique inner life of his own and respects the individuality of others; but yet where each does not lose but finds himself in others. God Himself is love and needs such a society (madbhaktaḥ me priyaḥ). Such at least is the teaching of the Gītā which declares the consummation of the divine purpose to be the establishment of such a divine society.

Accordingly the individuality is not a negligible feature of the world, but is necessary to its very idea. There is a room in the system of reality for individual beings possessing a certain measure of autonomy and capable of entering into personal relationship with God. God also is not the Absolute whose over-whelming omnipotence leaves no room for any will but His own. He, on the contrary, welcomes and inspires the free cooperation of the individuals in working out His plan. This God is not something away from the earth in a heaven, as Rāmānuja is sometimes mistaken to think, but He exists in us all in the form of an ideal tendency. The relation between God and the finite spirits should not be stated in terms of the relation of one finite being to another. To regard God as merely an individual caring for likes, praises and offerings of the finite is to fall far short of the highest insight alike of religion and philosophy. God should not be treated as one of the members of the divine society, rather He is the very source and substance of that society. He Himself is the divine society. When the Upaniṣads speak of 'entering into Brahman' they perhaps suggest that the individuals become members of this divine society which is a perfect society, a spiritual community, the family of God. This is the vision which the Vedic and Upaniṣadic seers had when they declared 'Tadviṣṇoḥ paramam padam sadā paśyanti sūrayaḥ' (Ṛgveda I.22.20; cf. Katha I.3.9). This perfect commonwealth of spirits is not so much an accomplished fact as an eventual consummation attainable through proper planning (jñāna), single-minded devotion (bhakti) and concentrated effort (karma).

From the foregoing consideration we conclude that despite God's absolute unity, finite selves as individuals preserve and attain their unique existence and meanings, and are not lost in the very Life that sustains them. This Life is real through them, and they are real through their union with that Life.

Rāmānuja and Pāñcarātra school — A Study in Contrast

As against Śankara, Rāmānuja is a staunch protagonist of the reality and inalienable existence of the individual self. His main target of polemic was all sorts of absolutism or singularism which was responsible for the denial of the reality and individuality of the finite self. The position of the Pāñcarātra school has very much come under the advaitic influence, and consequently we find that it is as far away as Śankara from the position of Rāmānuja. The uncompromising realism of Rāmānuja, his anxiety to refute the māyā doctrine, and his fight for the reality, individuality and inalienability of the individual self, are altogether absent in the Pāñcarātra school.

Though the Pāñcarātra school is very much wedded to advaitism, its instinctive theism did not allow it to rest contended with advaitism and the result is that it vacillates between advaitic and non-advaitic positions. As a matter of fact no efforts have been made to synthesise these two opposite positions which are placed side by side. But the problem is, since both the advaitic and non-advaitic tendencies are met with simultaneously, which one is original to this school. From the fact that in its theology and cosmology this school is manifestly advaitic we may believe that with regard to the individual self also its original and official view is advaitic and that the non-advaitic tendency is a later intrusion. The Pāñcarātra school, like many other systems of Indian thought, is not a product of one age or one generation, but has a long history whose major part is unknown to us. It may be that the Proto-Pāncarātra school was thoroughly advaitic, but when the advaitic school came under the disfavour of the rank and file because of its māyāvāda, the Pāñcarātra school also modified its strictly advaitic position and made a compromise with the non-advaitic tendencies. But even though the Pāñcarātra school reached a compromise with the non-advaitic (mainly viśiṣṭādvaitic) tendencies, it did not give up its original advaitic position. That is why we find that though Rāmānuja whose position is viśiṣṭādvaitic has some points in common with the Pāñcarātra school, he differs widely from the latter. From the few points of similarity one need not be hurried to conclude that the positions of the Pāñcarātra school and Rāmānuja are identical. The following comparative account of the two positions will substantiate our thesis.

The individual self in the Pāñcarātra school, unlike in Rāmānuja, is not an independent existence. It is declared to be a part of Lakṣmī which, like the māyā of the Advaita school, is a principle of differentiation, and which ontologically has no independent status, as it is merely Brahman's will. The concept of Lakṣmī in the Pāñcarātra school is more an assumption to explain the manifoldness than an existence. Phenomenally it is said to have a separate existence but transcendently speaking it is nothing but

Brahman Itself. Just as in the Advaita school the individual self is Brahman only conditioned by māyā, so in the Pāñcarātra school it is none else but a fulguration of Brahman caused by Lakṣmī. It has, therefore, no independent existence of its own, nor has it got any ontological status. To explain as to how the individual selves come to exist, the Pāñcarātra school very often used three well-known advaitic similies, viz., the pot in air, the pot in water, and one figure reflected in many mirrors.

The Pāñcarātra school, unlike Rāmānuja, further maintains that the individual self has no permanent existence. Since it has no independent existence of its own, but is merely a fulguration of Brahman, it is destined to be reabsorbed in It. The view that the individual self is not an imperishable entity, is a logical consequence of the pure monism of the Pāñcarātra thinkers according to whom the Supreme Self is the only reality. The Absolute of the Pāñcarātra thinkers, really speaking, is an Impersonal One for whom the individual selves count for little. The natural consequence is that the thought that Brahman is the Supreme Real, easily led them to think that It is the only Real. This is very often the position they adopted with regard to Brahman in relation to the individual self. It is undoubtedly true that to some of them the individual self was too sensibly real to be dismissed as unreal. Under the assumption of commonsense and perhaps also under the influence of the Viśiṣṭādvaita they did not carry their advaitic views to their logical consequences and admitted the eternal existence of the individual self. Nevertheless the dominant thought of the Pāñcarātra school is that the individual self is identical with the Supreme Self. It is only under this assumption that in the first chapter of the Ahirbudhnya Sāmhitā in Nāιada's hymn (as also in XXXV. 81-91) Ahirbudhnya, a bound soul, is praised as the Absolute One (Svatantra), Ever-satisfied One (Nityatṛpta), Creator and Destroyer of the universe etc.

Further, the relation between the individual self in the state of release and Brahman is described in the Pāñcarātra school in a thoroughly advaitic language with a manifest tendency to regard the two as identical. The state of release is very often denoted by the phrases like 'ekībhavati', 'abhinnam brahmaṇi sthitam', 'viśet param', 'Brahmabhāvāpatti', 'apunarbhavatā' etc. Again like the Advaita school, the Pāñcarātra school also admits the concept of gradual liberation (krama mukti) in which the individual self finally loses its individuality, and the concept of Jivana mukti. Both these concepts, on the contrary, have been severely criticised by Rāmānuja.

The Pāñcarātra school is advaitic not only in its description of the state of release, but also in its account of the means of emancipation. It declares that the knowlege of identity with Brahman leads one to liberation from bondage and the result is coalescence with Brahman. 'Brahmabhinnāt tato jñānāt Brahma samyujyate param' (Jayākhya IV. 50). Since the individual self is nothing else but Brahman, what is necessary is to realise this fact, and that is why identity-consciousness is regarded as the means of emancipation. Besides knowledge, yogic discipline is also emphasised as a means of emancipation, only because it is helpful in annihilating the sense of individuality.

Another point of difference between Rāmānuja and the Pāñcarātra school is that while the former insists that the individual self is necessarily atomic, the latter very often holds that essentialy it is all-pervasive and only in the state of bondage it is reduced to atomic size by the nigraha power 'of the Lord. Rāmānuja urges that the individual self in all the states is atomic only. This he does in order to safeguard the reality and inalienable individuality of the finite self. He wages a severe polemic against Śankara who regards the individual self as all-pervasive. The Pāñcarātra school also like Śankara describes the individual self as all-pervasive, which again is a consequence of its advaitic tendency. The individual self in the state of yoga is described as sarvaga, sarvabhūta etc., which all indicate its all-pervasiveness.

The unique contribution of Rāmānuja to the Vedānta philosophy is his view that the individual self is an eternal part or body or attribute of Brahman. This is the central doctrine of Rāmānuja's philosophy and is based on the Upaniṣad and the Gītā. This central doctrine is altogether absent in the Pāñcarātra school. As a matter of fact no attempt has been made in the Pāñcarātra school to put forth a systematic theory about the relation of the individual self to Brahman.

In the Pāñcarātra school we find a peculiar concept of Kūṭastha Puruṣa, an aggregate of souls, which is altogether absent in Rāmānuja. There is a mention of it in the Gītā and if Rāmānuja were a Pāñcarātrin he would have incorporated it without any fear of being sectarian, a fear which is attributed to Rāmānuja by Prof. Kumarappa. But the fact that this important Pāñcarātra concept has remained untouched by Rāmānuja, testifies that Rāmānuja was not an advocate of the Pāñcarātra school. Further, the multiplicity of the individual selves is recognised by Rāmānuja as an ontological fact, but in the Pāñcarātra school this multiplicity comes into existence from the Kuṭastha Puruṣa long after in the process of creation at the lower secondary stage. Not only that, the distinctness of the individual selves from Brahman and their plurality seem to be purely verbal in the Pāñcarātra school, as is evident from the nature of release which consists in union with Brahman.

From the foregoing account it has become quite clear that Rāmānuja is as far away from the Pāñcarātra school as far he is from Śankara, and therefore it would be far from truth to say that Rāmānuja was influenced by the Pāñcarātra school. Prof. Kumarappa, perhaps unmindful of the above fact, has tried to maintain that Rāmānuja got his views on the nature of the individual self and its relation to the Supreme Self from the religious experiences of his sect, i.e., Pāñcarātra and Śrīvaiṣṇavism. For maintaining the above position he has not put forth any argument or evidence in the support of it. He has simply argued that Rāmānuja was motivated to refute the advaitic view of the identity of Brahman and the individual self in order to safeguard the intense religious experiences of his sect. But he forgets that the Pāñcarātra school, on which the alleged sect of Rāmānuja is based, does not hesitate in maintaining the identity doctrine, rather it supports it. In that case how can it serve as an impetus for Rāmānuja to refute identity doctrine of Śankara ?

Prof. Kumarappa, for whom Rāmānuja is a disguised Pāñcarātrin, as it were, has further maintaind that Rāmānuja has got all the materials regarding the nature of the individual self and its relation to the Supreme Self from the religious experiences of his sect. He further contends that Rāmānuja did not draw upon them directly, for that would have made his philosophy sectarian. But this argument is vitiated with many flaws. We have doubted the very authenticity of the sectarian affiliation attributed to Rāmānuja. This saps the very root of this argument. Secondly, it is based on an unwarranted imputation of ungratefulness and hypocrisy on Rāmānuja. Lastly, this thesis could have been substantiated had there been no basis for Rāmānuja's doctrines in the Prasthāna Trayī, or also, had there been an identity of thought in Rāmānuja and the Pāñcarātra school. But, as we have seen, neither is the case, and therefore we may legitimately conclude that Rāmānuja was not influenced by the Pāñcarātra school and that the Pāñcarātra school was very much influenced by advaitism, a doctrine to which Rāmānuja was deadly hostile.

References and foot-notes :

1. Tiruvaymoli, C.8.5.8.
2. Tiruviruttam, 16.
3. Śrī Bhāṣya, II.1.15
4. Ibid, I.1.1.
5. Ibid, II. 2.24
6. Ibid, II.1.22
7. Ibid, I.1.1.
8. Rāmānuja derives support for this view from the Chād. Up. VIII. 1.5; 12.3; Bṛh. Up., IV.5.15; See Śri Bhāṣya, II.3.19.
9. cf. Gītā, III.27; XIV.19.
10. Śrī Bhāṣya, II.3.34.
11. Ibid, II.3.39.
12. Ibid, II.3.20.
13. Ibid, II.3.22-23.
14. Ibid, II.3.32
15. Ibid, II.3.26-27
16. Gītā Bhāṣya, II.12
17. Ibid, II.18.
18. Śrī Bhāṣya, II.3.42-45
19. Ibid, II.3.15
20. Ibid, II.1.35
21. Gītā Bhāṣya, III.10
22. Śrī Bhāṣya, I.1.13

23. Ibid, II.1.9
24. Ibid, II.1.4,21
25. Ibid, 1.4.22
26. Ibid, I.1.1.
27. Ibid, IV.4.1
28. Ibid, IV.4.3
29. Ibid, IV.4.48
30. Ibid, IV.4.15
31. Ibid, IV.4.18
32. Ibid, I.1.1.; I.4.22
33. Ibid, I.3.7
34. Ibid, I.2.12
35. Ibid, IV.4.19
36. Ibid, IV.4.1
37. Ibid, IV.4.3
38. Ibid, I.1.1.; IV.4.4.
39. Ibid, IV.4.4.
40. Ibid, IV.4.20
41. Ibid, IV.4.14
42. Ibid, IV.4.22
43. For details, see my book, Loc.cit.

CHAPTER IV

MEANS OF MOKṢA

Introduction

The individual life in the worldly state is incomplete and broken and points beyond itself. It has a goal to achieve, a purpose to fulfil, and an end to realise. This goal is not a matter of direct realisation of something which is existent from eternity, though hidden from our view. It is, as we have seen, an establishment of a society of perfect individuals wherein the sorrows and sufferings of the world would cease to exist. This is what we mean by mokṣa or release. This release of the individual self from the travails of the present earthly life, is not effected by mere wish, nor is it an idle or ideal apprehension through abstract speculation. It is a realisation through proper endeavour. It requires a rigorous discipline, a course of sādhanā—moral, intellectual and spiritual —and the consequent mental make up on the part of the individual. In the following pages we shall consider the views of the Advaita school, Rāmānuja, the Pāñcarātra school and the Āḷvārs on the nature of the means of mokṣa.

Advaitic account of means of mokṣa

Broadly speaking the course of discipline which the Indian systems of philosophy prescribe for attaining the final goal of life is three-fold, viz., karma, jñāna and bhakti. Of this triple method the Advaita school recognises jñāna alone as the direct means of release. This system being predominantly knowledge-centred, viveka, i e., discriminative knowledge of the real from the unreal alone is regarded as the immediate cause of release. The ethical discipline and devotion to God do not directly lead to emancipation, but they are only accessories to intellectual penetration and discrimination. Since bondage consists in being ignorant of the true nature of the self which alone is real, it is discriminative knowledge alone that can bring about release. Karma and upāsanā may help us in urging to know the Real, and may equip us for that knowledge by purifying our mind, but ultimately it is knowledge which by destroying ignorance can enable us to be one with the Real.

According to Advaita school karma or properly regulated life in the light of śāśtric injunctions generally known as dharma, is inherently incapable of removing ignorance for it is itself life in ignorance. Mokṣa is not possible with an experience of difference and karma is not possible without an experience of it. According to the Mīmāmsā school it is not knowledge but the performance of actions in accordance with the Vedic injunctions which can bring about mokṣa. The advaitin, on the contrary, declares that karmakānda cannot lead to final release, for even the most meritorious conduct necessarily leads to new forms of embodied existence. Actions are prescribed in the scriptures only for those who are in ignorance and not for those who are enlightened.

The advaitin thus bifurcates the scriptures into jñānakāṇda and karmakāṇda, and declares that it is the former which alone is the means of mokṣa. In the jñānakāṇda again there are two different parts, those which deal with Saguṇa Brahman and those which deal with Nirguṇa Brahman. Devout meditation of the Saguṇa Brahman does not lead to mokṣa, but to the world of Saguṇa Brahman only. They alone obtain release whose self has been enlightened by the texts embodying the higher knowledge of the Nirguṇa Brahman, and who have attained identity-consciousness.

This identity-consciousness or knowledge of oneness is possible to only those who are equipped with the four requisites (sādhana catuṣṭya), viz., (i) viveka, (ii) vairāgya, (iii) śama, dama, uparati, titikṣā, śṛddhā and samādhāna, (iv) mumukṣutva. These four are the sine qua non to the inquiry into the nature of Brahman. A man possessing these requisites should try to understand correctly the true purport of the scripture (śravaṇa). He should try to strengthen his conviction about that purport by means of arguments in its favour (manana); and then by meditation (nididhyāsana), which includes all the yoga processes of concentration, he should try to realise the truth. The Advaita Vedānta thus covers up the ground of yoga; but while in the Yoga system mokṣa proceeds from realising the difference between Puruṣa and Prakṛti, in the Advaita school it comes by the dawn of right knowledge that Brahman alone is the true reality, one's own self.

Rāmānuja's account of the means of mokṣa

A difference in the basic conception of life and reality naturally demands a divergence of the discipline for mokṣa. Rāmānuja, unlike the advaitin, upholds the dynamic concept of Reality, which retains an element of difference, a difference not to indicate a division in Its integrity, but to allow a communion in love and service. Such a conception of give and take has no place in the Advaita school. If nescience is the root of the world-appearance and knowledge is the direct cause of its sublation, with the complete denial of nescience the goal is achieved. For Rāmānuja denial has no place, for nothing is or can be denied. The individual self continues to exist for ever. It is only required to be saved from the influence of avidyā and its travail of divided existence. It can transcend this divided life and can pass into unitive divine life, and be eternally saved.

Rāmānuja admits with the advaitin that the removal of nescience, which puts the soul under bondage, is release, and that it can be secured by the true knowledge of the Reality, but he controverts the view that this true knowledge is devoid of karma and bhakti. The basic difference between Śankara and Rāmānuja with regard to the means of mokṣa starts with the interpretation of the word 'atha' in the first aphorism of the Brahma Sūtras. This word significantly points out that the enquiry into the nature of Brahman is to be preceded by some preliminary. It implies that something must have gone before to which Brahmajijñāsā is invariably related. Śankara maintains that the preceding refers to sādhana catuṣṭya, whereas Rāmānuja declares that it refers to karma mīmāmsā which is an indispensable prerequisite to jñānamīmāmsā. According to Śankara what is finally required for release is mere intellectual illumination and therefore ethical conduct has little place in the final stage of the discipline which is necessary to attain release. But Rāmānuja urges that Śankara overlooks those scriptural texts which emphasise purity of conduct, devotion of heart and grace of God, which are as essential as knowledge of identity.

Accordingly Rāmānuja in his synthetic approach regards the three paths to liberation, viz. karma, jñāna and bhakti, not as exclusive, but as inclusive of one another. Karmayoga or moral discipline is a process of self-purification which develops into jñānayoga. Jñānayoga is a means of self-realisation which culminates in bhaktiyoga, which in its turn is a method of God-realisation. On the basis of the Chāndogya Upaniṣad VIII.7.1 Rāmānuja maintains that knowledge of the ātman combined with karmayoga leads to jñānayoga. Through jñānayoga one arrives at the true contemplation of the realising-ātman (prāptṛ-ātman). This contemplation again is propaedeutic to bhaktiyoga, through which alone one is capable of attaining mokṣa.[1]

Rāmānuja fully agrees with Śankara that knowledge is the only means of obtaining release, but this knowledge, he urges, is not devoid of karma and bhakti as Śankara has tried to maintain. Śankara has categorically declared that neither action, nor even knowledge in combination with action is of any avail with regard to the attainment of release.[2] It is true that Bādarāyaṇa has declared that release accrues from vidyā and not from action,[3] but this vidyā means meditation upon and devotion to God.[4] Rāmānuja is firmly of the opinion that knowledge must be wedded to devotion before self-realisation may develop into God-realisation.[5] Knowledge is thus quite inevitable for obtaining release, but by itself it is quite insufficient. He compares knowledge to a horse which though a means of conveyance for his master, requires attendants, groomings etc. The horse will of course carry its rider, but a smooth riding requires certain actions on the part of the rider too.[6]

Rāmānuja holds that the duties relating to various āśramas also are to be discharged by a man of knowledge because karma contributes to vidyā.[7] In this respect he differs from Śankara who affirms that there is no necessity of karma for a man of knowledge. Rāmānuja, on the other hand, maintains that actions, if rightly done, are not detrimental to release. Not only the daily and the accidental actions but also the desired ones can procure emancipation provided the agent surrenders his agency to God.[8] Gītā declares, 'svakarmaṇā tamabhyarca siddhim vindanti mānavāḥ' and accordingly Rāmānuja writes that the Lord has declared that faithful discharge of ones' own duties is itself the worship of God.[9]

The three-fold yoga, thus, marks the three successive stages in the progressive realisation of release. Karma and jñāna are preliminaries to bhakti which is a direct path to release. Besides this triadic process of human sādhanā, Rāmānuja emphasises the role of grace of God. The later metrical Upaniṣads unmistakably declare that God out of His grace grants to the finite self that knowledge which it requires for obtaining release. In this way Rāmānuja does full justice to all the scriptural texts by synthesising the various elements which constitute the means of release. For this Rāmānuja is mainly indebted to the Gītā where this synthesis is attempted. Lord Kṛṣṇa has declared that the different pathways are not ultimately distinct though they appear to be so. (VII.21). He has synthesised karma, jñāna, bhakti, yoga, grace of God etc., has shown the exact place and value of each, and thus he has preached the effectiveness of the combined effort. Rāmānuja has fully followed this lead of the Gītā.

Let us now see in details the place and value of each of these constituents of the scheme of release in the philosophy of Rāmānuja.

Karmayoga

The karmayoga or ethical discipline is the first step in the scheme of release. It is regarded as a pathway to self-realisation, and is preferred on account of its ease, naturality, efficacy and freedom from the fallacy of mistaking not-self for the self.[10] Rāmānuja lays great emphasis on the need of moral conduct and the performance of the duties of life.

Rāmānuja's emphasis on the karmayoga is entirely based on the Upaniṣads and the Gītā It is true that in the earlier Upaniṣads the emphasis was laid on knowledge but this does not mean that ethical discipline is altogether absent in them. It is given there due place[11] but it is specially emphasised only in the later Upaniṣads. For example, Katha Upaniṣad declares, 'Not he who has not ceased from bad conduct can obtain Him by intelligence.' (II. 24) 'He who has no understanding, who is unmindful and ever impure, reaches not the goal, but goes on to transmigration' (Ibid III.1). 'This soul is obtainable by truth, by austerity, by proper knowledge, by the student's life of chastity constantly practised (Mundaka. III.1.5.). The Śvetāśvatara Upaniṣad also dwells on the necessity of yogic practices whereby the individual becomes cleansed. In the Maitri Upaniṣad the method for attaining release is described thus, 'Study of the knowledge of the Veda,...pursuit of one's regular duty, in one's own stage of the religious life that verily is the rule...If one does not practise austerity there is no success in the knowledge of the soul, nor perfection of works. For thus has it been said : 'It is goodness (sattva) from austerity (tapas), and mind from goodness that is won; and from the mind soul is won, on winning whom no one returns.'[12]

In the Gītā also, on which the ethics of Rāmānuja is mainly based, ethical requirements are declared as essential, and several virtues are accordingly mentioned as leading to the 'Divine Estate' which alone enables one to attain release. Throughout the Gītā Kṛṣṇa urges upon Arjuna the necessity to control the senses and desires, and to do one's duty leaving the consequences unto God.[13] He declares that one's duties must be performed irrespective of the consequences. 'Therefore without attachment ever perform the work that thou must do, for if without attachment a man works he gains the Highest.' (III.19) One can have the redeeming knowledge only when his senses are held in check and he is perfect in control (IV.38-39). The earnest desire of God to see that righteousness should prevail, is the chief motive of incarnation in the Gītā. The ethical conduct and the performance of duties is not only binding on the individual, but God Himself, though perfect, also acts for the sake of the finite self, and thus sets an example.

On the basis of the above authorities Rāmānuja also emphasises the place of karmayoga. He urges that one who aspires after release must fulfil many practical requirements. It is first of all necessary for him to avoid sin for thereby he can have the real knowledge of the self. After this he is required to give himself to the pursuit of all the duties binding on his station in life, without any tinge of selfishness or desire for personal gain.[14] Rāmānuja writes, 'All daily (nitya) and incidental (naimittika) rites prescribed in the śāstras shall be performed.........As for the fructiferous rites (kāmya) even those shall be performed in the manner prescribed for the several castes (varṇa) and orders of life (āśrama), and according to one's ability; but resigning their specific fruits'.[15] 'The Deity is pleased and conciliated by the different kinds of acts of sacrifice and worship duly performed by the devotee day after day'.[16] God Himself says, 'The work of sacrifice, gift-giving, and austerities is not to be relinquished, but is indeed to be performed; for sacrifices, gifts and austerities are purifying to the thoughtful.' 'He from whom all beings proceed .. worshipping Him with proper works man attains to perfection.'[17]

Not only such sacrificial rites but also the duties connected with each āśrama have to be performed.[18] Those who are not within any āśrama should devote themselves to practices not exclusively connected with any āśrama, such as prayer, fasting, propitiation of the Deity and so on.[19] But better than to be outside the āśramas is the condition of standing within āśrama. The latter state may be due to misfortune; but he who can should be within an āśrama which state is the more holy and beneficial one.[20] Those who have fallen from the āśrama state owing to a lapse from chastity are not qualified for knowledge of Brahman.[21] The duties obligatory on the four varṇas are prescribed in the śāstras and these duties should be faithfully performed.[22]

Jñānayoga

In order that an individual may perform his duties properly and disinterestedly it is necessary for him to know his own essential nature. Since the root of all evil is nescience whereby the soul identifies itself with the body and gives itself to the pursuits of bodily ends, it is necessary for it to see that its own true nature is quite distinct from that of the body. Rāmānuja writes, 'Knowing ātmā to be that which is distinct from the body, uncontaminated with qualities pertaining to bodies, and to be that which is eternal, keeping the mind imperturbable under the varying conditions of pleasure and pain, gain and loss...and destitude of any wish for reward. In this wilt thou escape sin.'[23] Rāmānuja further holds that one must meditate on oneself as not only different from the body but also as having qualities similar to Brahman.[24] This is the state or condition of work-performance in an unselfish or disinterested manner, based on the knowledge of the eternal self. This method has for its aim the achievement of true wisdom.[25] Thus jñānayoga consists of knowledge of the ātman combined with karmayoga. In this way karmayoga presupposes jñānayoga and jñānayoga includes karmayoga. Karma and jñāna, thus, interpenetrate each other. The two can be distinguished but not separated. Hence there must be a blending (samuccaya) of the two.

Bhaktiyoga

The jñānayoga which consists of the knowledge of oneself as different from the body and as akin to the pure nature of Brahman, and the karmayoga which means the fulfilment of religious and social duties inculcated in the śāstras without any expectation of reward, are not sufficient to bring about release. What is needed is a whole-hearted devotion which demands the centering of one's thought entirely on God. The karmayoga and jñānayoga must be supplemented with bhaktiyoga, without which no emancipation can be achieved.

Rāmānuja admits that the jñānayoga by itself can also lead to mokṣa, but he points out that meditation on the soul is not within the easy reach of the ordinary man. Therefore he insists on bhaktiyoga which is quite an easy method.

The origin of the cult of bhakti in Hinduism is shrouded in mystery, but it is quite evident that its germs are found in the Vedic hymns. The doctrine of loving God is as old as the Vedas as is evinced in passages such as, 'yoṣājāramiva priyam' (Ṛg. IX.32.5). The hymns 'namo bharantā emasi' (Ṛg.V.1.1.), 'yasya viśvā upāsate;' (Yaju. 25.13), 'Mahaste viṣṇoḥ sumatim' bhajāmahe' (Ṛg.I.156.3) etc. suggest the consciousness of love and reverence to the Deity as the only means of the progress of man. Bhakti has been the trend even of the oldest phase of the Vedic religion. As B.N. Seal has remarked, 'The Vedic hymns are replete with sentiments of piety and reverence in the worship of God...The upāsanākāṇḍa of the Āraṇyakas and Upaniṣads lay the foundation ,of the bhaktimārga, the way of devotion and faith.'[26] Prof. Belvalkar is also of the same opinion when he writes, 'It is impossible to read some of the soul-stirring Vedic hymns to Varuṇa, Savitra and Uṣas, and not to feel therein the presence of the true bhakti, however, inadequate may have been its philosophical background.'[27]

In the Upaniṣads we find distinctly theistic tendencies gradually developing. Though the older prose Upaniṣads lay stress on knowledge as the way to release, the older metrical Upaniṣads like Katha, Mundaka, Śvetāśvatara etc. distinctly advocate the doctrine of bhakti. In the Śvetāśvatara we also find the doctrine of prapatti. Bādarāyaṇa also in his Brahma Sūtras refers to it as 'Samārādhana.'[28]

In the Gītā we find a systematic account of the cult of bhakti. God of the Gītā is not an abstract impersonal Absolute to whom the individual self counts for little. He is a personal God who loves the individual self and wishes to possess him completely. Consequently what He requires more than all else is whole-hearted devotion. It is this bhakti, a constant life-long contemplation on God and total dedication of oneself to Him, which the Lord names as madbhakti, madyajana, manmanana etc.

Accordingly Rāmānuja describes the devotion that is required of the individual self as chiefly contemplative involving the centering of one's thoughts on the Deity.[29] It is a devotion which requires the dedication of one's will[30] for it involves the performance of all one's own duties.[31]

Rāmānuja regards this bhakti as synonymous with upāsanā.[32] In the Vedic literature we find both these words used for devotion. Bhakti, derived from the root 'bhaj' appears in the Vedic passage 'Mahaste Viṣṇoḥ sumatim bhajāmahe' (Ṛg. I.156.3). The root 'as' with the prefix 'upa' is also used side by side with the root 'bhaja' as we find in the Yajurveda passage 'yasya viśvā upāsate'. (25.13)

Rāmānuja further maintains that this devotion is identical with redeeming knowledge. He explicitly declares that it is essentially a specific form of cognition.[33] It is not an unintellectual exuberance of feeling, or a fervent glow of emotion, or an unrestrained exhibition of erotic element, but it is thoroughly meditative and contemplative. He accordingly defines bhakti as 'a meditation on God accompanied by love'.[34] He elsewhere writes, 'That the knowledge intended to be enjoined as the means of final release is of the nature of meditation we conclude from the circumstance that the terms 'knowing' and 'meditating' are seen to be used in place of each other in the earlier and later parts of the Vedic texts'. He further writes that this is the view of the Vākyakāra as well, and quotes the following passage, 'Knowledge (Vedānta) means meditation (upāsanā) scripture using the word in that sense.'[35]

Bhakti as a loving meditation is also described by Rāmānuja as a 'steady remembrance'. He writes, 'Meditation means steady remembrance, i.e., a continuity of steady remembrance, uninterrupted like a flow of oil; in agreement with the scriptural passage 'On the attainment of remembrance all the ties are loosened'. (Chānd. VII.26.2). Such remembrance is of the same character (form) as seeing (intuition) for the passage quoted has the same purport as the following one, 'The fetter of the heart is broken, all doubts are solved, and all the work of that man perish when He has seen who is high and low (Mund. II.2.8). With reference to remembrance, which thus acquires the character of immediate presentation and is the means of final release; scripture makes a further determination, viz., in the passage (Katha II.23) 'That Self cannot be gained by the study of the Veda (reflection), nor by thought (meditation), nor by much hearing. Whom the Self chooses, by it may be gained.' Now a 'chosen' one means a most beloved person, the relation being that he by whom that Self is held most dear is most dear to the Self. That the Lord Himself endearvours that this most beloved person should gain the Self, He Himself declares in the following words, 'To those who are constantly devoted and worship with love I give that knowledge by which they reach me' (Gītā. X.10), and 'To him who has knowledge I am dear above all things, and he is dear to me.' (VII.17) Hence he who possesses remembrance marked by the character of immediate presentation (sākṣātkāra), and which itself is dear above all things since the object remembered is such; he, we may say, is chosen by the highest Self, and by him the highest Self is gained. Steady remembrance of this kind is designed by the word 'devotion' (bhakti); for this term has the same meaning as upāsanā (meditation).

'Hence we conclude that the knowledge which the Vedānta texts aim at inculcating is a knowledge of the sense of sentences, and denoted by 'dhyāna', 'upāsanā' (i.e. meditation), and similar terms. With this agree scriptural texts such as 'Having known it, let him practise meditation' (Bṛh. IV.4.21)...all these texts, must be viewed as agreeing in meaning with the injunction of meditation contained in the passage quoted from the Bṛhadāraṇyaka Upaniṣad and what they enjoin is therefore meditation.'[36]

In this way Rāmānuja makes it quite clear that the knowledge which is a means to release, is not mere vākyārtha jñāna (knowledge of mere sense of the sentences), but it is of the nature of contemplation and direct intuition of Brahman. Thus by equating bhakti with jñāna Rāmānuja gives to bhakti a predominantly meditative significance on the one hand, and on the other, regards the redeeming knowledge taught by the Upaniṣads as neither something purely intellectual nor as something to be accomplished once and for all, but as a meditative devotion daily practised and constantly improved by repetition throughout one's life, and culminating in a mystic intuition of the Deity. The system of Rāmānuja from this point of view culminates in a lofty mysticism in which the soul finds its highest life in the intellectual love of God.

Though Rāmānuja describes devotion as chiefly contemplative, he does not underrate the emotional side of it lest it should become a matter of head only. Accordingly he gives recognition and due place to the emotional experiences of the devotees.[37]

The account of the state of an ardent devotee given by Rāmānuja (which occurs once only in all his works) is, no doubt, an emotional attitude of worship and devotion, but it is not a blind intensity of feeling or an unreasoned ecstasy divorced from knowledge and the duties of practical life. In this respect this slight emotional element in the meditative and ethical bhakti of Rāmānuja cannot be compared with or traced to the highly emotional bhakti of the Āḷvārs who would reject jñāna and even karma and would regard the ecstatic passion of the erotic nature as the only essential.

It is further to be noted that the bhakti in Rāmānuja is not an outer form of worship, as it has become in the Pāñcarātra cult, but it is an inner spiritual attitude produced and enriched by virtues. It is not an emotionalism but a training of the body, will and intellect. This bhakti is the ripened fruit of karma and jñāna, and is not possible without them. Rāmānuja writes, 'Sacrifices and similar works being performed day after day have the effect of purifying the mind, and owing to this, knowledge arises in the mind with ever increasing brightness.'[38] 'Hence in order that knowledge may arise, evil works have to be got rid of, and this is effected by the performance of acts of religious duty not aiming at some immediate result (such as the heavenly world and the happy life), according to the text 'By works of religious duty he discards all evil'. Knowledge which is the means of reaching Brahman thus requires the works prescribed for the different āśramas.'[39]

For the careful discipline of the mind and will Rāmānuja, following the Vākyakāra, prescribes a seven-fold scheme of self-discipline. Without undergoing this no one can be granted the redeeming knowledge by the Deity. The seven constituents of the scheme are viveka (abstention from impure food), vimoka (absence of attachment to desires), abhyāsa (continued practice), kriyā (performance of Pañcamahāyajñas), kalyāṇa (virtuous conduct), anavasāda (freedom from dejection) and anuddharṣa (absence of exultation).

The bhakti which is the result of this sādhana-saptaka has three stages and nine phases. The three stages are dhruvānusmṛti (firm meditation), asakṛdāvṛtam (frequent repetition) and darśana samānākāratā (orison of union). Its nine phases are as follows : stuti (glorification), smṛti (remembrance), namaskṛti (homage), vandana (salutation), yatana (mortification), kīrtana (exaltation), guṇaśravaṇa (listening to the attributes of the Lord), vacana (narrating the attributes), dhyāna (meditation), arcana (adoration) and praṇāma (prostration).[40]

Does Rāmānuja advocate the doctrine of Prapatti ?

It has been maintained by many scholars[41] that Rāmānuja has accepted and incorporated the Pāñcarātra doctrine of prapatti which teaches an absolute surrendering of oneself to the Deity and leaving the work of mokṣa to be done by Him, as a means independent of and superior to bhakti, or as the only requisite for mokṣa. But there is no evidence in his works to support this contention. We shall substantiate our point by considering three of his works, viz. Śrī Bhāṣya, Gītā Bhāṣya and Vedārtha Saṃgraha. His other two works, viz. Vedānta Sāra and Vedānta Dīpa need no separate consideration, as they are mere condensed forms of the Śrī Bhāṣya. Another work, Gadya-trayam, is also ascribed to him, but its genuineness is yet to be established.

The word 'prapatti', as far as I know, does not occur in the Śrī Bhāṣya. Nowhere in his works Rāmānuja has said that the individual self can lay aside its responsibility for salvation and entrust this work to the Deity, or that the Deity requires nothing from the self beyond complete surrender. Nor has he said that the Deity plays a leading role and the individual self has to play only a subordinate role. Far from maintaining that mokṣa is entirely the work of God, or it is due to the 'sole agency' of God, or that all that is necessary is to flee to the Deity for refuge, Rāmānuja insists that no one can get mokṣa unless one becomes purified by devout works and strenuous discipline. He makes it quite clear that the 'saving knowledge' which is the effect of God's grace is not possible except to one who has undergone thorough preparation ethically, intellectually and spiritually. A methodical training of body, intellect and will through karmayoga, jñānayoga and bhaktiyoga is an indispensable prerequisite to it. He declares, 'It is impossible that the capability of performing meditation on Brahman should belong to a person not knowing the nature of Brahman and the due modes of meditation, and not qualified by the knowledge of the requisite preliminaries of such meditation, viz., recitation of the Veda, sacrifices and so on. Mere want or desire does not impart qualification to a person destitute of the required capability'.[42] At so many places Rāmānuja emphatically declares that the grace of God is not arbitrary, but acts in accordance with the law of Karma.[43]

Prof. Kumarappa, who maintains that Rāmānuja has advocated the doctrine of prapatti, also admits that the tenets of this doctrine are not present in the Śrī Bhāṣya. He writes, 'Since grace functions then only when the soul has elaborately prepared itself by Vedic instruction, performance of śāstric duties, intellectual knowledge of Brahman, and desire for release, there can be no talk of the Deity either overriding the individuality of the soul or permitting a violation of His laws. This is the view consistently maintained throughout the Śrī Bhāṣya.'[44]

From the above it is quite clear that the tenets of the doctrine of prapatti are in flagrant contradiction to the declared teachings of the Śrī Bhāṣya, and hence it would be far from truth to say that Rāmānuja has accepted it.

In the Vedārtha Samgraha also the distinctive tenets of this Pāñcarātra doctrine are conspicuously absent. In one of the various recensions of the Vedārtha Samgraha the word 'prapatti' occurs thus, 'Eteṣām samsāra mocanam bhagavat-prapattimantareṇa nopapadyeta.'[45] This sentence is not at all found in the palm leaf manuscript of the Mysore Oriental Research Institute Catalogue No. A.2409. In the palm leaf manuscript of the Mysore Government Oriental Research Institute Catalogue No. Gr. 878 instead of 'prapatti' the word is 'pratipatti'. In some manuscripts it is 'bhagavatprāptim'.[46] Since the word 'prapatti' occurs in one recension only and there too we are not quite certain about the sense in which it is used, it may be contended that this recension has come to be distorted by the later sectarians.

In the Gītā Bhāṣya also no where Rāmānuja has maintained that the redeeming knowledge can be bestowed on any one irrespective of the moral considerations. He has never suggested that the redeeming grace works in such a way as to annul the law of Karma. He has, on the contrary, always tried to emphasise that in the operation of Divine grace both the individuality of the finite self and the moral consistency of Brahman are preserved. He has declared that the individual must fulfil many conditions if it is to obtain release. Indeed, even devotion which the Deity requires as the supreme condition for release is possible only to one who has through efforts achieved merit. He writes, 'Those whose self-acquired merits have led them to come to me as their asylum, whose bond of sin has been broken down and who partake of the divine nature are noble-souled'. (IX. 13). 'It is only to one who is entirely cleansed of all his sins that I become the object of love.' (XII. 11). 'Thus, then, in conclusion thou shalt carry on all thy worldly duties and scriptural duties occupying thyself daily. Thus, in devotion of the aforesaid description thou shall reach Myself.' (IX. 34). From these references to the Gītā Bhāṣya it is quite obvious that the Deity through His grace grants release only to those who have fulfilled the necessary condition of knowledge, duty and devotion.

As a matter of fact the centıal idea of the prapatti doctrine is present in the Gītā passages such as 'mām prapadyante' (IV. 11) 'māmeva ye prapadyante' (VII. 14) 'tameva śaraṇam gaccha' (XVIII. 62) 'māmekam śaraṇam vraja' (XVIII. 66) etc. The word 'prapatti' occurs at many places in the Gītā. But no where Rāmānuja has interpreted it in the Pāñcarātra sense of prapatti. In VII. 19 it is described as an approach to the Lord which presupposes the true knowledge of the ātman that its sole essence is to be a śeṣa of God. In this way it is a means of self-realisation. In XVIII. 62 it is explained as 'anuvartasva' i.e. obey the commands of the Lord. He interprets 'prapadyante' as 'samāśrayante' (IV. 11, VII. 20) or as 'upagamya' (XV 4-5) or as 'upāsate' (VII.10), none of which has the Pāñcarātra sense. Besides Rāmānuja refers to it as an activity which leads to bhakti.[47]

Thus no where the word 'prapatti' has been used in the sense in which it is used in the Pāñcarātra school, as a complete surrender of the devotee to the Deity who moved by devotee's utter desolation lifts him to beatitude by a mere act of grace. Though in the Gītā it is maintained that prapatti stimulates God's grace, there is no evidence to prove that Rāmānuja believed that prapatti alone would suffice for this. On the contrary, it becomes quite clear that he does not consider pıapatti a separate, let alone superior, means apart from bhakti but only a preliminary to it.

Though the position of Rāmānuja is quite clear on this point, Kumarappa feels that on this topic Rāmānuja's teaching in the Gītā Bhāṣya differs from his teaching in the Śrī Bhāṣya. Kumarappa agrees that the doctrine of prapatti could not find its expression in the Śrī Bhāṣya, but he argues that 'the religion of devotion to which he belonged seems to lead him in the Bhagvad Gītā Bhāṣya to assert that the Deity requires nothing from the soul beyond complete surrender (prapatti)'.[48] In order to support his conclusion he cites Rāmānuja's commentary on the Gītā XV. 4. But here he attaches importance to a varient reading which Rāmānuja mentions but does not accept. First of all Rāmānuja gives his own interpretation and then in the second place he gives only a varient reading by saying 'iti vā pāṭhaḥ'. Kumarappa cites only this varient reading, perhaps because it serves his purpose. He further quotes the Gītā XV. 5 and here also he is misled by Govindācārya's faulty translation of the phrase, 'matprasādāt' as 'through my sole agency', whereas it really means 'by my grace'. Besides he refers to Śaraṇāgati-gadya, whose authorship is very much disputable.

Further, Kumarappa quotes Rāmānuja's commentary on the famous śloka XVIII. 66. Here again he gives greater emphasis to the latter half portion of the explanation. Rāmānuja gives here two different explanations. The first explanation is perfectly in keeping with his general views, and is preferred by him. The second one, though ambiguous, does not mean that taking refuge in God is 'solely' enough for release. As to why Rāmānuja has given two different explanations, it may be said that though Rāmānuja did not subscribe to the views prevalent at his time he did not want to exclude them from his Bhāṣya. In the first explanation, which alone is acceptable to him, he interprets 'renouncing' (parityajya) not as 'absolute surrendering of oneself to the Deity and leaving the work of salvation to be done by him', but as 'performing one's duties without attachment to fruits etc.' The declaration 'I will deliver thee from all sins' is interpreted by him to mean that the Deity will 'remove the obstructions caused by the past sins.' Here Rāmānuja makes it quite clear that the Lord would only remove the obstructions and it would be the sole responsibility of the individual self to strive for mokṣa.

Thus viewed, Rāmānuja has rather rejected the unconditional surrender to God and together with it the exclusive responsibility for the mokṣa of the individual self on God. This is a clear evidence to show that the doctrine of prapatti was not accepted by Rāmānuja.

It would be interesting to note here that in the Gadyatrayam, which the sectarians attribute to Rāmānuja, there is a passage in which Rāmānuja is made to confess his omission of not referring to this doctrine in his other works.[49] The very wording of this passage betrays the imposition of this doctrine on Rāmānuja. No reasons have been given why Rāmānuja concealed it in his other works, and why he deemed it fit to reveal it in the Gadyatrayam. As many sectarian doctrines have been attributed to Rāmānuja by his Śrīvaiṣṇava followers with a view to find support for their sect in his philosophy, this also seems to be an instance of the same. As a matter of fact had Rāmānuja been an advocate of the doctrine of prapatti he would have unfailingly utilised the Gītā passages for this purpose, which, as we have seen, are very much inclined towards the prapatti mārga. Moreover, we find many references to this doctrine in the recognised scriptural works as well, and it would have been least sectarian had Rāmānuja dwelt upon it.

From the foregoing considerations the conclusion we arrive at is that the Pāñcarātra doctrine of prapatti, wrongly maintained to have been accepted by Rāmānuja, has found no expression in his works, and is also in opposition to his declared teachings.[50]

Divine grace as a means of Mokṣa

According to Rāmānuja God is not only a Creator and a Sustainer but a Redeemer as well. He has always regarded God as eminently loving. He bears an immense love for His devotees. This has been the teaching of the Gītā, and Rāmānuja, therefore, rightly draws upon it for this idea. While commenting on the Gītā VIII.18 he writes, 'As for the jñāni, I deem him as my own self, i.e., my very life depends on him. He cannot live without Me—his highest goal—I cannot live without him'. Similar are the interpretations of Rāmānuja of many other devotional passages of the Gītā.

The origin of the ideas of God of love and God of grace has been attributed to Vaiṣṇavism, but in the Upaniṣads we find a growing tendency to regard the Supreme Being as 'eminently loving' and as the Redeemer who by his grace leads man to mokṣa. In the Śvetāśvatara (I.6, III.20) the Supreme Being is referred to as

'Kindly One'. In the Katha II. 20 it is declared that one becomes free from sorrow, i.e., gains release, 'when through the grace of the Creator he beholds the greatness of the self. Further the same Upaniṣad declares,"This self (Ātman) is not to be obtained by instruction, nor by the intellect, nor by much learning. He is to be obtained only by the one whom He chooses; to such a one that Self (Ātman) reveals His own person." (cf. Mundaka III.2.3.) In the earlier Upaniṣads the redeeming knowledge was something philosophical or intellectual, but in the later Upaniṣads it was transformed into something religious. It came to be believed that this knowledge is not so much the product of one's own efforts as it is a gift of God's grace.

This thought is further developed in the Gītā. Here the individual is not left alone to work out his own mokṣa by work, knowledge and devotion, but is assisted by God whose grace he can procure easily. But this grace is not bestowed without any consideration of merit. It befalls only on those who are righteous. In the Gītā we come across some passages which appear to declare that the loving God is not unwilling to extend His grace to the most undeserving, but all such passages are immediately followed by other passages which remove this ambiguity. God is loving but He is also righteous, and does not wish that His all-forgiving love should lead to unrighteousness.

On the basis of the above authorities Rāmānuja also advocates the doctrine of grace. His favourite texts in this connection is Katha II.23. He writes that God protects all irrespective of their differences. He is the refuge of all beings high and low irrespective of their differences of caste (jāti) figure (ākāra), creed (jñāna) and nature (svabhāva).[51] Though the Deity showers His grace without any discrimination of such sort, this grace is never unmerited. The redeeming knowledge is granted only to him who has rid himself of all evils. Further if the grace operates unconditionally, that would nullify the freedom of will of the individual self and also the doctrine of Karma. Rāmānuja is very particular about preserving the individual freedom and initiative, and therefore he can never accept any such idea which may involve cessation of individual freedom and initiative.

In the operation of grace God simply carries to fruition the meditation the devotee adopts for reaching Him. He wards off the obstacle which may hamper him in his progress in meditation. Lastly He generates in him the intense love and affection for Him.[52] This much alone is the role of God and the rest all is to be done by the individual self only. This is the view of Rāmānuja in the Śrī Bhāṣya as well as in the Gītā Bhāṣya. Kumarappa has misunderstood the position of Rāmānuja in the Gītā Bhāṣya. Under the supposition that Rāmānuja has advocated the doctrine of prapatti, Kumarappa feels that in the Gītā Bhāṣya Rāmānuja has maintained that mokṣa is entirely a work of God and the soul has no part to play except that of absolute self-surrender to God. But we have already cleared this misunderstanding.

Thus, according to Rāmānuja, release is always a gift of God's grace and involves God taking the necessary steps to this end, but it is not possible except to one who has undergone a thorough preparation involving a rigorous training of the body, intellect and will. There can be no possibility of God either over-riding the individuality of the soul or permitting a violation of His laws. That is why Rāmānuja maintains that release is not possible for a śudra[53]. But this does not imply any partiality on the part of God, because He is to abide by the law of Karma.[54] All His favours or disfavours are always in accordance with His law that the souls shall be dealt with in the light of what they deserve.

According to Rāmānuja there is no opposition between the grace of God and the law of Karma. Both are the divine modes of action. The law of Karma is merely instrumental for the grace of God. It determines the operation of the grace. This is the interpretation Rāmānuja puts[55] on Kauśītakī Upaniṣad, III.8. This way of relating the two preserves the individual freedom and initiative of the finite, as well as the perfect and just nature of the Infinite.

In this way this triadic process of karma, jñāna and bhakti provides the aspirant for release the needed discipline of knowledge, feeling and will. Thus equipped, the individual self is granted the redeeming knowledge by God out of His grace. This redeeming knowledge is different from the path of knowledge. The path of knowledge is a sort of self-realisation, a knowledge of one's own true self, whereas the redeeming knowledge is the knowledge of one's true relation with God and the world. It is the latter which removes the avidyā and the consequent bondage.

Pāñcarātra account of means of Mokṣa[56]

The Pāñcarātra school prescribes two major ways to attain mokṣa viz., yoga and devotion. Though a distinction is made between these two methods, and though the latter one is regarded as superior, it has been emphasised that a devotee must also be initiated into the yogavidhi. It seems that the yoga method is regarded as a preliminary to the path of devotion.

In some of the Pāñcarātra samhitas the details of Ṣadāṇga Yoga and Aṣṭāṇga Yoga are also discussed. The methods of karmayoga and jñānayoga are also mentioned but in a different sense. Karmayoga is defined as performance of action with firm devotion. Similarly, jñānayoga is defined as acquisition of knowledge without being anxious of the result.

The Samhitās also abound with passages which declare knowledge as the only means of mokṣa. This knowledge is named as 'Vedānta jñāna' and it is the same as the identity-consciousness of the Advaita Vedānta.

The path of devotion is regarded as the earliest and hence preferable means of mokṣa. It is named as 'prapatti', the keynote of which is to flee to God for salvation. It emphasises an absolute and unconditional surrender to God and leaving the work of salvation to be done by Him. It also suggests that God can grant salvation irrespective of moral considerations.

Apart from these various methods the Pāñcarātra school emphasises the importance of the grace of God. Out of love for devotees God assumes five-fold forms and seeks to free his worshippers from the bonds of the world.

Although God thus works for the individual's salvation the latter also has to play his part. He has to approach God through a teacher, who initiates the individual in the method of worshipping God. God has to be worshipped through His idols (arcās). The worship should always be conducted through the mantras in the strict Pāñcarātra manner.

Means of mokṣa in the religion of Āḷvārs

The Āḷvārs are not philosophers but ardent devotees of Viṣṇu, and therefore, their whole outlook towards life and other related problems is marked with the devotional tinge. The Āḷvārs regard the earthly life as full of horrors and, therefore, we find in them an utter hatred for it.[57] The reason for wishing to flee from the earthly life is not merely that it is itself evil, but also that it separates the soul from God, whereas the Āḷvārs long to be with Him or to be merged in Him. The worldly existence comes in the way of their achieving this end, and therefore, they desire to get rid of it. A day in samsāra seems to them like a dark painful night of a thousand ages, for it separates them from the Lord, for whom they become pale and languish.[58]

Union with God—the end of life

The intensity of devotion and love that finds expression in the hymns of the Āḷvārs reflects an earnest appeal of a longing for union with God. Kulaśekhara Āḷvār, for example, will not rest content with anything short of entering into God.[59] Nammāḷvār realises that 'it is difficult to enter into Him', and, therefore, he impatiently cries, 'I do not know when I shall be able to join the company of His servants.' He imagines himself a love-sick maiden, weeping day and night, and wasting away for her lover, and expresses the yearning of his heart to be united with the Lord.[60]

The stories connected with some of the Āḷvārs[61] relate that they merged in this fashion into God. Thus it is said of Āndāl that in the presence of all assembled she, 'ascending the soft Śeṣa bed of the Lord, more and more pressed on to His side; and lo! where was she ? She had passed into Him. Her distinct person was no more cognizable to mortal ken. Glory merged in glory'.

But the state of merger is left here quite ambiguous, and it is difficult to decide whether it is total absorption or mere communion. At times the former is clearly suggested for by merger they mean total annihilation of individual's personality. But at many more times the latter tendency is dominant for in this process of merger the soul retains personal identity, since this union is not identification or extinction, but only an intimate association. For example, Tirumangai prays that he may never leave God.[62] At the end of the Tiruppallandu it is hoped that all the souls will gather round God and there 'Namo nārāyaṇa' will be the unceasing chant.

Grace of God as a means of mokṣa

The above mentioned state of communion with God or mokṣa from the Samsāra, can be attained only through the grace of God. As we have seen it is the loving and condescending nature of God and His acts of grace that chiefly appeal to the Āḷvārs, evoke their devotion and determine their conception of God. Accordingly for reaching the goal of their life, viz., communion with God, neither asceticism nor ceremonial conduct, neither knowledge nor high birth is required. Tirumangai, who belonged to the thief caste and could not claim any of these distinctions—not even the distinction of a virtuous life—is loudest in proclaiming God's mercy which stoops to accept the simple devotion of even the most degraded. Thus, e.g., in Periya Tirumoli he dwells with great feeling on God's grace shown at sundry times to those of low state.[63] In a similar vain, Tondaradipodi declares that even the lowest of the low, if they have devotion, are dearer to God than men of high caste deep in learning.[64]

When such simple devotion is found God in His infinite mercy destroys all sin and takes the soul to Himself. 'First He cuts off the two kinds of sin in me. Then He wipes off the residue. Then He leads the mind towards Him by degrees. Then He gets the heaven decorated and takes me there.'[65]

The Ālvārs, conscious as they are of their own weakness and unworthiness, are apt to ascribe all the work of transformation and redemption to God's grace. Thus Tondaradippodi who was lost in a life of sin till God Himself intervened and redeemed him from it, speaks of grace as operating on him in spite of himself. His heart's devotion, he declares, was forced out of him.[66] Nevertheless in living the life of a true devotee great effort was also necessary on the part of the Āḷvār, as is shown by his earnest prayer for grace to negate his sins.[67] Nammāḷvār declares that God takes the initial step in the work of salvation. 'It is not on my request He comes and resides in my mind. He took abode there of His own accord......First He infused His spirit into my flesh, then into my life, and became one with my soul.'[68] Residing in the soul, He will not allow the five senses of His refugee to go in their own way. He takes up all souls of all places to the higher and higher state of goodness gradually. He destroys all the cruel sins in the period of a moment, and drives away the ignorance of the devotee. He produces the love which He requires of the worshipper.

Moral virtues pre-requisite of Divine grace

Although God seeks in all these ways actively to redeem the soul it would appear that His grace is not irresistible for 'He leaves him who goes away desiring other things.'[69] In order to win the grace of God along with single-minded devotion moral qualities are necessary, and without them no man can be a true worshipper of God. 'To leave off wicked deeds and the blackest sins, and to be engaged in good deed and to rise, is to go to the grove where God resides !' 'Go to the Lord, rooting out all ideas of you and yours completely.'[69] Āndāl regards austerities, control of appetite, abandoning of self-love and vain glory etc. as equally necessary[70] along with good deeds and charity. Tondaradippodi holds that so long as one is steeped in sin, he cannot attain communion with God.[71]

Although victory over sin and leading of virtuous life are necessary for mokṣa, the sinner and the degraded ones are not rejected by God.[72] Though a man who is steeped in sin is thus accepted by God and is forgiven, once he becomes a devotee he is required to flee from sin, and to practise righteousness. As a matter of fact the very act of worship has a purifying effect if it is done with all sincerity. The very thought of the Lord suffices to make one renounce evil.[73]

Devotion as means of securing grace

Āḷvārs, as we have said, were in the fullest sense God-intoxicated, God-enamoured and God-absorbed mystics. Their hearts were as if welling with a genuine, unalloyed and devoted love of an intense degree. It is, therefore, quite evident that the chief characteristics of the religion of Āḷvārs was a passionate devotion to God. They believed that a single minded devotion to Viṣṇu in the simplest form possible was the most efficacious means for the attainment of mokṣa.[74]

The passionate devotion to God in the Āḷvārs culminates in the spirit of total surrender and a feeling of clinging to God as one's all. Their ardent devotion deepens into prapatti the key-note of which is a state of prayerfulness of mind to God associated with deep conviction that He alone is the saviour and that there is no other way of attaining His grace except by such self-surrender. The only requisite for gaining the grace of God is a change of heart, a sense of utter humiliation and an absolute surrender. It is not a possession of any merit or wisdom but a sense of humility and sinfulness.[75]

In their all-absorbing devotion the Āḷvārs are so much dedicated that every drop of their blood, every beat of their heart and every thought of their mind are surrendered to God the soul of their souls.[76] Such ekalakṣaṇatva, i.e., placing oneself entirely at the disposal of God, is the essence of the devotion of the Āḷvārs. This highest form of devotion further demands a sincere dedication to God of everything that the devotee as an individual separate from God possesses. This total renunciation of earthly things is found in the case of Kulaśekhara who renounced his kingdom to be an Āḷvār.[77]

The devotion in the Āḷvārs further expresses itself in the worship of God. The Āḷvārs are particularly fascinated by God's manifestation in the arcā form. They dwell with love not only on God as an incarnate in individuals like Kṛṣṇa, but also as incarnate in images. They are deeply touched with His infinite mercy in making Himself easily accessible to men in their form. They feel His immediate presence in the shrines and are moved to tears in the contemplation of His attributes. They gaze at the image, and with hearts filled with emotion they shed tears of joy.[78]

Out of intense love they dress and adorn the image and dwell on the infinite perfection of God it represents, on the beautiful shape it possesses, on the radiance of its countenance, on the brilliance of its ornaments etc. Āndāl and other Āḷvārs love to go to the shrine even before the temple doors are opened to wake God and to greet Him with flowers. Their single-minded devotion expresses itself in worshipping at the shrine, offering flowers to

God, singing His praise, joining with others in uttering His names, gazing at His image, reciting His great and glorious deeds of grace, meditating on His incarnations till finally the soul is filled with ecstatic joy.[79]

So dearly do they love the temple in which the image is enshrined that Kulaśekhara Āḷvār declares that rather than be a king in this world or in heaven, he would prefer to be a crane or a fish in the temple-tank, a tree in the temple-garden, a road upon the temple-hill, a step at the threshold of the temple, or anything whatsoever so long as he is in the vicinity of the shrine.[80]

Though the Āḷvārs worship the arcās, they repudiate elaborate ritualism involving various articles of worship. They believe that what God desires from His devotees is their whole hearted devotion, expressing itself in loving worship at the shrine, uttering His names, meditating on His act of grace, and joining with others in singing His praise.[81]

The sum and substance of the entire teachings of the Āḷvārs is condensed in the opening verse of the Prabandham in which the Āḷvār exhorts his soul to be devoted to the active worship of the Lord who by His grace cleanses and purifies the mind and the heart of the devotee. The religion of the Āḷvārs, therefore, is marked with an undivided devotion and unreserved surrender to God. It was the sentiment of bhakti, a continuous flow of emotional religiosity ranging from the worship of idols to the most exalted mysticism of love for and surrender to God that pervaded and animated the religious life of the Āḷvārs.

Appraisal of Advaitic and Rāmānuja's accounts of means of mokṣa.

All systems of Indian philosophy, except the Cārvāka and the allied schools, maintain that the ultimate end of human life is to transcend the mundane life of travails and traversities. But they differ widely with regard to the nature of the life attained after this transcendence, and also with regard to the means by which this transcendence can be attained. They agree that the means to mokṣa involves a course of sādhanā, but what are the constituents of this sādhanā, and which constituent is more or less important is a matter of great dispute. A traidic process of sādhanā consisting of karma, jñāna and bhakti has been usually recognised in most of the schools.

Of this traidic process the Advaita school recognises jñāna alone as the final means. This is the logical conclusion of the advaitic metaphysical position. For the advaitin emancipation is not something to be attained, but it is only to be realised or known. Ignorance is bondage and knowledge is mokṣa. Accordingly he prescribes jñāna as the only final requisite for this purpose. According to Rāmānuja, on the other hand, bondage is undoubtedly due to ignorance, but it cannot be negated by mere intellectual enlightenment. It is not something to be realised, but rather to be attained through a disciplined endeavour. Accordingly, he regards karma, jñāna, bhakti and grace of God as the constituents of the process leading to mokṣa.

In the previous chapter we have tried to suggest that by mokṣa we should not mean annihilation of the individuality of the self, dissipation of its personality and identification with Brahman. On the contrary it stands for the perfection of the individual self, an establishment of a society of perfect selves. This end, then, is not something to be realised only, but it is to be attained. The establishment of such a society requires a rigorous effort, an all-round development of individual's personality.

The human being is a complex of cognitive, conative and affective elements, and therefore, any sādhanā, worth the name, must have in view a balanced development of all the three faculties. The whole man must rise up, awake and fight against the limitations, imperfections and finitude. Karma, jñāna and bhakti are the three different, though integrally united, processes relating to conative, cognitive and affective aspects respectively. These three are not to be regarded as three independent forms of sādhanā in the sense that only one of them is sufficient for the attainment of mokṣa.

This fact that all the three aspects are intimately interconnected is very well emphasised in the Gītā. We call them different because they represent three different aspects of the personality, but all the three are always present together though we may give more or less emphasis to each of them at different stages of spiritual development. A karmayogī, thus, far from being devoid of bhakti and jñāna, must necessarily be a jñānī and bhakta at a certain stage of his development. Similar is the case with a bhakta or jñānī. The natural bent of mind or aptitude determines the particular line of sādhanā for every particular sādhaka, but it is never to be forgotten that the particular line is merely a main support for the development of the different aspects. The difficulty arises only when this aspect of mutual cooperation is lost sight of, and undue importance or unmerited neglect is accorded to one or the other of them.

Karma, jñāna and bhakti, then, are the three disciplines suiting to different stages in the course of the development of the sādhaka. From which of these three the starting is to be made will depend upon his aptitude and bent of mind but at one stage or the other he will have to undergo the remaining stages. The easiest method is that one should start with karmayoga, and through jñānayoga should subsequently reach to bhaktiyoga. This appears to be the teaching of the Chāndogya passage 'āhāraśuddheḥ sattva śuddhiḥ sattvaśuddheḥ dhruvāsmṛtiḥ'. (VII.26.2) First of all there should be purity in all that is gathered through the senses. This would result in transperance of the intellect. The latter in turn produces constant and continuous recollection. Let us now see the place of each one of these constituents in the scheme of sādhanā.

Karmayoga

There has been a general agreement among all schools of Indian thought that the realisation of the highest end is impossible unless one is purified in mind and body, and that this purification can be brought about only through karma. But they differ with regard to the utility of karma in the later stages of the course of sādhanā. Śankara maintains that karma has only secondary significance in so far as it is accessory to intellectual penetration and discrimination. An advanced sādhaka should cease from all sorts of karmas, since all karmas proceed from ignorance. Pūrva mīmāmsā, on the other hand, maintains that jñāna alone can never yield liberation, but must be joined with karma for attaining the same. It, however, rejects niṣiddha and kāmya karmas, and prescribes nitya and naimittika karmas. Rāmānuja on the authority of the Gītā goes a step further and declares that all sorts of activities are to be performed. He takes karma in the widest sense.

The most striking teaching of the Gītā is that in no circumstances karma should be renounced. Activity is the law of life.

Conation is an essential factor of consciousness. Cessation from karma in thought, words, or deed is a psychological impossibility.

The liberated soul also cannot be free from activity. That the liberated soul should perform actions is evident from the passage of the Gītā where the Lord Himself is said to perform actions. (III.22-3). When the liberated soul acts, he always acts that which is good. In order to do the good, he is not required to make any effort, for good actions come out of him automatically and spontaneously. This circumstance is very well expressed by Kant when he writes, 'No imperatives hold for the Divine will, or in general for a holy will. 'Ought' is here out of place, because the volition is already itself necessarily in unison with the law.'[82]

Thus karma is quite indispensable both for the released as well as for the aspirant for release. Karma alone confers the required all round growth and development. The individual contains within himself immense potentialities which when fully developed and properly cultured open up the centre of infinite energy, unbounded expansion and limitless bliss. Since even an individual is an element in the whole and has no existence and hence no function apart from the whole all the functions performed by the parts need to be dedicated to the whole. Then only he can feel in him the centre of infinite energy, unbounded expansion and limitless bliss. In this state the individual identifies his whole essence with the universal centre of energy and feels himself as only an instrument through which the universal centre of energy is manifesting itself. No longer does he feel his limited existence as a separate individual possessing a limited source of energy, limited span of consciousness and a limited degree of enjoyment.

This attainment of the feeling of oneness with the Infinite is possible only when the actions are performed without attachment. In the Vedic literature there is a very apt word used for such type of action. The universe, according to the Ṛgveda, is a mahāyajña (great sacrifice) on the part of the Infinite. It is visṛṣṭi or visarga, a giving out or sacrificing oneself. By self-sacrifice alone God multiplies Himself and produces the universe. This sacrifice alone is the divine action, the true action. The individual should join hands with the Lord in performing such action. Through this alone the universe is sustained and through this alone the universe can develop. This alone restores the equilibrium and reestablishes the lost harmony. By this alone the world-cause and the purpose of God can be served. This is the real worship of God.

Thus karmayoga preaches renunciation in action and not renunciation of action. We must not seek freedom from action but only freedom in action. We must not abandon the deed but the selfish motive in performing the deed. The performance of such a deed would be a process of self-realisation through self-sacrifice. This is the burden of the teaching of the Iśopaniṣad and the Gītā.

Jñānayoga

The value and importance of jñāna in the scheme of sādhanā is clearly emphasised in the Upaniṣads and the Gītā. At places they declare that by jñāna alone one can attain mokṣa. It is very difficult to understand exactly what they mean by the term 'jñāna'. This much is clear that it is not an ordinary ratiocinative knowledge, but something intuitive and immediate (aparokṣānubhūti). Both Śankara and Rāmānuja agree that this knowledge in the form of aparokṣānubhūti is a means to mokṣa but they differ with regard to the nature of this knowledge. According to Śankara it is a realisation of one's own self by the self (ātmabodha). For him this is both the means and the end, for the individual self is identical with the Absolute. But for Rāmānuja by attaining ātmabodha the process does not come to an end. The knowledge of the true nature of the self must ripen into a sort of intellectual love or intellectual sympathy for the cosmic self.

Bhaktiyoga

The karmayoga must develop into jñānayoga because the proper performance of one's actions need a true knowledge of one's own potentialities and the ways of expressing them. Since every individual is a part, he must know his station in the whole and the duties pertaining to that station. He must know that he has no separate existence of his own apart from the cosmic whole and his true good and well-being lies in the well-being of the whole. This feeling of sympathy for other is nothing short of devotion to the cosmic end, *i.e.*, the perfection of the whole universe. This feeling is well expressed by Royce by the term 'appreciation'.[83] It is realising a thing exactly as a part of one's own experience. When the finite self feels itself identified with the Infinite self, it can be said to possess appreciative knowledge.

Śankara cannot speak of such a world of mutual appreciation for there is no such a thing as a society of perfect selves in his philosophy. Mokṣa for him is nothing but a flight of the alone to the alone. He talks of a state of experience where there is not a society of selves, but the Only Self, one without a second, pervading the whole of cosmos and resting in Its own glory. In the philosophy of Rāmānuja there is much scope for this mutual appreciation among souls, which alone is a pre-requisite of perfection, peace and plentitude. This is how Rāmānuja should have understood the concept of bhakti. He is wrong in maintaining that the conative part of devotion lies in bhajana, kīrtana etc. only. At some places Rāmānuja has become anthropomorphic in his account and we must repudiate such elements in his philosophy.

Besides these three constituents of the scheme of sādhanā, unlike Śankara, Rāmānuja emphasises the role of divine grace which is a crowning achievement of this endeavour. This alone can ultimately deliver one from bondage. Because of his theological leaning Rāmānuja has taken grace as something coming from above but it should be understood in the sense of an awakening of an ideal tendency in the heart. That is, the mutual appreciation among the souls must become instinctive and a part and parcel of the life. Here again Rāmānuja has given vent to his anthropomorphic accretions and mythological fancy.

Rāmānuja and Pāñcarātra school-A Study in contrast

Our comparative studies in the philosophy of Rāmānuja and the Pāñcartāra school in the previous chapters have shown that the doctrines of Rāmānuja differ widely from the Pāñcarātra doctrines and that the latter approach very near to Advaitism. Our comparative studies on the topic of the means of mokṣa would further confirm this finding.

The fundamental difference between Rāmānuja and the Pāñcarātra school is that the synthetic approach of Rāmānuja, under which he coordinates karma, jñāna, bhakti and grace of God as integral constituents of the same course of sādhanā, is conspicuously absent in the Pāñcarātra school. Though these concepts do occur in the Pāñcarātra sādhanā, the meaning put to them is quite different. Unlike Rāmānuja, the Pāñcarātra school advocates two different lines of sādhanā, the relation between which has been left undescribed. It seems that the two are regarded as independent and separate means. The one form of sādhanā consists of jñāna and karma, with a basis of yoga. This form is mainly advaitic in nature. Rāmānuja also recognises karma and jñāna as the stages in the scheme of sādhanā, but they are not given independent status. They are merely preliminaries to bhakti. In the Pāñcarātra school, like the Advaita, karma is helpful to the attainment of jñāna and it is jñāna alone which is the direct means to release. Further by karma Rāmānuja means niṣkāma karma as taught in the Gītā, whereas in the Pāñcarātra school karma is understood as performance of action with complete concentration. Similarly jñāna in Rāmānuja stands for the true knowledge of the individual self as different from the body etc. In the Pāñcarātra school knowledge is understood, as in the Advaita school, as identity-consciousness, *i.e.*, the consciousness of oneself being identical with the Absolute. The means of developing such a knowledge are vairāgya and samādhi, which are again the means recognised in the Advaita school.

Through the Advaita school the whole process of Pāñcarātra sādhanā has very much come under the influence of Yoga system. Here the Yoga process has occupied such an important place that an aspirant for release is required to be a yogī. The Pāñcarātra not merely borrowed the Yoga sādhanā but also has made substantial improvement upon it.

The other line of sādhanā recognised in the Pāñcarātra school is that of bhakti, or more properly, prapatti. In Rāmānuja jñānayoga must ripen into bhaktiyoga and bhakti alone evokes grace of God which results into release. But in the Pāñcarātra school jñāna not only does not develop into bhakti but also does not stand in need of the grace of God for the attainment of release.

Further, the whole theory and practice of bhakti in Rāmānuja is essentially different from that of the Pāñcarātra school, so much so that psychologically speaking they may be said to be just the opposite. In the Pāñcarātra school bhakti moves in an indefinite haze of mythology (in the Nārāyaṇīya) and occultism (in the Samhitās) with a strange combination of sentimentalism. In Rāmānuja, on the contrary, it is set forth not only with a systematic philosophic background, but also with an intellectual seriousness and ethical nobility. In the Pāñcarātra school bhakti, as a matter of fact, is nothing else than prapatti, a spirit of absolute and unfliching surrender to God, leaving aside all other scriptural duties, technically called avidhigocaratva. But in Rāmānuja the concept of prapatti, as we have seen, is not only altogether absent, but it is also in flagrant contradiction to his declared teachings. The bhakti of Rāmānuja is contemplation of God, but the prapatti of the Pāñcarātra school is an utter self-surrender to God. The goal of bhakti is realisation of God but the goal of prapatti is servitude to God. It is true that the Pāñcarātra bhakti does not have that much of exuberance of feeling, erotic element and unintellectual emotionalism as we find in the Āḷvārs, yet it is not completely free from these elements. In Rāmānuja, on the contrary, bhakti is essentially qualified by karma and jñāna, is very much restrained, and consists of calm meditation and serene contemplation. In Rāmānuja it stands for intuitive realisation or immediate presentation but such a sublime concept is far from the ritualistic bhakti of the Pāñcarātra school. In the Pāñcarātra school bhakti has sometimes come to assume a mechanical and ritualistic outer form, mere heartless repetition of mantras, but in Rāmānuja it is essentially an inner spiritual attitude enriched by virtues and disciplined by rigorous effort. The bhakti in Rāmānuja is a result of sādhana saptaka whereas in the Pāñcarātra school it is mere spontaneous and unrestrained exhibition of the feeling of surrender. Lastly, the bhakti of Rāmānuja takes full regard of the factors of freedom and initiative of the individual and moral responsibility of God, but both these factors are absent in the Pāñcarātra concept of prapatti.

Rāmānuja and the Pāñcarātra school recognise the grace of God as the culminating result of the triadic process of karma, jñāna and bhakti, which involves a training of the body, intellect and will. In the Pāñcarātra school out of the two processes recognised for release, it is only the bhakti mārga which stands in need of the grace of God, and not the jñāna mārga. In the bhakti mārga, too, the grace of God, unlike in Rāmānuja, is quite unmerited, and is showered irrespective of the conduct and character of the subject. Not only they differ with regard to the stimulus for grace, but they also differ with regard to the function of grace. In the Pāñcarātra scheme the individual has to play no role except that of self-surrender. The Deity requires no efforts on the part of the individual. But in Rāmānuja the grace of god merely removes the obstacles in the path of devotion caused by past sins and generates a tendency towards devotion, the rest is to be done by the individual only. In Rāmānuja the grace of God operates in accordance with the law of karma, but in the Pāñcarātra school even the karma can be annulled by the grace.

Another point of difference between Rāmānuja and the Pāñcarātra school is that unlike the former the latter is very much wedded to the worship of idols (arcā). Almost half of the Pāñcarātra literature consists of the elaborate process of worship, recitation of mantras and other related things. The worship of idols may be regarded to be one of the most important characteristics of the Pāñcarātra school. It is regarded as almost indispensable for a devotee. In order that one may be entitled to perform worship he is required to undergo initiation through the teacher. All these processes of worship and initiation have very much come under the influence of tāntrism. The worship of idols, ceremony of initiation in the sect and consequent importance to the teacher and the predominance of tāntric element are altogether absent in Rāmānuja. As a matter of fact Rāmānuja does not belong to any particular sect, though his philosophy has very much influenced the Śrī Vaiṣṇava sect.

Rāmānuja and Āḷvārs-A Study in Contrast

It has been very often maintained that in his concepts of bhakti and grace of God, Rāmānuja chiefly draws upon the rich religious experiences of the Āḷvārs.[84] The fact that Rāmānuja nowhere mentions or alludes to the Āḷvārs, and that some people regard Āḷvārs as the successors of Rāmānuja, obliges us to examine the truth of this contention. A comparative study of the concepts of bhakti and grace of God will show that there seems to be no truth in the above contention.

As a matter of fact, the meditative and ethical bhakti of Rāmānuja can not be compared with, or traced to, the highly emotional bhakti of the Āḷvārs who would reject jñāna and even karma, and would regard the ecstatic passion of the erotic nature as the only essential. For the Āḷvārs the bhakti is the alpha and omega of spiritual life, whereas for Rāmānuja it is only one of the constituents of the scheme of means to release. In Rāmānuja bhakti is a feeling accompanied by intellectual sympathy, devoid of exciting emotional attitude. It is an expression of divine life in knowledge and immensity with sublime touches on feeling. It is an intellectual communion with silent devotion, free from the heights of violent emotional outbursts. The reverse is the case with the Āḷvārs. Psychologically speaking a contradiction is manifest between these two attitudes. One is characterised by the intellectual serenity and meditative calmness, whereas the other has the deep expression of love-consciousness, with a maddening experience of the sweetness and beauty of the Lord. In Rāmānuja the heightening in intellectual love and enjoyment has the effect of quietening down the love impulses whose flashes are so manifest in the Āḷvārs. This sort of delirious, rapturous and ravishing love and the consequent maddening intoxication associated with ecstacy in the Āḷvārs are perhaps due to the impact of the Bhāgvata Purāna. Rāmānuja is absolutely uninfluenced by the Bhāgavata Purāna, perhaps because the latter was either not written down in his times or because by then it did not receive canonical recognition.

The Āḷvārs dwell with great feelings on the grace of God, which to them is His most endearing quality. The legendary acts of helpfulness shown by God at sundry times, especially to those of the low caste, appeal to the Āḷvārs the most. Rāmānuja also accepts the concept of the grace of God, but for him the grace of God is only a means to release and not the end of spiritual life.

This acceptance of the idea of grace of God by Rāmānuja and the Āḷvārs has led some scholars to presume that Rāmānuja has borrowed this idea from the Āḷvārs. But this position can hardly be substantiated. It is true that the Vaiṣṇava religion had always spoken of the gracious Deity, helping man in various ways, especially in his efforts for release. In the history of Hinduism Viṣṇu, as the God of grace, has come down right from the Vedic period. The fact that Āḷvārs speak touchingly of the divine grace which stoops to rescue even the meanest and the most unworthy does not provide us with any valid reason to think that this idea was an innovation of the Āḷvārs. This idea has been deeply rooted in Hinduism from antiquity and is not peculiar to any one particular sect or denomination. If Rāmānuja also advocates this doctrine because it is an accepted notion of the Upaniṣads and the Gītā, why should he be attributed with any sectarian motive ? There is no ground whatsoever for saying that Rāmānuja did so only because this doctrine is given very important place in the Vaiṣṇava sect. If any upaniṣadic doctrine is advocated by Rāmānuja and if the same doctrine is found in the Vaiṣṇava sect as well, there is no point of justification in saying that Rāmānuja accepted it, just because it is taught in the Vaiṣṇavism. This has been the argument of Kumarappa throughout his work.

Another point of difference between Rāmānuja and the Āḷvārs is that unlike Rāmānuja the Āḷvārs are very much given to the worship of idols. It is true that the idea of a personal God satisfies the deepest yearning of all religious people all over the world. And therefore, no religion can escape from symbolism and icons. The finitude and the emotional nature of man require some definite object of worship and adoration, help and protection. The idol worship also has the advantage of creating the belief that the real presence of the so called transcendental Lord is possible. It also shows symbolically some of the attributes of the Lord. It produces godliness, inspires piety and love and enables one to concentrate on God. So far as it remains a means to these it goes well. But the moment the idols themselves are regarded as God, or as actual incarnations of God (arcāvatāra) and not mere symbols, it results in low idolatory. Then people come to believe not in one God, but in many gods, quite independent of one another, residing in separate places, having particular days, articles, and modes of worship etc. This is nothing but a fall of religion. In the Āḷvārs we do appreciate the sincerity of feeling but we do not find favour with this sort of narrow idolatory. Rāmānuja is free from such idolatory, though he has fallen in the trap of anthropomorphism which we had an occasion to disapprove.

References and foot-Notes

1. Introduction to the chapter III of the Gītā Bhāṣya.
2. Gītā Bhāṣya, p. 449.
3. III.4.1.
4. Śrī Bhāṣya, IV.1.1.

5. Ibid, the introductory verse ; cf. Introduction to the Gītā Bhāṣya.
6. Ibid, III.4.2.
7. Ibid, III.4.12 ; Gītā Bhāṣya, XVIII.5.
8. Gītā Bhāṣya, XVIII.56.
9. Śrī Bhāṣya, IV.4.22.
10. Introduction to the chapter V of the Gītā Bhāṣya.
11. Chānd, VII.26.2 ; VIII.4.3 ; VIII.5 ; VIII.15.1 ; Tait, 1.9 ; I.11 etc.
12. Cf. Iśopaniṣad, XII.
13. Cf. 11.2.55-71.
14. Gītā Bhāṣya, II.37.
15. Ibid, II.41.
16. Ibid, III.9.
17. Ibid, XVIII.54-56 ; Śrī Bhāṣya, III.4-26.
18. Śrī Bhāṣya, III.4.32.
19. Ibid, III.4.36.
20. Ibid, III.4.39.
21. Ibid, III.4.42-43.
22. It should be noted that among these scriptures enumerated by Rāmānuja there is no mention of the Pāñcarātra works.
23. Gītā Bhāṣya, II.38.
24. Śrī Bhāṣya, III.3.52.
25. Gītā Bhāṣya, II.52.
26. Comparative Studies in Christianity and Vaiṣṇavism, p.8.
27. History of Indian Philosophy, volume II. p. 409.
28. Śrī Bhāṣya, III. 2. 24.
29. Gītā Bhāṣya, VIII. 7.
30. Ibid, IX. 27.
31. Ibid, IX. 34.
32. Śrī Bhāṣya, I. 1. 1.
33. Vedārtha Samgraha, 144.
34. Gītā Bhāṣya, VII. 1.
35. Śrī Bhāṣya, I. 1. 1.
36. Ibid, I. 1. 1.
37. Gītā Bhāṣya, IX-14.

38. Śrī Bhāṣya, III. 4. 35.
39. Śrī Bhāṣya, I. 1. 1.
40. Vedārtha Samgraha, 149 ; all these elements are met with but not conjointly in the Vedic scriptures. See K.D. Bharadwaja, 'The Philosophy of Rāmānuja' p. 178.
41. Kumarappa, loc. cit., p. 306 ff.
42. Śrī Bhāṣya, I. 3. 32.
43. Ibid, II. 3. 41.
44. Loc. cit., 296-97.
45. Section 45.
46. See Buitenen's translation of the Vedārtha Samgraha, p. 116.
47. VII. 14.
48. loc. cit., 305-306.
49. quoted from K.D. Bharadwaja, loc. cit., p. 205.
50. See Rajagopalachariar, 'Vaiṣṇavite Reformers of India', p.5; Satyavrata Sinha, 'Vedānta Deśika- a study, p. 87 ; Buitenen 'Introduction to the English translation of the Gītā Bhāṣya p. 24 ; Grierson, Journal of Royal Asiatic Society, 1912, p. 718 ; K.D. Bharadwaja, loc. cit., p. 199.
51. Gītā Bhāṣya. IX. 29.
52. Ibid, VIII. 14.
53. Śrī Bhāṣya, I. 3. 32.
54. Ibid, II. 3. 47.
55. Ibid. II. 3. 41.
56. See for details my book on the Pāñcarātra, Loc. cit.
57. Periya Tirumoli, XI. 8. 2-3.
58. Tiruviruttam, 70.
59. Perumal Tirumoli, C. 5. 8.
60. Tiruvaymoli, C. I. 7. 10 ; II. 3. 10 ; II. 4.
61. Govindacarya, Holy Lives of the Āzwārs pp. 39-54 and 144.
62. Periya Tirumoli, V. 8. 6.
63. Ibid, I. 1. 8.
64. Tirumalai, 39.
65. Tiruvaymoli, C. I. 5-10 ; Tiruppavai, 5.
66. Tirumalai, 16 ; 26.

67. Ibid, 29, 30, 32, 33. 35 etc.
68. Tiruvaymoli, C. I. 7. 7 ; I. 7. 2 ; I. 7. 4 ; II. 3. 3.
69. Ibid, C. I. 7. 10. I. 2. 3.
70. Tiruppavai, II.
71. Tirumalai, 16-17.
72. Tirumalai, 4.
73. Ibid, 40.
74. Tiruvandadi. II. 38.
75. Tirumoli, C. V. 5.
76. Tiruvaymoli, C. II. 3. 4.
77. Tirumoli. C. III. 1.
78. Tirumal, V. 18.
79. Tirupalli yeluchi, 10 ; Tiruppallandu, IV. 5, Tiruvaymoli, C. II. 6. 4, 6 ; X. I ; X. 2.
80. Tirumoli, C. IV.
81. Tiruvandadi, II. 39.
82. Metaphysics of morals, Watsons' selection, p. 31.
83. The Spirit of Modern Philosophy, p. 286.
84. Kumarappa, loc. cit. p. 294.

CHAPTER V

CONCLUDING REMARKS

After having dealt in a comparative and critical manner with the views of Rāmānuja, Advaita school, Pāñcarātra school and the Āḷvārs we may now offer a few observations by way of concluding remarks.

To start with the Advaita school and Rāmānuja, our comparative study has shown that whether we consider the interpretations of Śankara and Rāmānuja on the basis of their faithfulness to the Prasthāna-trayī, or independently of that, Rāmānuja's interpretation seems to be more satisfactory.

Among the Prasthāna-trayī, so far as the Upaniṣads are concerned they speak with a double voice and hence both Śankara and Rāmānuja could successfully draw upon them for their basis. Therefore it is difficult to maintain that they consistently imply either the views of Śankara or of Rāmānuja. But with regard to the Gītā and the Brahma-sūtras it appears that they do not teach the doctrines of Advaita in the characteristic sense of the school. They do not seem to suggest the higher and the lower knowledge of Brahman and the consequent distinctions of the higher and the lower Brahman. Nor do they seem to afford any evidence of their having held the doctrine of māyā, and the consequent phenomenality of the world, in the form in which it is advocated in the Advaita school. Further, they do not seem to teach the doctrine of complete identity of the individual self and the Supreme.

Śankara's interpretation of the Brahma-sūtras reveals that very often than not he feels the necessity of supplementing his interpretation by certain additions and reservations of his own for which the text gives no occasion. Rāmānuja, on the contrary, is able to take the Sūtras as they stand. This suggests that the doctrines of Śankara are not present to the mind of the author of the Sūtras. The fact that the Sūtrakāra should begin and end with the Sūtras which can on no account be reconciled with Śankara's esoteric doctrine, leads one to suppose that there is a flaw in his reasoning so far as his faithfulness to the Sūtrakāra is concerned. Further, there is a series of ancient commentators (of whom Śankara also takes cognisance) on whom Rāmānuja looks as authorities in the interpretation of the Sūtras and the Vedānta philosophy. The fact that these commentators did not teach the Advaita philosophy, as is acknowledged by Śankara himself, suggests that the Advaitic interpretation of the Sūtras was not favoured by many ancient authorities on the Vedānta.

Considered independently of the Prasthāna-trayī, again, Rāmānuja's system appears more satisfactory. Granted the premises of Śankara's system, his philosophy appears to be the most compact systematic and logical. His system affords the best example of the philosophy of identity ; but mere logicality is not the Alpha and Omega of life. Man is a sythesis of cognitive as well as affective elements, both of which demand their fuller satisfaction. In the organicismic view of Rāmānuja we find a more balanced, more comprehensive and more pacifying satisfaction of the demands of reason and the deep cravings of feeling. Another feature of his philosophy is his uncompromising insistence on safeguarding the inalienable individuality of the finite self and the reality of the world of matter, by assigning them proper places and value in the unifying conception of an all-embracing Reality without in any way destroying Its unity and supreme perfection. Though we thus appreciate the general drift of his system, we do not feel at home with the crude anthropomorphism that has found its way deep into his philosophy, specially in his concept of God and his account of nature and means of release.

With regard to Rāmānuja, the Pāñcarātra school and the Āḷvārs we have undertaken their comparative study with a view to examine the opinion held by many scholars that the theism of

Rāmānuja is an outcome of his conscious effort to blend the Vedāntic metaphysics with the Vaiṣṇavite religion of the Pāñcarātra school and the Āḷvārs.[1] On the basis of our comparative study we feel that the trend of thought in the works of Rāmānuja does not seem to support this view. Not only all the characteristic doctrines and dogmas of the Pāñcarātra school and the Āḷvārs are conspicuous by their absence in the works of Rāmānuja, but there are also fundamental and far-reaching doctrinal differences between them. From this we may conclude that the alleged impact of the Pāñcarātra school and the Āḷvars on Rāmānuja cannot be substantiated. Our conclusion can further be confirmed from the following considerations.

First of all we propose to consider as to how far it is true that Rāmānuja was born in the spiritual lineage of the Śrī-Vaiṣṇava sect[2], and that 'his study of the Āḷvārs and his training by the Śrī-vaiṣṇava ācāryas helped him to develop elements which otherwise would have remained latent in the Upaniṣads and the Brahma-sūtras'.[3] This contention is based on the Śrī-vaiṣṇava tradition whose reliability has been doubted by many scholars.[4] Therefore, in the absence of any tangible evidence it is not proper to attribute his theistic interpretation to the so-called sectarian training, simply because he maintained that the Brahma-sūtras set forth one philosophical view rather than the other.

Further, from the writings of Rāmānuja we get nothing to infer of his affiliation to any sect. The spirit as well as the contents of his works lend themselves to a non-sectarian interpretation and one may naturally doubt whether the alleged sectarian affiliation attributed to him is well-founded and justified or not. Nowhere in his works he mentions or quotes any of the Pāñcarātra Samhitās except once under Brahma-sūtras II.2.39-42 which, as the tradition goes, contain more than one and a half crores of verses. Nor does he mention or quote the works of the Āḷvārs and the Śrī-vaiṣṇava ācāryas. Not only this while describing the scriptures which are authoritative to him he does not even mention the Pāñcarātra Samhitās or the Nāḷayira-prabandham. Whatever he asserts or denies, confirms or refutes, he derives support for that from the Vedāntic scriptures and not from the works of the Śrī-vaiṣṇava sect.

Moreover, he does not even allude to the Śrī-vaiṣṇava ācāryas whom the tradition regards as his spiritual teachers. When he enumerates the 'ancient teachers' on whom he relies upon not infrequently, he does not mention any of these Śrī-vaiṣṇava ācāryas. It is true that he begins the Vedārtha Samgraha and the commentary on the Gītā by paying his tribute to Yāmuna. Frequently he draws upon the Siddhi-traya and the Gītārtha Samgraha of Yāmuna and generally follows their line of argument. But this Yāmuna does not seem to be the author of the Āgama-prāmāṇya and other sectarian works ascribed to him. It may be that the arguments of Rāmānuja in favour of the Pāñcarātra put forth in the Śrī Bhāṣya were elaborated in the Āgama-prāmāṇya by a later hand and then this work was attributed to Yāmuna to get association with his name. Such a phenomenon is not infrequent in Indian literature. Or it may be that there were two Yāmunas, one the philosopher and the other the Śrī-vaiṣṇava. The Yāmuna who is paid tribute to by Rāmānuja may be the philosopher Yāmuna and not the Śrī-vaiṣṇava one. As the tradition itself holds that Rāmānuja did not meet the Śrī-vaiṣṇava Yāmuna, the latter cannot be his guru. Even if for the sake of argument we regard the Śrī-vaiṣṇava Yāmuna who has championed the cause of the Pāñcarātra school to be his guru this does not provide us with sufficient reason to conclude that Rāmānuja must also have done so. Even if we further admit that being born in the Śrī-vaiṣṇava lineage he must have been indirectly influenced this does not prove the thesis of 'conscious synthesis'.

From the above it seems that Rāmānuja was not a follower and an advocate of Śrī-vaiṣṇavism. Had he been so he would have championed its cause as vigorously as the author of the Āgama-prāmāṇya did. All the scholars who allege the influence of the Pāñcarātra school and the Āḷvārs quote nothing from his works to substantiate their thesis. They derive support only from the Yatīndramatadīpikā, Tattvatrāya etc. which are the works of his followers. All these prove that the contention of these scholars does not have any ground.

We may now consider another question, viz., does Rāmānuja in his treatment of the Pāñcarātra school declare himself a follower of the Pāñcarātra ?[5]

As regards the allusion to the Pāñcarātra school under Brahma-śūtras II.2.39-42 and Rāmānuja's favourable attitude towards it, one should interpret what he says only in the light of the particular context. Rāmānuja regards the Mahābhārata as an authority which, according to him, is composed by the Sūtrakāra himself. In the Mahābhārata the Sūtrakāra has upheld the validity of the Pāñcarātra teachings by saying that they are of divine origin, and therefore, Rāmānuja contends, the Śūtrakāra cannot impugn the same in the sūtras. Rāmānuja of his own accord does not plead for the orthodoxy of the Pāñcarātra school, but is motivated to do so by Śankara's rejection of its validity, which to Rāmānuja is a clear case of going against the verdict of the Sūtrakāra stated in the Mahābhārata. Śankara has rejected the validity of the Pāñcarātra school on the ground that it teaches the origination of the soul and the plurality of gods. Rāmānuja tries to repudiate the Śankarite contention by presenting a view which he deems correct. Only in order to elucidate his point Rāmānuja refers to the doctrines of Vyūhas and the three-fold manifestations of God. But this does not mean that he has imbibed and assimilated these doctrines in his philosophy. From his treatment of this school it cannot be concluded that he was its follower and had accepted its doctrines. If he were to advocate its doctrines, he should have done so in the first sūtra of the first chapter.[6]

It will not be out of context to discuss here as to how far Rāmānuja's interpretation of these four sūtras is tenable. It is quite evident, as all the commentators agree, that the tone of the first two sūtras is combative. The difference of opinion is with regard to the interpretation of the last two sūtras. In the second sūtra, according to Rāmānuja, the use of the particle 'vā' is indicative of the change of side in the argument. One can find such instances in the third pāda of the third chapter. But in the present context this does not seem to be warranted. It is true that the Sūtrakāra while refuting the origination of the soul in the preceding sūtras, has in this sūtra used the word 'vā' which indicates that here he is not refuting some of the Pāñcarātra doctrines. But this need not necessarily mean that it is a change of side. It may be that in the sūtra he has given an alternative which though true may not be worthy of importance. Or it may be that in the preceding sūtras after refuting the origination in the present sūtra he has given an alternative that if by 'mana' we mean knowledge which arises from jīva, then this is not to be refuted. In the Upaniṣads also various forms of knowledge are referred to as mana. The word 'vā' may suggest two alternatives; if the first is accepted, then the Pāñcarātra school is worth condemnation, and if the second is accepted, then it is not to be refuted. In this respect the interpretation of Rāmānuja does not seem to be correct.

Further, in the same sūtra Rāmānuja interprets the word 'vijñānādi' as Brahman which does not seem to be proper because no where the Sūtrakāra has used this word in this sense. He always uses it in the sense of mana or buddhi. Nor is this word a technical term in the Pāñcarātra school.

From the interpretation of the last sūtra it is quite evident that Rāmānuja has twisted its meaning. Here he explains 'vipratiṣedhācca' as 'and because the origination of the individual soul is contradicted in this śāstra', saying thereby that the objection raised in the first sūtra is out of question since the Pāñcarātra school does not hold this view. But this interpretation is not at all happy. Here not only he explains away the question of origination, but also commits the fallacy of inconsistency. This becomes evident when we compare it with the sūtra II. 2. 9, where the same phrase is interpreted by Rāmānuja to mean that contradictions in the Sāmkhya system make it unacceptable. The interpretation of Rāmānuja that in the Pāñcarātra school itself the origination of the jīva is refuted and therefore the Pāñcarātra school is regarded as valid by the Sūtrakāra, would have been correct provided in the sūtra instead of 'vipratiṣedhācca' there would be simply 'pratiṣedhācca'. Vipratiṣedha means mutual contradiction and this is accepted by Rāmānuja in II. 2.9.

So far as the negation of origination is concerned, it is found in some sections of the Pāñcarātra followers, but there must have been some section which accepted and preached origination, as is testified by Kṣemarāja in the Pratyabhijñā Hṛdaya. Though the alleged doctrine is not present in the modern Pāñcarātra works, and hence the above criticism of the Sūtrakāra is not now applicable to it, yet the fact remains that the interpretation of Śankara is not incorrect. Moreover, Rāmānuja while defending the Pāñcarātra school quotes the Parama Samhitā (II. 19), but, in that Samhitā this verse, 'Vāsudevāt samkarṣaṇo nāmajīvo jāyate, does not occur. It seems that by the time of Rāmānuja those Pāñcarātra works which held the doctrine of origination must have become non-prevalent.

The argument of Rāmānuja that the Sūtrakāra is also the author of the Mahābhārata, has no sound historical support. Secondly, in the Mahābhārata itself at some places the Pāñcarātra school is regarded as outside the pale of Vedic orthodoxy. Lastly, in the Mahābhārata the Sāmkhya is also praised, but here in the Sūtras it is condemned. The defence of Rāmānuja that the Sāmkhya is condemned because of its human origin does not seem to be a sound one.

As a matter of fact, the 'tarkapāda' is meant to refute rival theories, as Rāmānuja himself accepts it (parapakṣa pratikṣepo hyasmin pāde krīyate II. 2. 10). In the whole of this section the Sūtrakāra is on the offensive, refuting through reasoning only, without recourse to the scriptural texts. Here he refutes those schools of thought which were regarded as outside the sphere of the Vedas. The Pāñcarātra was also regarded so and therefore we cannot reasonably expect Bādarāyaṇa to have accepted the Pāñcarātra view. Had he intended to do so, he should not have dealt with it in the tarkapāda. The best place for this would have been II. 3. 18, where on the authority of the scriptures he negates the origination of the soul and propounds its eternity. Moreover, if the Sūtrakāra wanted to defend the Pāñcarātra school he could have done so in a far less ambiguous manner.

The arguement of Thibaut that it is not unnatural to end the tarkapāda with the defence of a doctrine which is to be viewed as true, is without any force, since the exposition and the defence of the true doctrine is the object of the whole book and not of one single adhikaraṇa. What is more important is that we do not come across in the whole work any characteristic doctrine of the Pāñcarātra school. The fact that this doctrine is refuted last of all can be explained by the circumstance that it is most allied to the Vedānta doctrine, as is admitted by Śankara and Bhāskara as well.

We may now turn to the consideration of another question, viz., is there not a Vedāntic tradition of long antiquity which Rāmānuja follows in toto ? The school which Rāmānuja professes to follow has a long standing ancestry commencing almost from the times of the author of the Sūtras. There is sufficient evidence to prove that the theistic interpretation by Rāmānuja was no innovation nor does it betray any non-Vedāntic influence. In fact his philosophy seems to be a faithful representation of the Vedānta teachings enshrined in the Prasthāna-trayī.

In the Upaniṣads we find distinctly theistic and devotional tendencies gradually developing. Further the Brahma Sūtras furnish us with indications of the existence already at an early time of essentially different Vedāntic systems. In the Sūtras we find Vedāntic doctrines of teachers like Ātreya, Āśmarathya, Auḍulomi, Kāśṇajini, Kāsakṛtsna, Jaimini, Bādari etc. being quoted by Bādarāyaṇa himself. Among the passages where diverging views of these teachers are recorded and contrasted three are of particular importance, namely, I.4.20-22 ; III.4.7-14 ; IV.4.5-7. An analysis of these Sūtras will clearly indicate that even before Bādarāyaṇa composed the Sūtras there were different views about the teachings of the Upaniṣads and that the theistic view was one of the dominant ones.

Turning next to the Śānkara Bhāṣya we there meet with the indications that the Vedāntins were divided among themselves on some fundamental points. Śankara more than once refers to the opinion of 'another' commentator of the sūtras, and at several places Śankara's commentators explain that this stands for Bodhāyana whom Rāmānuja expressly follows. There are two remarks of Śankara which are of great importance in this connection. The first is as follows, 'some declare those sūtras which I look upon as setting forth the siddhānta view to state merely the purvapakṣa'. This clearly indicates that Śankara's interpretation was not acceptable to other ācāryas who perhaps were more inclined towards the theistic tendency. Another instance we find under I.3.15 where Śankara after having explained at length that the individual soul as such cannot claim any reality, but is real only in so far as it is identical with Brahman, adds the following words, 'Apare tu vādinaḥ pāramārthikameva jīvarūpamiti manyante asmadīyā ca kecit' i.e., 'other theorisers, again, and among them some of ours are of the opinion that the individual soul as such is real.' The term 'ours' here stands only for the Vedāntins. From this it appears that Śankara himself was willing to class under the same category himself and other philosophers who—as n the later times Rāmānuja—looked upon the individual soul as real in itself.

Yāmuna, the author of Siddhi-traya and Gītārtha Samgraha, mentions a series of authors who preceded him and composed works explanatory of the Sūtras. They are Bhāṣyakṛta (perhaps Dramiḍa), Śrī Vatsānka, Ṭanka, Bhartṛprapañca, Bhartṛhari, Brahmadatta, Śankara and Bhāskara. The first three belong to the school of Rāmānuja.

Rāmānuja also at the very outset in his Śrī Bhāṣya claims to follow the authority of Bodhāyana which was upheld by 'ancient teachers'. In the Vedārtha Samgraha we meet with the enumeration of the following authorities of his school who preceded him. They are Bodhāyana, Ṭanka, Dramiḍa, Guhadeva, Kapardin and Bharuci. Quotations from the writings of some of them are not infrequent in the Vedārtha Samgraha and the Śrī Bhāṣya.[7]

From the foregoing it appears that the theistic interpretation of the Brahma-sūtras and the Upaniṣads by Rāmānuja was no innovation, nor does it betray any foreign influence. There had been great names among the Vedāntic precursors of the Viśiṣṭādvaita philosophy of Rāmānuja and Rāmānuja at no place countenances departure from the tradition established by them.

Having given the account of the Vedāntic tradition followed by Rāmānuja we may now consider the antiquity of theism. The origin of theism, as we have seen, can be traced back to the Vedic hymns which are replete with the sentiments of piety and reverence. In the Upaniṣads we find distinctly theistic and devotional tendencies. This may be partly due to the innate theistic strain in the Upaniṣads themselves and partly due to the compromise reached between the high speculations about the impersonal Brahman and the popular faiths gathering round the devout worship of personal gods. The epics though recognised the unconditioned aspect of Brahman as superior, the conditioned one was invested with a distinct personality for love and worship. The Gītā also absorbs a great deal of the monistic ideas of the Upaniṣads and reinterprets them with a clearly theistic and devotional attitude. The theistic ideas were already there in the Upaniṣads, but they were so scattered that it was necessary for practical purposes to work them up into a system. This syncretic theism of the Gītā, which was lost under the spread of Buddhism and Advaita vedānta, was restored by Rāmānuja through the help of the Viṣṇu Purāṇa. The Gītā provided

Rāmānuja with the spirit of his theism and it was clothed by the Viṣṇu Purāṇa. Thus the theism of Rāmānuja is not an innovation, and there is no ground to trace its impetus to the Śrī-vaiṣṇava school.

Before coming to a close we may do well to consider the possible causes for the misconception that Rāmānuja was influenced by the Pāñcarātra school and the Āḻvārs.

First of all, there is a strong tendency among the writers on Rāmānuja to regard his Viśiṣṭādvaita as identical with Śrī-vaiṣṇavism, which seems to be of a later origin and which is highlighted by his followers.[8] This confusion is due to a failure to dissociate the Viśiṣṭādvaita of Rāmānuja from the Viśiṣṭādvaita of his followers. It is true that the Viśiṣṭādvaita professed and practised by his followers is identical with Śrī-vaiṣṇavism, but on this ground it cannot be said that the same must be the case with regard to the Viśiṣṭādvaita of Rāmānuja. The Viśiṣṭādvaita of Rāmānuja is poles apart from the Śrī-vaiṣṇava cult which is sectarian in character practising ritualistic externalism enjoined by the Pāñcarātra school.

Secondly, it is only the Śrī-vaiṣṇava tradition (whose reliability is very much doubtful) which mentions Rāmānuja in the spiritual lineage of the Āḻvārs and the Śrī-vaiṣṇava ācāryas. Some of the followers of Rāmānuja, who perhaps established this tradition, could not resist the allurement of being the devoted disciples of their master and at the same time accepting the enamouring utterances of the Āḻvārs and the ācāryas. Therefore they tried to associate the two by dragging Rāmānuja within the fold of Śrī-vaiṣṇavism. They attributed to Rāmānuja those doctrines of their sect which are not found in his works and which he would never have accepted. Referring to this circumstance Macnicol remarks, '...even the well-knit fabric of Rāmānuja's system did not prevent his followers from wild and dangerous aberrations.'[9] Monier Williams writes, 'After Rāmānuja's death his numerous followers corrupted his teachings in the usual manner introducing doctrines and practices which the founder of the sect had not enjoined and would not have sanctioned.'[10] Prof. Srinivas Aiengar observes, 'The modern Viśiṣṭādvaita is a school of eclecticism blending the Rāmānuja Vedānta philosophy and Āgama cosmology and practices. Rāmānuja himself, though the ācārya par excellence of this sect and though he pleaded for the orthodoxy of the Pāñcarātra books, expounds only the Vedānta philosophy and discipline. But his followers have neglected the Vedānta philosophy and brought into prominence Āgama doctrines and practices'.[11]

Lastly, there have been vigorous attempts made by the advocates of the Pāñcarātra school which is non-Vedic in origin and anti-Vedic in attitude—to secure Vedic basis for their doctrines and practices. They tried to prove their ancestry from the Vedic passage, 'Nānyaḥ panthā ayanāya vidyate'. They named themselves as Ekāntins and tried to identify their sect with the Ekāyana sect of the Kāṇva śākhā of the Śukla Yajurveda. A similar effort was made to misappropriate the meaning of the word 'pāñcarātra-satra' of the Śatapatha Brāhmaṇa (XIII. 61). The shelter-seeking advocates of the Pāñcarātra school further found in the Śrī-Bhāṣya of Rāmānuja a clue to secure the needed Vedāntic support. They tried to associate his authority with their sect so as to enhance its dignity and to get rid of the reproach of unorthodoxy etc. which had dogged their sect up to that time. In order to drag Rāmānuja within the fold of the Pāñcarātra sect they even did not spare Yāmuna, the author of the Siddhi-traya and the Gītārtha Samgraha. They further described Rāmānuja as an incarnation of Samkarṣaṇa, the Vyūha emanation of God (Bṛhad-samhitā II.7.66 ff.)

From all the foregoing considerations we may conclude that the Pāñcarātra school, though recognised in passing as an orthodox system, is not at all utilised by him to corroborate his system of Vedānta. As regards the Āḷvārs he does not even allude to them. Therefore there is no ground for the contention of the scholars that the theism of Rāmānuja is an outcome of his conscious effort to blend the Vedāntic metaphysics with the Vaiṣṇavite religion of the Āḷvārs, Śrī-vaiṣṇava ācāryas and the Pāñcarātra Samhitās. As a matter of fact, we do not find any element in him which may be regarded as non-Vedic.

References and foot-notes

1. See Indian Antiquary, XVIII, pp. 189-90, June, 1889; Collective works of R. G. Bhandarkar, Vol. IV. p. 80; Journal of the Royal Asiatic Society, 1910, p. 566; P. N. Srinivasachari—The Philosophy of Viśiṣṭādvaita, Introduction, p. XXXIV. B. Kumarappa, loc. cit, pp. 149, 103 n, 250, 314

etc., Roy Chaudhary—Early History of Vaiṣṇavism, p. 31 ; Macdonall, India's Past, p. 149 ; Das Gupta, loc. cit., pp. 24, 80 etc. ; Radhakrishnan, loc. cit., Vol. II, p. 667 ; Hiriyanna, loc. cit., p. 409.

2. See my paper 'Did Rāmānuja Advocate Pāñcarātra and Śrīvaiṣṇavism ?', Philosophical Quarterly, April, 1963.
3. Radhakrishnan, loc. cit., p. 667.
4. See T. A. Gopinath Rao, History of Śrīvaiṣṇavism.
5. See my paper 'Did Bādarāyaṇa favour Pāñcarātra ?', Philosophical Quarterly, April, 1965.
6. See the opinions of Prof. Kane in 'The History of the Dharmaśāstras' Vol. V. pt. II. pp. 955 N, 957 N ; and Buitenen Vedārtha Samgraha, Introduction, pp. 36-39.
7. See my paper 'The Vedāntic Precursors of the Viśiṣṭādvaita Philosophy of Rāmānuja', Poona Orientalist, April, 1965.
8. See P. N. Srinivasachari, loc. cit., p. 503 ; R. G. Bhandarkar, who among the modern scholars first promulgated this view, based his account of Rāmānuja upon the Artha-pañcaka and the Yatīndramatadīpikā. This makes it quite evident that this view has come to be held in indifference to Rāmānuja's own works. (Indian Antiquary, Vol. XVIII, June 1889, pp. 189-90 ; Journal of the Royal Asiatic Society, 1910, p. 565.)
9. Indian Theism, p. 111.
10. Religious Thoughts and Life in India, p. 124.
11. Loc. cit., pp. 185, 95.

SELECT BIBLIOGRAPHY

1. Aiyangar, N. K. — A Free Translation of the Tiruvāymoḷi of Śaṭhakopa, Trichinopoly, 1925.
2. Aiyangar, S. K. — Early History of Vaiṣṇavism in South India, Madras, 1920.
3. Aiyangar, P. T. S. — Outlines of Indian Philosophy, Benaras, 1909.
4. Bhandarkar, R. G. — Vaiṣṇavism, Śaivism and Minor Religious Systems, Strasburg, 1913.
5. Bharadwaja, K. D. — The Philosophy of Rāmānuja, Delhi, 1958.
6. Buitenen, J. A. B. Van — Rāmānuja on the Bhagavadgītā, Gravenhage, 1953.
7. Buitenen, J. A. B. Van — Rāmānuja's Vedārtha Saṃgraha, Poona, 1956.
8. Das Gupta, S. N. — A History of Indian Philosophy, Vol. III, Cambridge, 1952.
9. Duessen — The System of the Vedānta, Chicago, 1912.
10. Ferquher, J. N. — An Outline of the Religious Literature of India, London, 1920.
11. Gopinath Rao, T. — The History of Śrīvaiṣṇavas—Sir Subramanya Lectures, 1923.
12. Hiriyanna, M. — Outlines of Indian Philosophy, George Allen & Unwin, 1958.

13. Kumarappa, B. The Hindu Conception of the Deity, London, 1934.

14. Padmarajiah, Y. J. Jain Theories of Reality and Knowledge, Bombay, 1963.

15. Radhakrishnan S. Indian Philosophy, George Allen & Unwin, 1951.

16. Rajagopalacharya The Vaiṣṇavite Reformers of India, Madras, 1909.

17. Rangacharya, M. Translation of the Śrī Bhāṣya, Madras, 1899.

18. Schrader, F. Otto Introduction to the Pāñcarātra and Ahirbudhnya Samhitā, Adyar, 1916.

19. Sirkar, M. N. Comparative Studies in Vedāntism, Oxford, 1927.

20. Srinivasachari, P. N. The Philosophy of Viśiṣṭādvaita, Adyar, 1943.

21. Srinivasachari, S. M. Advaita and Viśiṣṭādvaita, Bombay, 1961.

22. Teliwala, M. T. Discuss how far Śankara truly represents the views of the author of the Sūtras, Bombay, 1918.

23. Thibaut, G. S. B. E. Series. Vol. XXXIV

24. Thibaut, G. S. B. E. Series. Vol. XXXXVIII

25. Yamunacharya Rāmānuja's teachings in his own words, Vidya Bhawan Series, 1963.

Sanskrit Texts

26. Śrī Bhāṣya Rāmānuja

27. Gītā Bhāṣya Rāmānuja

28. Vedārtha Saṃgraha Rāmānuja

29. Siddhi-traya Yāmunācārya

30. Gītārtha Saṃgraha Yāmunācārya

31. Gītā

32. Mahābhārata

33. Ahirbudhnya Saṃhitā

34. Īśvara Saṃhitā
35. Jayākhya Saṃhitā
36. Lakṣmī Tantra
37. Nārada Pāñcarātra
38. Parama Saṃhitā
39. Pārameśvara Saṃhitā
40. Parama Prakāśa Saṃhitā
41. Padma Tantra
42. Viṣṇu Saṃhitā
43. Viṣṇu Tilaka
44. Viśvakṣena Saṃhitā.

INDEX